PRINCIPLES AND PRACTICES
OF CASE MANAGEMENT IN
REHABILITATION COUNSELING

ABOUT THE EDITOR

E. Davis Martin, Jr., Ed.D., C.R.C., N.C.C. is professor, Department of Rehabilitation and Special Education, College of Education, Auburn University, where he serves as the coordinator of the Rehabilitation Counseling Program. He was formerly executive vice president of Sinsabaugh Consulting Services, PC, Richmond, Virginia; emeritus professor of rehabilitation counseling, professor of rehabilitation counseling, interim chairman, and director of clinical practice, Department of Rehabilitation Counseling, Virginia Commonwealth University (VCU); collateral professor of special education, School of Education, VCU; acting dean, School of Community and Public Affairs, VCU; and director of continuing studies, School of Allied Heath Professions, Medical College of Virginia, VCU; and has served in various rehabilitation counseling, supervisory, and administrative positions in the state-federal vocational rehabilitation program. He has served as a fair hearing officer for the Virginia Department of Rehabilitative Services and for the Virginia Department for the Blind and Visually Impaired. Dr. Martin has authored/ co-authored/edited five major textbooks and has been a frequent contributor to the rehabilitation literature. He currently serves as the editor of the *Journal of Forensic Vocational Analysis,* a leading journal for the forensic vocational expert. Dr. Martin previously served as a vocational expert for the Office of Hearings and Appeals, Social Security Administration for 25 years and has provided expert testimony in numerous civil suits involving occupational injury, accidental injury, disability retirement, and issues of product liability involving injury. Dr. Martin's primary research interests have focused on advocacy, leadership, inclusion, and empowerment for persons with disabilities. He has consulted with local, state, and federal agencies as well as with organizations in the private sector. Dr. Martin has been repeatedly recognized for his outstanding leadership and service by the receipt of many awards and commendations from professional, governmental, and private agencies including appointment to significant state boards and councils. He served as a member of both the Statewide Independent Living Council and the State Rehabilitation Council, which he chaired, in Virginia, and currently serves on Alabama's State Rehabilitation Council. Dr. Martin is a licensed professional counselor (Virginia), certified rehabilitation provider (Virginia), certified rehabilitation counselor, and national certified counselor and has attained Diplomate status with the American Board of Vocational Experts.

Second Edition

PRINCIPLES AND PRACTICES OF CASE MANAGEMENT IN REHABILITATION COUNSELING

Edited by

E. DAVIS MARTIN, JR., ED.D., CRC, NCC

Professor of Rehabilitation Counseling
Auburn University

With a Foreword by

PHILIP BROWNING, PH.D.

Wayne T. Smith Distinguished Professor and Head
Department of Rehabilitation and Special Education
Auburn University

CHARLES C THOMAS • PUBLISHER, LTD.
Springfield • Illinois • U.S.A.

Published and Distributed Throughout the World by

CHARLES C THOMAS • PUBLISHER, LTD.
2600 South First Street
Springfield, Illinois 62704

© 2007 by CHARLES C THOMAS • PUBLISHER, LTD.

ISBN 13 978-0-398-07697-9 (hard)   ISBN 10 0-398-07697-9 (hard)
ISBN 13 978-0-398-07698-6 (paper)   ISBN 10 0-398-07698-7 (paper)

Library of Congress Catalog Card Number: 2006045671

With THOMAS BOOKS *careful attention is given to all details of manufacturing
and design. It is the Publisher's desire to present books that are satisfactory as to their
physical qualities and artistic possibilities and appropriate for their particular use.*
THOMAS BOOKS *will be true to those laws of quality that assure a good name
and good will.*

Printed in the United States of America
MM-R-3

Library of Congress Cataloging-in-Publication Data

Principles and practices of case management in rehabilitation counseling / edited
by Ed. Davis Martin, Jr., with a foreword by Philip Browning–2nd ed.
p. cm.
Includes bibliographical references and index.
Contents: Rehabilitation policies and perspectives–Rehabilitation
approaches to case management–Psychosocial case studies.
ISBN 0-398-07697-9 – ISBN 0-398-07698-7 (pbk.)
1. Rehabilitation counseling. 2. Vocational rehabilitation. I. Martin, E.
Davis.

HD7255.5.P75 2007
361'.06–dc22

2006045671

For
my much beloved daughter
Michele Martin Murmer,
a shining light in my life
and
my esteemed students
past and present,
a guiding force in my life

CONTRIBUTORS

Philip Browning, Ph.D.: Dr. Browning received his B.A. degree in psychology from Howard Payne University in Texas and an M.A. degree from Texas Tech University in counseling psychology with a major in rehabilitation. He earned his Ph.D. degree in 1969 in rehabilitation and special education from the University of Wisconsin and then spent the next 21 years at the University of Oregon. He initiated and directed an interdisciplinary doctoral program in rehabilitation, mental retardation, and research that produced 23 Ph.D. graduates. In addition, at different times, he served as both the training and research director for the national Rehabilitation Research and Training Center in Mental Retardation. In 1989, he joined Auburn University as head of the Department of Rehabilitation and Special Education. Since his arrival at Auburn, he has received several honors, including the College of Education's *Outreach Award* (1994) and *Research Award* (2002), Alabama's *Outstanding Special Educator of the Year Award* (1996), and Auburn University's annual *Excellence in Faculty Outreach Award* (2005). In 2000, he co-founded the Auburn Transition Leadership Institute and became its first director. Dr. Browning, who holds a Wayne T. Smith Distinguished Professorship in Education, was honored in 2003 with the National Council on Rehabilitation Education's *Distinguished Career Award in Rehabilitation Education.*

Rebecca S. Curtis, Ph.D., C.R.C.: Dr. Curtis is assistant professor of rehabilitation counseling, Department of

Rehabilitation and Special Education, Auburn University. She formerly was assistant director in the Andrew Young School of Policy Studies at Georgia State University, Rehabilitation Continuing Education Program for Community Rehabilitation Providers for the Rehabilitation Services Administration, Region IV. She has served as an adjunct faculty member for San Diego State University and the University of North Texas in association with the Consortium for Distance Education in Federal Rehabilitation. Dr. Curtis has served with the Rehabilitation Research and Training Center in Learning Disabilities, University of Georgia/Roosevelt Warm Springs Institute for Rehabilitation and has worked as a behavior specialist at Roosevelt Warm Springs Institute for Rehabilitation and as a psychiatric specialty counselor at the University of Pittsburgh Medical Center, Western Psychiatric Institute and Clinic. Dr. Curtis was a Mary Switzer Memorial Scholar, one of twenty persons from the United States chosen for the twenty-third annual Switzer Memorial Seminar, a think tank on issues in vocational rehabilitation. She is a certified rehabilitation counselor.

J. Chad Duncan, M.S., C.P.O., C.R.C.: Mr. Duncan is coordinator of clinical practice and a doctoral student, Department of Rehabilitation and Special Education, Auburn University. Formerly, Mr. Duncan worked in the field of prosthetics and orthotics, where he distinguished himself as client-focused practitioner. His rehabilitation research interests are in assistive technology, distance education technology, life care planning, and crisis management. Mr. Duncan has presented at many national professional conferences on such topics as the O*NET, ethics and supported employment, assistive technology, and distance education as well as prosthetics and orthotics.

Gerald L. Gandy, Ph.D., C.R.C., N.C.C.: Dr. Gandy is emeritus professor of rehabilitation counseling, Department of Rehabilitation Counseling, Virginia Commonwealth University (VCU). Formerly, he was professor,

Department of Rehabilitation Counseling, VCU; president of the faculty, School of Community and Public Affairs, VCU; Director, Rehabilitation Services Education Program, VCU; chief, Counseling and Rehabilitation Services, Veterans Administration Regional Office, Columbia, South Carolina; counselor, University of South Carolina Counseling Center; and captain, United States Army Medical Services Corps. Dr. Gandy has either authored or co-authored/co-edited five major textbooks and contributed numerous articles to the professional literature. He has been active in local, national, and international professional activities and has received various awards and recognition for his service. Dr. Gandy is a licensed professional counselor (Virginia), licensed clinical psychologist (Virginia), certified rehabilitation counselor, and national certified counselor. He is registered with the National Register of Health Service Providers in Psychology and holds the Association of State and Provincial Psychology Boards Certificate of Professional Qualification in Psychology. Dr. Gandy is also a Fellow and Diplomate in Professional Counseling of the International Academy of Behavioral Medicine, Counseling and Psychotherapy.

Richard E. Hardy, Ed.D.: Dr. Hardy is emeritus professor and chair of rehabilitation counseling, Department of Rehabilitation Counseling, Virginia Commonwealth University. Formerly, he was chief psychologist and supervisor of professional training, South Carolina Department of Rehabilitation; rehabilitation advisor with the Rehabilitation Services Administration, Washington, DC; and rehabilitation counselor with the Virginia Commission for the Visually Handicapped. He also served on the South Carolina Board of Examiners of Psychology and taught part-time in the Psychology Department at the University of South Carolina. Dr. Hardy has consulted extensively internationally on mental health and rehabilitation. He has published many books and articles used worldwide, and over 100 reviews of them have been published thus far in professional journals of other countries. Several national organizations have named him a Fellow, and he has received both national and international awards.

George R. Jarrell, Ph.D.: Dr. Jarrell is emeritus professor of rehabilitation counseling, Department of Rehabilitation Counseling, Virginia Commonwealth University (VCU). Formerly, he was professor and coordinator of the Work-Study Program, Department of Rehabilitation Counseling, VCU; assistant dean, School of Community and Public Affairs, VCU; and rehabilitation counselor, South Carolina Department of Vocational Rehabilitation. Dr. Jarrell previously served as vocational expert consultant with the Office of Hearings and Appeals, Social Security Administration. He has written a number of articles on the role of the vocational expert. He is widely known in the legal profession and is frequently asked to lecture on the utilization of vocational experts in personal injury cases. Dr. Jarrell was a licensed professional counselor (Virginia), certified rehabilitation counselor, and national certified counselor.

Karen Rabren, Ph.D.: Dr. Rabren is an associate professor in the Department of Rehabilitation and Special Education and director of the Auburn Transition Leadership Institute, Auburn University. She has devoted most of her career to an area of study known as transition, which focuses on the preparation practices and supports needed for youth and young adults with disabilities. Dr. Rabren's research interests are in postschool outcomes for students with disabilities, secondary curriculum, and transition program development, implementation, and evaluation. Prior to joining Auburn University, Dr. Rabren directed Alabama's five-year systems change grant project in transition. Her university responsibilities include teaching undergraduate and graduate courses in areas of disability, as well as conducting research and training through the Auburn Transition Leadership Institute.

Allison E. Shipp, M.B.A., M.Ed., C.R.C., A.T.P.: Ms. Shipp is assistive technology associate, Program for Students with Disabilities, Auburn University, and doctoral student, Department of Rehabilitation and Special Education, Auburn University. Ms. Shipp coordinates the alternate format services for the Program for Students with Disabilities. She reviews documentation to determine eligibility, supervises workers in the Assistive Technology Lab, and trains college students with disabilities to use assistive technology. Ms. Shipp travels extensively, providing training to other postsecondary disability support services on topics such as accessible Web design, electronic text production, making distance education accessible, producing Nemeth Braille and tactile images, and developing accessible electronic training materials. Ms. Shipp also conducts assistive technology assessments and consultations for primary and secondary school systems.

Larry L. Sinsabaugh, Ph.D., C.R.C.: Dr. Sinsabaugh is chief executive officer of Sinsabaugh Consulting Services, PC, specializing in private sector rehabilitation and forensic practice. Dr. Sinsabaugh has extensive rehabilitation counseling experience in both state (Virginia, Maryland, North Carolina, West Virginia, and Ohio) and federal (Veterans Administration and Department of Labor) rehabilitation programs. He served for many years as an adjunct faculty member, teaching career development, occupational analysis, and placement courses in the Department of Rehabilitation Counseling, Virginia Commonwealth University; and has previously served in various managerial positions in the private sector of rehabilitation. He currently serves as associate editor of the *Journal of Forensic Vocational Analysis,* a leading journal for the forensic vocational practitioner. Dr. Sinsabaugh is member of the board of directors for the American Board of Vocational Experts, where his service has been acknowledged with the receipt of the President's Award twice. He has previously been awarded the Outstanding Rehabilitation Counselor Award from the Virginia Rehabilitation Counseling Association. In addition to Dr. Sinsabaugh's forensic practice, he is an adjunct professor with Bluefield College, and Central Michigan University. Dr. Sinsabaugh is a Licensed Professional Counselor (North Carolina, Virginia, and West Virginia), and a certified professional counselor (Maryland), certified rehabilitation counselor, national certified counselor, certified disability management specialist, certified case manager, and certified employee assistance professional. He has attained Diplomate status with the American Board of Vocational Experts.

Keith C. Wright, M.S.: Mr. Wright is emeritus professor of rehabilitation counseling, Department of Rehabilitation Counseling, Virginia Commonwealth University (VCU). Formerly, he was professor, Department of Rehabilitation Counseling, VCU; research analyst, West Virginia Division of Vocational Rehabilitation; and counselor and research analyst with the United States Public Health Service. Professor Wright served for many years as chair of the Board of Professional Counselors for the Virginia Department of Health Regulatory Boards. He also served as president of the Virginia Rehabilitation Association, president of the Virginia Easter Seals Society, and president of the Faculty of the School of Community and Public Affairs at VCU. He has received many awards and honors for his distinguished community service. Professor Wright has contributed numerous articles and book chapters on a variety of topics to the rehabilitation literature. He previously was a licensed professional counselor (Virginia), certified rehabilitation counselor, and national certified counselor.

FOREWORD

Chapter 1 of this book is properly placed, for it provides the learner with an important foundation for the remainder of the text. Its substance lies in an assemblage of landmark legislation that now assures people with disabilities of their human and civil rights as *abled citizens*. In addition to presenting the infrastructure for civil rights, the chapter also reflects a philosophical and best practices framework that serves as a standard and guideline throughout the book. What follows in this foreword is a historical backdrop to this chapter. Subsequent attention is devoted to the following chapters in their order of appearance.

The lives of people with disabilities have been dramatically affected over the past forty-plus years, a time span that parallels this country's unfolding journey toward human and social change. Joining in this awakening were movements of society at large, including civil rights, the consumers' marketplace, equal rights for women, and social welfare reform. Civil rights for people with disabilities, which did not take hold until the 1970s, was preceded by the Civil Rights and Voting Rights Acts in the 1960s. African-Americans marched on Washington in 1963, the Poor People March on Washington occurred in 1968, and four years later people with disabilities traveled the same route for the same reason. And, that same year, women were given equality of rights under the law. These reforming crusades advocated many dramatic changes for racial minorities, women, the poor, and people with disabilities. A window to this period of social enlightenment is captured by such slogans as *Nader's Raiders, Citizen Participation, We Shall Overcome, I Have a Dream,* and *The Times They Are A' Changin'.*

The year 1970 was a significant year for people with disabilities in that the Developmental Disabilities Act was signed into law and, five years hence, became the "bill of rights" for their integration into our communities. This national declaration set in motion the dismantling of our institutions while building for these individuals a foundation for normalization. Alongside this was the Rehabilitation Act of 1973 that provided them, including those with *severe* limitations, many employment services and civil rights mandates. Within the same time frame, the passage of the All Handicapped Children Act would permanently change this country's educational philosophy, programs, and practices for students with disabilities. The year 1990 was yet another dramatic year in that an amendment to the earlier education act, now known as the Individuals with Disabilities Education Act, provided all students with disabilities equal educational opportunities and the most appropriate services in an inclusive setting with students without disabilities. A final cornerstone was laid that same year with the passage of the Americans with Disabilities Act, which extended the federal civil rights laws that apply to women and minorities to all Americans with disabilities. In the words of President George H. W. Bush, who signed the Act on July 26, 1990, ". . . every man, woman and child with a disability can now pass through once closed doors into a bright new era of equality, independence and freedom." In summary, these five legislative landmarks ensured people with disabilities of the rights and opportunities entitled to all U.S. citizens. They provided a foundation of permanent social change by safeguarding rights to education, to the workplace, and to the community.

Since the 1960s, one essential change that has emerged for people with disabilities is their assimilation into a world ever more welcoming to diversity. While their integration into our schools, the work force, and communities has been borne out of larger social influences, their inclusion in American life has been spearheaded by the enactment of the above legislation. A congressional sponsor noted, for example, that the Americans with Disabilities Act was their "emancipation proclamation." The 1992 Rehabilitation Act underscores this claim by inscribing Independent Living to "maximize the leadership, empowerment, independence, and productivity of individuals with disabilities, and the integration and full inclusion of individuals with disabilities, into the mainstream of American society" (Rehabilitation Act, 1992 amendments, PL 102-569). Chapter 1 provides a framework that underlies the concepts and practices of integrated residential living, mainstreaming in education, inclusion in the work force, and independent living in the community. Clearly, the assimilation of people with disabilities into society's mainstream is a philosophy that navigates contemporary practice.

Related to assimilation is the person-centered concept that grew out of this nation's consumer movement and is now embedded in the cited legislation. In the 1960s, people in all walks of American life began to express and organize their rights as consumers. Buyers in the marketplace, for example, led to Nader's Raiders, recipients of social services led to the National Welfare Rights Organization, and those with disabilities led to the founding of the American Coalition of Citizens with Disabilities. This crusade of social reform manifested a climate of consumer assertion of special interests, rights, and citizenship for groups facing discrimination. Growing out of these consumer crusades led by racial minorities, the poor, women, and people with disabilities inspired person-centered slogans such as *Power to the People, Citizen's Advocacy, Women's Lib,* and *People First.*

Legislative safeguards for individual rights and opportunities, coupled with the consumerism movements, have resulted in persons with disabilities increasingly asserting their rights and becoming self-advocates for their own interests. Central to this self-directed principle is the concept and practice of choice-making. For too long, consumer-choice, self-determination, and self-advocacy were absent from our thinking and practice. The field in its earlier years, and society for that matter, operated primarily on a deviancy model that highlighted the "limitations" of people with disabilities. The significance of this practice is especially telling when we referred to persons with severe cognitive impairments as individuals who were not capable of even making a decision, much less the right one! As an alternative to the definition of functional limitations, a sociopolitical definition of disability has now entered the professional scene. Disability, from this vantage point, is not a personal defect or deficiency but instead is a product of a disabled environment such as attitudes, lack of opportunities, and environmental constraints.

Rightfully so, we continue to move from viewing people with disabilities as being passive recipients of services to that of active participants who are capable of making their own choices, and mapping-out and steering their own future. Parent's (1993) words tell it all:

> . . . consumers should have the opportunity to choose their jobs, the
> places they would like to live, the activities in which they would like to

participate, the community environments they would like to access, and the friends they would like to have, as well as the opportunity to alter their decisions as preferences, needs, and desires change. Having the ability to control the direction and outcomes in one's life is a critical factor in achieving personal satisfaction and quality of life. (p. 36)

These are indeed self-empowering experiences that greatly enhance one's level of human pride and sense of self-worth. They are experiences that help people with disabilities become the masters of their own lives. The significance is far reaching. Not only is it right for one to have control over one's own choice-making, but research shows that individuals (with disabilities or without) tend to participate more and experience greater benefit from those happenings in which they can experience choice and control over their outcomes.

The 1980s and 1990s (and beyond) can be partly characterized by the host of best practices that began to be articulated. The identification and proclamation of these practices are due largely to three inter-related factors—societal values, legislation, and the profession. Legislation reflects society's values; the profession is influenced by it; and, in turn, the profession—through its philosophy, research, and clinical practice—provides a basis for legislative policy change. The best practices presented in this book are considered contemporary in that they are based on a growing body of knowledge in rehabilitation and are in congruence with societal, professional, and legislative values. A sample of the best practices that are intertwined in the cited legislation, and are articulated (or implied) throughout the book, are advocacy, consumer involvement, consumer choice, empowerment, self-determination, individualized plans, independent living, community integration, competitive employment, collaborative services, to name a few. I consider these to be some of the more important principles and practices upon which this book (and the profession) is based. It is within the context of these introductory remarks that I will now briefly speak to each of the chapters.

Chapter 2 is a much-welcome addition to the book's second edition. Both education and rehabilitation legislation recognize the nature and importance of the transition-age group, which represents some 2 million students with disabilities between the ages of 14 and 22. In 1984, Madeleine Will, then assistant secretary of the U.S. Department of Education, set in congressional motion transition from school-to-work as a national priority. While in office, she wrote the "bridges model," in which she identified three optional bridges for the successful crossing from school to adult roles. Of these, Bridge Two requires "time-limited services" that lead to eventual employment, and partners rehabilitation counseling services with the educational system. Interestingly, the idea for this partnership is over forty years old. In the 1962 National Action to Combat Mental Retardation Report prepared for President John F. Kennedy, one of the recommendations was: "It is clear that the first line of attack is through the educational system, and that vocational rehabilitation for the mentally retarded must be coordinated with our secondary education system" (p. 125). Rehabilitation must have a partnership role with education to provide time-limited services to assist many of our nation's youth with disabilities in becoming responsible and productive citizens.

The living words presented in Chapter 3 underscore the human pain and suffering that can be associated with disabilities. Free of professional jargon, technical writing, literature citations, and research statistics, the stories constitute a clear and emotional understanding of what it means to have a disability. With that acknowledgment, I wish to make three points. First, we must be careful not to totally excuse ourselves from their states of helplessness and powerlessness. In other words, such reactions experienced by them not only may be due to the physical and psychological limitations or impairments resulting from the disability itself but also may be aided by external sources such as service providers, social institutions, and society at large. Second, as consumers, we must view them as our allies, not only as consumers and clients. We must allow them to be partners in the rehabilitation mission. We have much to learn from them; they have much to teach us. And finally, let us be reminded that, in addition to hardship tales, there are also literally thousands of triumphant stories of how individuals have captured the American Dream. And herein lays the mission of rehabilitation.

I suspect that the readers of this book are rehabilitation counselors in-the-making. Therefore, they should find Chapter 4 to be especially germane to their career aspirations. While counselors are at the heart of the rehabilitation profession, it is important to note that they represent more than just service providers who simply assist people with disabilities to enter, or re-enter, the world of work. In essence, they manifest a belief in the spirit of the human being, a value in their independence, and a commitment to the ideals of inclusion in all walks of life. While best practices are the tools to be applied in our rehabilitation practice, best values should serve as a decision-making foundation for their application as discussed in Chapter 7. The values of *independence* (having choice and control of one's life), *productivity* (working in the primary labor market), and *inclusion* (to live, work, and play in one's community of choice) drive the ideals of rehabilitation counseling and that of its practitioners. It is through this legislative, philosophical, and best practices window that the counselor must be prepared to assist persons with disabilities toward a more complete and satisfying life. The counseling itself is expressed in the dialogue between the client and counselor, in the trust that emerges from the relationship formed between the rehabilitation counselor and client, and in the nonintrusive manner in which men, women, and youth learn to become independent, self-sustaining members of our American democratic society.

Over the past thirty years, functional assessment has emerged as a best practice in which information is obtained for developing, designing, implementing, and evaluating specific interventions for the individual. By contrast, traditional assessment is often agency-oriented (e.g., disability diagnosis, service eligibility, classification, record keeping). Traditional assessment typically uses norm-based, psychometric tests that compare a person's test performance to the test performance of his or her peers. It relies on the individual's prior learning. Unfortunately, persons with developmental disabilities who are subjected to this "prior learning" assessment are uniquely vulnerable to inappropriate judgments because, by definition, they are deficient in their background, knowledge, and experience. Also, for people with severe cognitive disabilities, standard low scores most often prove to be rather redundant for what we already know about their performance level. Functional assessment, which relies on an array of less formal measurement tools such as self-reports, observational checklists, and situational assessments, addresses the individual's current learning. A typical functional assessment standard is the criterion-based measure that assesses the performance in terms of what and how well the individual learns, without comparison to the norm standard of others. The rehabilitation agency's traditional assessment practice has been to determine vocational capability and then attempt to predict success (or failure) in the work setting, often using standard norms. Instead of attempting to predict one's potential for work, or to use standard scores to underserve (or exclude) persons, especially those with significant disability, from programs and services, assessment concerns should direct the focus toward intervention strategies needed for the individual to achieve the goal of employment. In this regard, assessment as a best practice in rehabilitation hás expanded from being agency-oriented to person-oriented.

The purpose of employing best practices in rehabilitation is to ensure that clients with disabilities will be well prepared and enabled to independently and successfully meet the demands of their needs and preferences, especially in the occupational world. In addition to best practices, however, *best values* also should be considered for their potential effect on the client's outcomes. Thus, where best practices are the tools to be applied in our rehabilitation trade, best values should serve as a decision-making foundation for their application. In other words, just as the rehabilitation counselor must be equipped with a set of professional attributes (e.g., best practices), he or she should also possess a set of personal attributes as they pertain to a philosophy, the values inherent in that philosophy, and a commitment to those values. It would be one thing for the counselor simply to solicit the client's interests in developing the individualized work plan because it is legislatively required. It is quite another, however, when the counselor is committed to the value of consumer empowerment and therefore truly believes that the *Plan* must come from, and belong, to the client. I say commitment because one's philosophy and values are not enough in and of themselves. There must be a commitment to what one believes for, in its absence, a claimed philosophy and its related values are limited, at best. Finally, values can serve as standards that guide and significantly influence the entire rehabilitation service delivery process, including the formulation of objectives, the search for alternatives, and the choices among them. Through the process of value identification and clarification, rehabilitation counselors will make their decisions among alternatives in current modes of practice and choose which rehabilitation path to travel in order to reach the goals for which his or her clients strive. The phrase "to travel" is significant because a value is not just a matter of what one believes to be desirable but also entails what he or she does about that belief. As such, a commitment to a value requires a prescriptive action that leads toward some desired goal, such as a client's desire to positively affect his or her quality of life through the world of work.

The importance of facilitating entry into the primary labor market should not be underestimated, nor should the fruits of participation in the primary labor market be diminished; that is, employment that has a career ladder, which progresses in terms of emoluments and benefits, helps to pave the way to the American Dream. I will never forget when I first met a young man who was the co-author of a best selling book entitled *Count Us In: Growing Up with Downs Syndrome.* I invited him as the keynote speaker for an annual conference and had prepared for his arrival by reading his book and becoming familiar with his portfolio. Even though he had an impressive work record, the number of jobs he had held caught my attention since he had done so well in each. In the course of our becoming acquainted, I asked him why he had elected to leave so many jobs, given that he was successful in each preceding one. Without pause, he informed me that these were not just "jobs" he had held. Rather, they served as important vocational experiences that in turn allowed him to develop a career. "Dr. Browning," he said, "where I worked was more than just a job." To paraphrase our continued conversation, his work experiences in multiple settings were stepping stones to his career-in-the-making. Through my restrictive lens I saw a job and disability; through his expansive lens he saw a career and pride! I will always be grateful to Levitz for teaching me so much on that day. I embarrassingly learned what I should have known already, that his vocational hopes and aspirations were no different than mine and yours and those of most all other people.

Parts 1 and 2 provide the learner with a person-centered philosophy and substantial knowledge base in case management, whereas the opportunity to begin applying this comprehensive foundation is presented in Part 3. By analyzing the thirteen psychosocial case studies, the learner will be challenged to examine his or her philosophy and identify and clarify the values derived from that philosophy, better understand the social and psychological concepts in rehabilitation practice, and get in closer touch with the meaning and importance of "best practices" and "best values" in case management. Representing an array of physical, mental, cognitive, and sensory disability conditions, these cases will require the application of a wide array of information, ranging from medical to psychological, from counseling to occupational analysis and career planning, and from job development to job placement, with disability rights serving as the common thread throughout.

Undertaking this final section will prove to be the most exciting, yet difficult and challenging, part of the book. Exciting, in that it will provide the learner with a simulated experience in professionally serving people with disabilities, and what a rewarding experience that should prove to be. Difficult, in that it will require the learner to engage in a critical decision-making process as he or she identifies and interprets the necessary parts to be assembled and integrated into the case management portfolio. And, challenging, in that the goal will be to facilitate each individual in achieving full utilization of his or her potential and to advocate on his or her behalf the fair and equal opportunities necessary to live a productive, responsible, and satisfying life in the mainstream of America.

PHILIP BROWNING, PH.D.
Wayne T. Smith Distinguished Professor and
Head Department of Rehabilitation and Special Education
Auburn University

REFERENCES

Parent, W. S. (1993). Quality of life and consumer choice. In P. Wehman (Ed.), *The ADA mandate for social change* (pp. 19–44), Baltimore: Paul H. Brookes.

Report to the President. (1962). *A proposed program for national action to combat mental retardation.* Washington, DC: The President's Panel on Mental Retardation. Author.

PREFACE

This edition of the text represents a major revision and update of *Rehabilitation and Disability: Psychosocial Case Studies* originally published in 1990. Similarly, the purpose of this edition of the text is to provide a realistic perspective of the role and function of the rehabilitation counselor relative to the utilization of effective principles and practices of case management from the vantage point of the vocational rehabilitation process. The text has been written and designed so multiple aspects of the vocational rehabilitation process may be examined, and differing paradigms of intervention can be applied for the benefit of recipients of these services. While this text has been developed principally for use in graduate rehabilitation counseling programs, it has great utility for in-service or short-term training programs and may be employed in related psychological and social service educational programs where an understanding of the vocational rehabilitation process may be facilitated from a client centered perspective. The benefit for such professionals is an in-depth knowledge of the vocational rehabilitation process, where such knowledge and understanding have the capacity to yield great benefits relative to referral and advocacy for persons with disabilities to the state-federal program of vocational rehabilitation. The ultimate goal of the vocational rehabilitation process for persons with disabilities is the opportunity to access the American Dream; that is, to live, work, and play in the community of their choice. A unifying theme in each case study presented is to emphasize the holistic nature of people.

The new *Principles and Practices of Case Management in Rehabilitation Counseling* contains some material from the previous edition, although new material regarding the vocational rehabilitation process is reflected in the various chapters in Parts 1 and 2 of the text relative to transition, adaptation to disability, vocational evaluation, assistive technology, and ethics. Within this edition, the reader will find significant updating of original material and expansion and reorganization of material related to service priority and legislation, the rehabilitation process, and career and occupational information. Part 3 of the text contains thirteen case situations, although not exhaustive of all disabilities, they are, however, representative of major disabilities. The case studies in this section of the text are composites of various individuals representing reality concerning the challenging circumstances that people with disabilities, family members, and others close to the person with a disability confront daily.

An outstanding group of contributors were selected to co-author or to author the various chapters, providing an added dimension of excellence to the finished manuscript. These contributors have achieved a balance in their academic training, professional experience, community service, publications, and credentialed status ranging from a lifetime of service to those in the beginning stages of their careers. Their collective achievements have included agency-executive leadership, university professorships, state, national, and international committee and consultative activities, extensive publications in the form of books, refereed articles, and other media. These talented and giving persons represent a blending of mentors, colleagues, and students, all who have given their time, energy, and commitment for the development of educational and rehabilitative systems that provide *equality of opportunity* for persons with disabilities. These are persons who live and reflect the values of *independence, productivity,* and *inclusion* for all people.

A special debt of gratitude is extended to my former colleagues in the Department of Rehabilitation Counseling at Virginia Commonwealth University, who initially assisted Professor Jerry Gandy and me in the development of the original case management text. This influence remains an integral part of this second edition. Professors Keith Wright, George Jarrell, and Warren Rule deserve particular recognition and appreciation for so generously giving their time, expertness, and commitment to the ideal of rehabilitation counseling that not only is reflected in this text but resides in all those persons who studied with these masters. Professor Gandy belongs in this elite group of professional colleagues; he is, as well, a master teacher, superb colleague, and great friend. Professor Dick Hardy, chairman of the Department of Rehabilitation Counseling for more than twenty-five years, who continuously provided emotional and financial support as well as sound advice and counsel to all of the above-noted persons in the development of this and many other writing projects, deserves special recognition and appreciation for his superb leadership. Dr. Hardy is a master teacher, an ideal colleague, and leader.

Professor Jerry Gandy was the coauthor of the original text, *Rehabilitation and Disability: Psychosocial Case Studies,* and while choosing not to continue in the role of co-author for this edition, is, nevertheless, a prime collaborator and contributor to the development of the thirteen cases presented in Part 3 of the text. Dr. Gandy and I believe that an important aspect of the professional content of the assessments for each case is the nature of the information that provokes the types of discussion questions identified at the end of each case study. In some instances, this information may be sufficient and relevant to the resolution of the case; in other situations, the discussion questions help to suggest additional information or other interpretations that may be needed to contribute to an improved rehabilitation outcome. In prefatory material in this section of the text, instructions and a structure are provided that will facilitate case resolution.

Dr. Larry L. Sinsabaugh deserves recognition as a talented academic and professional colleague, former doctoral student, former employer, and great friend who has taught me much about career and occupational information. As a prominent private sector rehabilitation practitioner, his thoughts regarding the rehabilitation process are tempered from the perspective of the public sector, private sector, and the nonprofit private sector that have resulted in a particularly insightful commentary regarding the practice of rehabilitation counseling. He, too, is a master teacher and superb colleague.

Special recognition and appreciation are extended to my colleagues at Auburn University, particularly to Dr. Phil Browning, Wayne T. Smith Distinguished Professor and head of the Department of Rehabilitation and Special Education, for his support of this project and his insightful foreword, and especially to Dr. Becky Curtis, Dr. Karen Rabren, Ms. Allison Shipp, and Mr. Chad Duncan for their participation and involvement in the development of this edition of the text. Drs. Rabren and Curtis' chapter on the partnership between special education and vocational rehabilitation regarding the transition of youth with disabilities from the secondary school system is particularly relevant and timely given the emphasis placed on this group within current federal legislation. Dr. Curtis provides an insightful perspective on the nature of values in the chapter on ethics she coauthored. Ms. Shipp provides a very useful and insightful perspective on assistive technology in the chapter focusing on disability assessment. Ms. Shipp and Mr. Duncan each provide a narrative approach to case resolution and a sample case resolution that are highly instructive and illustrative for use by readers and students.

I am grateful to all of my students, at both Auburn University and Virginia Commonwealth University, who, over the years, have taken the case management course and persevered in the development of realistic case resolutions that allowed entry or approximation to the primary labor market and, more importantly, for the persons they have served to this end in the state-federal vocational rehabilitation program and elsewhere–kudos to each and everyone, for you bring reality to the ideal of vocational rehabilitation and to our profession of rehabilitation counseling.

I am especially indebted to Ms. Altamese Stroud-Hill for her knowledge of APA style, and her usual thoroughness, good humor, and word processing ability in formatting the final manuscript for transmission to the publisher, Charles C Thomas. Similarly, appreciation is extended to the Learning Resources Center within the College of Education at Auburn University and to Dr. Susan Bannon, the director of this unit, for the provision of this service to faculty members of the college.

Finally, a special tribute of gratitude is extended to my wife and children, Ruth, Richard, Michele, and Matthew, for their support and assistance throughout each phase of writing and editing of the manuscript and for their enduring patience–four persons who make my life especially meaningful and fulfilling.

War Eagle!

E. Davis Martin, Jr.
Auburn, Alabama

CONTENTS

PART 3:
PSYCHOSOCIAL CASE STUDIES
E. Davis Martin, Jr. and Gerald L. Gandy

PRINCIPLES AND PRACTICES OF CASE MANAGEMENT IN REHABILITATION COUNSELING

PART 1

REHABILITATION POLICIES
AND PERSPECTIVES

Chapter 1

DISABILITY IN AMERICA: ISSUES, SERVICE PRIORITY, AND LEGISLATIVE RESPONSE

E. DAVIS MARTIN, JR.

D isabilities that are regarded as significant have been given increasingly greater emphasis since the passage of the historic 1973
Rehabilitation Act and, in fact, selection priority in the delivery of
vocational rehabilitation services. The Rehabilitation Act amendments
in 1992 and 1998 have continued and expanded this mandated priority. Programs and activities created by these legislative events have
moved the delivery systems toward a client or consumer perspective
with greater control vested in the person with a disability regarding
choice. The Americans with Disabilities Act (ADA), for instance, mandated that educators, employers, businesses, and governmental agencies were to provide goods and services to persons with disabilities
from a posture of anti-discrimination. The major difference articulated
in the ADA when compared to Section 504 of the 1973 Rehabilitation
Act is its effect on the private sector of the economy. Similarly, the
education of children and youth with disabilities has moved from seg-
regated self-contained classrooms to mainstreaming to full inclusion
through passage of P.L. 94–142 to the now entitled Individuals with
Disabilities Education Improvement Act (IDEA 2004). IDEA 2004,
for example, calls for greater coordination in the transition of youth
with disabilities from secondary schools to that of further education or
work through a partnership with vocational rehabilitation for those
students who meet the vocational rehabilitation agency's eligibility cri-

teria (note Chapter 2 for a detailed discussion of transition programming and vocational rehabilitation).

The purpose of this chapter will be to review the historic legislative events that originated during the 1970s, most notably the 1973 Rehabilitation Act and its subsequent amendments, denoting the changes over the course of the past three decades. The human service delivery systems, principally the vocational rehabilitation program and the public educational systems that were mandated to provide services as a result of these legislative events, will be analyzed from the perspective of the consumer of those services. The decade of the 1970s produced three of the most significant legislative accomplishments of the twentieth century: the Developmental Disabilities Services and Facilities Construction Act (P.L. 91–517), the Rehabilitation Act of 1973 (P.L. 93–112); and the Education for All Handicapped Children Act (P.L. 94–142). Each of these legislative events and subsequent amendments continuing to the present represented a paradigm shift that signaled an increased voice and influence for persons with disabilities regarding vocational, educational, and independent living choices.

Developmental Disabilities Legislation

With the passage of P.L. 91–517, the Developmental Disabilities Services and Construction Act of 1970, the term *developmental disability* first came into use (Kiernan & Schalock, 1995). The term *developmental disability* was defined to include the following specific disabilities: mental retardation, epilepsy, and cerebral palsy. Onset of the developmental disability was to have occurred at birth, or prior to age eighteen, and have imposed severe limitation in the child's or person's ability to function. The act established a formula grant program in which the states were encouraged to develop coordinated services for persons labeled as having a developmental disability. Braddock, Hemp, Parish, and Westrich (1998) noted that the ". . . states were required to establish interagency councils representing numerous state government agencies relevant to the delivery of developmental disabilities services . . . [that would develop] . . . every three years . . . formal state plans to set goals and improve the delivery of services" (p. 7).

In 1975, amendments to the Developmental Disabilities Services and Construction Act re-titled the act as the Developmental Disabilities Assistance and Bill of Rights Act (P.L. 94–103). Categorical groupings of disabilities were maintained and the disabilities of autism and dyslexia (with some qualifications) were added. The 1975 amendments also specified essential services that should be available as basic rights to persons defined as having a developmental disability. Those services specified, among others, were residential services, employment services, treatment, transportation, and leisure services. These services were considered to be basic rights. These amendments were greatly influenced by ". . . a series of class-action law suits in which the courts ruled that the mentally retarded [*sic*] in institutions had constitutional rights to treatment, services, and habilitation that 'maximize the developmental potential of the person and are provided in the setting that is least restrictive of the person's personal liberty'" (Berkowitz, 1987, p. 207). Most notable of these class-action suits were *Wyatt v. Stickney* (344 F. Supp. 378, M.D., Alabama, 1972) and *New York State ARC v. Rockefeller* (357 F. Supp. 752, 1973), often referred to as the *Willowbrook* case.

The 1978 amendments, now titled as the Rehabilitation, Comprehensive Services, and Developmental Disabilities Act (P.L. 95–602), broadened the definition of developmental disability from the existing categorical basis to a functional basis; that is, a definition that no longer specifically denoted a particular mental or physical condition, e.g., mental retardation and epilepsy, but a chronic and lifelong mental or physical condition that impeded substantial functional limitations in the performance of major life activities. Of the seven characterized major life activities, at least three must present substantial limitations to the person:

1. Self-care
2. Receptive and expressive language
3. Learning
4. Mobility
5. Self-direction
6. Capacity for independent living
7. Economic self-sufficiency

Braddock et al. (1998) moreover, reported that the 1978 amendments established the Protection and Advocacy Program ". . . thus completing the triad of Developmental Disabilities Act funded organ izations: university affiliated programs (UAPs), state planning councils, and advocacy agencies" (p. 7).

The 1973 Rehabilitation Act and Amendments

The passage of the 1973 Rehabilitation Act (P.L. 93–112) was, perhaps, one of the most significant events of the twentieth century; in particular, the effect and impact that Section 504 would have upon American society and for the rights of persons with disabilities. The major focus of the 1973 Rehabilitation Act dealt with equality of opportunity through provisions relating to (a) consumer involvement, (b) emphasis on persons with severe disabilities, (c) creation of the now-named National Institute on Disability and Rehabilitation Research (NIDRR), (d) emphasis on program evaluation, and (e) the advancement of the civil rights of persons with disabilities. The 1973 Rehabilitation Act represented a mandate to serve persons with severe disabilities.

Emphasis on Persons with Severe Disabilities

While the emphasis was to serve persons with severe disabilities, the creation of independent living rehabilitation options in the 1973 Rehabilitation Act was omitted, in large part, because President Nixon had vetoed two previous rehabilitation bills in 1972 that contained a provision related to independent living (Rubin & Roessler, 2001). The Nixon administration, as noted by Rubin and Roessler (2001), ". . . did, however, agree to a compromise–a Comprehensive Needs Study (CNS; Section 130 of the Act) to determine the rehabilitation needs of individuals who 'cannot reasonably be expected to be rehabilitated for employment but for whom a program of rehabilitation would improve their ability to live independently or function normally within their family and community'" (p. 46). It would not be until the 1978 amendments that the independent living rehabilitation program would be authorized.

Title VII of the 1978 amendments contained three parts that provided the basis for independent living rehabilitation options:

- *Part A*–authorized comprehensive services that would enhance the person's ability to function in employment or the home.
- *Part B*–authorized grants for the establishment of centers for inde-

pendent living that would provide a wide range of services inclusive of peer counseling, independent living skills, assistance with housing and transportation, and personal assistance services.
- *Part C*–authorized independent living services to older blind persons.

DeJong (1979) stated that for the first time in more than fifty years professional rehabilitation leaders were joined in these efforts by an increasingly visible and effective leadership from people with disabilities. People with severe disabilities were representing a growing and vigorous constituency: a most assertive and, at times, a more militant group who were insistent on change.

In addition to independent living services, the 1978 amendments authorized the creation of a grant program to serve American Indian tribes on reservations, the establishment of the now-named National Council on Disability, Rehabilitation Research and Training Centers, the Helen Keller Center for Deaf-Blind Youths and Adults, and Comprehensive Rehabilitation Centers.

Consumer Involvement

The essence of the rehabilitation process is the relationship between the counselor and the client. The 1973 Rehabilitation Act stressed the nature of this relationship as one of joint involvement and responsibility that should pervade the rehabilitation process from beginning to closure. Throughout the process, the consumer or client was to be informed of decisions that may have an impact (that may be perceived by the client as adverse) and given an opportunity to appeal those decisions. Eligibility, for example, was one area that may be subject to disagreement. Initially, no formal or organized programs were available to assist clients who questioned the decisions of counselors or supervisors. Client assistance projects were first authorized in the 1978 amendments, and ultimately client assistance projects would be required for each state in order to ensure due process (the 1984 amendments).

The Individual Written Rehabilitation Program (IWRP) represented a real opportunity for the client and counselor to mutually plan a sequence of services that would enable the client to enter into employment. The basic intent of this planning process was the mutual involvement and subsequently joint formulation of a rehabilitation program that would have the capability to change the client's (and his or her family's) life. Such a momentous event required nothing less than mutual respect and involvement in decision-making.

Subsequent amendments to the 1973 Rehabilitation Act in 1978 and 1984 created the National Council on the Handicapped in 1978 and six years later renamed the National Council on Disability in 1984. This fifteen-person council, appointed by the president of the United States and confirmed by the United States Senate, is an independent federal agency whose overall purpose is ". . . to promote the policies, programs, practices, and procedures that guarantee equal opportunity for all individuals with disabilities, regardless of the nature of the severity of the disability; and to empower individuals with disabilities to achieve economic self-sufficiency, independent living, and inclusion and integration into all aspects of society" (National Council on Disability, 1996, p. 187). This council represents, perhaps, the zenith in consumer involvement from a policy perspective.

Creation of the National Institute on Disability and Rehabilitation Research

The 1973 Rehabilitation Act provided for the continued funding of innovation and expansion grants, rehabilitation research and training centers, and other types of demonstration grants. The 1978 amendments established as well the, then named, National Institute of Handicapped Research. Rubin and Roessler (2001) noted that the National Institute of Handicapped Research ". . . was established to direct the research thrust in rehabilitation, particularly that of the Rehabilitation Research and Training Centers . . ." (p. 51) and to:

(a) disseminate information on ways to increase the quality of life of individuals with disabilities;
(b) educate the public about ways of providing for the rehabilitation of individuals with disabilities;
(c) conduct conferences concerning research and engineering advances in rehabilitation; and
(d) produce and disseminate statistical reports and studies on the employment, health, and income of individuals with disabilities (p. 51).

Emphasis on Program Evaluation

Meaningful consumer involvement in the rehabilitation process also required that the outcomes of that process be assessed. Program evaluation to be undertaken by state agencies, as noted by Rubin and Roessler (2001), ". . . meant that state rehabilitation agencies would be held accountable for providing information on

(a) the percentage of the existing target population being served,
(b) the timeliness and adequacy of their services,
(c) the suitability of the employment in which clients are placed and the sustention of that employment, and
(d) client satisfaction with rehabilitation services" (p. 50).

Needs assessments occurring on a three-year cycle (CFR 361.29) and client/consumer satisfaction surveys are now a defined component of the state rehabilitation agency. For each state-federal vocational rehabilitation agency, the State Rehabilitation Council (created by the 1992 Rehabilitation Act amendments) monitors this process.

Advancement of the Civil Rights of Persons with Disabilities

Sections 501, 502, 503, and 504 of Title V of the 1973 Rehabilitation Act addressed the following areas of concern, respectively: nondiscriminatory federal hiring (501), accessibility (creation of the Architectural and Transportation Barriers Compliance Board) (502), affirmative action (503), and prohibition of discrimination against persons with disabilities in terms of programmatic and physical accessibility in schools and institutions of higher education, hospitals, and other institutions that receive federal financial assistance (504).

Increased awareness of persons with disabilities and of the environmental and attitudinal barriers encountered by persons with disabilities is generally credited as a major impetus for the passage of the 1973 Rehabilitation Act, and the subsequent 1978 amendments. These legislative events signaled a change in public policy patterned largely after the Civil Rights Act. No longer were employers, or potential employers, asked on the basis of moral grounds to hire persons with a disability, but rather to take affirmative action in hiring as well as to assuming a posture of nondiscrimination. Admission to schools and institutions of higher education, likewise, was addressed by Section

504 of Title V. This section noted:

> No otherwise qualified handicapped [*sic*] individual in the United States, as defined in section 7 (7), shall, solely by reason of his handicap [*sic*], be excluded from the participation in, be denied the benefits of or be subjected to discrimination under any program or activity receiving Federal financial assistance or under any program or activity conducted by any Executive agency or by the United States Postal Service.

Section 504 was originally envisioned as an anti-discrimination provision that would have more impact as a symbolic statement and not necessarily as a mandate (Percy, 1989). Blanck, Hill, Siegal, and Waterstone have noted that Section 504 was "the first explicit Congressional statement recognizing 'discrimination' against people with disabilities" (2004, p. 1:9). The origins of 504, as noted by Percy (1989), can be:

> . . . traced to Senator Hubert Humphrey and Representative Charles Vanik, who introduced bills in Congress to amend the Civil Rights Act to include protections for persons with disabilities. While this strategy produced little result, it set the groundwork for Section 504 to be included, quietly and without fanfare, in the Rehabilitation Act as the legislation was being marked up by staff members from the Senate Committee on Labor and Public Welfare and the House Committee on Education and Labor. (pp. 225–226)

Senator Humphrey's advocacy for what ultimately became Section 504 stemmed, in part, from his experiences as a grandparent of a child with a disability.

Another powerful reason for inclusion of Section 504 in the 1973 Rehabilitation Act, as noted by Scotch (1984) and reported in Percy (1989), was:

> Staff members were concerned that, when disabled [*sic*] individuals completed their training in the VR [vocational rehabilitation] system and were ready to enter the workplace, many employers appeared reluctant to hire them. Staff members felt the final goal of the VR program, getting disabled [*sic*] people into the mainstream of society, was being blocked by negative attitudes and discrimination on the part of employers and others. (p. 53)

The definition of disability was modified by the 1974 amendments to be much broader and inclusive than the original definition, which was employment based (Percy, 1989). Broadening the definition allowed for inclusion of children with disabilities, older persons with disabilities, and persons with severe disabilities. A person with a disability according to this definition was defined as a person who:

1. has a physical or mental impairment that substantially limits one or more of such a person's major life activities;
2. has a record of such impairment;
3. or is regarded as having such impairment. (p. 65)

An additional concept that originated from Section 504 (and was applicable to Section 503 as well) was that of reasonable accommodation. Reasonable accommodation was defined ". . . with reference to examples that included making employee facilities readily accessible to and usable . . . job restructuring, modifications in work schedules, changes in equipment, and provision of readers and interpreters. A limitation on mandated accommodations was included through the modifier 'reasonable'" (Percy, 1989, p. 76). An employer did not have to make an accommodation if it was deemed to create an "undue economic hardship." Little guidance was provided in the interpretation of what was reasonable or unreasonable. Because of this lack of specificity and the nature of individualized accommodations, compliance became a case-by-case situation that sometimes was confusing and controversial. Perhaps most notable was *Davis v. Southeastern Community College* (442 U.S. 397, 1979) in which the Supreme Court reversed an earlier favorable decision by the 4th U. S. Circuit Court of Appeals. *Davis* was the first real test of Section 504. Davis, a licensed practical nurse, had applied for admission to the college's nursing program and had requested accommodations on the basis of her hearing impairment. The college denied her admission on the basis of safety (that Davis would not be able to lip read in clinical situations where masks were worn) and that to admit her would force the college to lower its standards. The Supreme Court found in favor of Southeastern Community College, noting that this was a case about affirmative action, not an anti-discrimination case. Consequently, the issue of equality of opportunity and reasonable accommodation was sidestepped. Many regarded this decision as a continuing pattern of bias and prejudice against people with disabilities. In any event, it noted that the effectiveness and powerfulness of Section 504 may not be what were envisioned, particularly by persons with disabilities and other advocates.

Prior to the 1978 amendments, persons who pursued a legal course of action were not allowed to collect attorney fees in litigation in which they prevailed. Section 505 was added to the 1978 amendments, which corrected this situation as well as allowing for the same rights, procedures, and remedies as outlined in Title VII of the Civil Rights Act of 1964 (Percy, 1989).

Toward the end of the decade of the 1980s, the National Council on Disability observed that the current status of existing nondiscrimination laws, such as Section 504, was:

> . . . extremely important and have engendered much progress. [But] (in) an overall context, however, our Nation's laws provide inadequate protection from discrimination for people with disabilities. Current statutes are not comparable in their scope of protection against discrimination afforded racial, ethnic, and religious minorities and women under civil rights laws. (Percy, 1989, p. 224)

As a result of this finding, the National Council on Disability championed the development and passage of new legislation in 1990–the Americans with Disabilities Act (ADA). The ADA, it was thought, would bring together and strengthen nondiscrimination policies for all persons with disabilities.

Individuals with Disabilities Education Act (IDEA)

Prior to the passage of P.L. 94–142, the Education for All Handicapped Children Act of 1975, children with disabilities, particularly those with significant disabilities, had few programs that were designed to accommodate instructional needs that differed from the mainstream. Parents and parent-based groups, the National Association of Retarded Children [*sic*], and the Council for Exceptional Children lobbied the federal government for programs to educate children with disabilities. A major, although small, gain was realized through this advocacy with the establishment of the Bureau for Education of the Handicapped [*sic*] within the Office of Education, which took as its focus the development of training programs for special education teachers and initiated research programs on how to effectively teach children with disabilities (Percy, 1989). It would ultimately, however, be the courts to conclude that the state educational systems in America had failed to provide an education for children with disabilities (Tucker & Goldstein, 1992).

Two court cases, in particular, provided the foundation for the creation of P.L. 94–142: *Pennsylvania Association for Retarded Citizens v. Commonwealth of Pennsylvania* (343 F. Supp. 279, 1972) and *Mills v. Board of Education of the District of Columbia* (348 F. Supp. 866, 1972). In the *PARC* case, children who were labeled as mentally retarded

> . . . sued the state claiming that they were denied the right to a public education . . . [on the basis of] . . . three claims: (1) a violation of due process because there was no notice or hearing provided before retarded [*sic*] children were excluded from public school or their educational assignments were changed; (2) a violation of equal protection due to the lack of a rational basis for assuming that mentally retarded [*sic*] children were uneducable and untrainable; and (3) a violation of due process because it was arbitrary and capricious to deny mentally retarded [*sic*] children a right to the education guaranteed by state law. (Tucker & Goldstein, 1992, p. 2:14)

The *Mills* case, similarly, centered on the denial of a publicly supported education and involved not only children labeled as mentally retarded but children with other disabilities as well. Both the *PARC* and *Mills* cases demonstrated (*PARC* through a consent agreement and *Mills* through a summary judgment) that children with disabilities were entitled to a free and suitable public education based on the constitutional rights extended by the Due Process and Equal Protection clauses of the Fourteenth Amendment (Tucker & Goldstein, 1992).

The Education for All Handicapped Children Act was passed and signed into law by President Gerald Ford in 1975, and regulations were finalized less than two years later. P.L. 94–142 mandated that each child with a disability be provided with a "free, appropriate public education" (FAPE).

The concept of a "free appropriate public education" was welcomed, in particular, by parents of children with disabilities. Free appropriate public education from a parental perspective means the best educational situation for any child to succeed. However, this was not exactly the meaning of free appropriate education as ultimately noted by the Supreme Court. Amy Rowley, a young girl who had minimal hearing, was an excellent speech reader. She was in the first grade, had been provided with a hearing aid, receiving speech therapy, and had a tutor for the deaf. Academically, Amy was doing well in her studies (upper half of her class) and passing. However, Amy's parents, who were deaf, felt that she was missing too much classroom instruction and requested that the school provide Amy with a sign language interpreter. The school refused, however, and an administrative hearing officer and the state upheld the school's decision. The Rowleys filed suit in the federal courts and won at the district court level, which was appealed by the school board. The Rowleys again won at the Court of Appeals for the Second Circuit and the school board appealed to the Supreme Court. The Supreme Court in its decision in *Board of Education of the Henrick Hudson Central School District v. Rowley* (458 U.S. 176, 102 Sup. Ct. 3034, 1982) ruled in favor of the school board. The Supreme Court concluded that since Amy had access to and was benefiting from her educational program, this met the intent of free appropriate public education. In other words, it did not matter that she may achieve more with the provision of a sign language interpreter. Tucker and Goldstein (1992) noted that:

> Thus the Supreme Court in *Rowley* set forth a two-prong test, one procedural and one somewhat substantive, for courts to apply in determining whether children with disabilities have been provided a FAPE. The Court indicated that the individual needs of the child, as determined by an IEP, are the appropriate focus. Furthermore, the Court held that children with disabilities do not have an enforceable right to achieve their maximum potential, but rather are entitled only to receive some educational benefit, the sufficiency of which is to be left to a case-by-case analysis. (pp. 16:5 and 16:6)

Amendments in 1986 to the Education for All Handicapped Act (P.L. 99–457) authorized early intervention programs for preschool age children with disabilities. In 1990, the act was amended and titled the Individuals with Disabilities Education Act (IDEA) of 1990. In addition to changing the title of the act, IDEA represented a shift in thinking about children/youth with disabilities. IDEA abandoned the use of the terminology "handicap" and "handicapped" to describe children and youth with disabilities and adopted person-first language, a much sought-after change that had the potential to reduce negative attitudes or stereotypes of what, mostly, children with disabilities could not do. Children and youth with disabilities are, however, still labeled with such negative terms as educable mentally retarded, trainable mentally retarded, emotionally disturbed, severely and profoundly handicapped, or disabled among others. IDEA also required the development of an Individual Transition Plan (ITP) for each student with a disability that would facilitate transition from school to post-school activities, e.g., work, training, further schooling, independent living. Rehabilitation professionals have a significant role to play in this transition. Hayes, Bain, and Batshaw (1997) have noted that the provisions of the Individualized Education Plan (IEP) should require:

1. The process to be outcome oriented,
2. Students to be meaningfully involved in the process,
3. Students' needs to be projected beyond one year,
4. Schools to work with external agencies responsible for the provision of services or funding, and
5. Schools to provide extensive community-based instruction. (pp. 761–762)

Moreover, Hayes et al. (1997, p. 762) observed that not all school systems are providing these services because ". . . educators believe that these requirements go well beyond the school's responsibilities or capabilities" (p. 762). The potential effect or reality is that some youth will not receive transition services and may likely "fall through the cracks" and end up at home watching television while awaiting services from unknown agencies (note Chapter 2, which details the working relationship between these two agencies relative to the role of the rehabilitation counselor).

Other Significant Legislation Passed in the 1980s

The 1986 amendments to the 1973 Rehabilitation Act emphasized the use of rehabilitation engineering services, supported employment services for persons with severe disabilities, and mandated a gradual reduction in federal financial assistance to the state programs from the current 80 percent to an anticipated 75 percent matching ratio in 1993 (Rubin & Roessler, 2001).

The Technology-Related Assistance for Individuals with Disabilities Act of 1988 (P.L. 100–407) had as its purpose to improve access to technology devices and services for individuals with disabilities. Kurtz and Harryman (1997) noted that the tech act was to

> . . . support not only the purchase or lease of equipment but also a range of services to ensure success with their use. . . . [Moreover] . . . (t)hese [services] include 1) evaluation of the child's technological needs, 2) maintenance and repair of equipment, 3) training in the use of the devices, and 4) coordination of technology with other therapy services. (p. 719)

The tech act encouraged the states to engage in a competitive grant process that would allow the development of a consumer responsive system of technology services that would be accessible.

The importance of assistive technology cannot be understated. Assistive technology has the capacity to lessen or reduce the effects of disability, which then allows for participation in education, employment, and activities of daily living; that is, participation in the work and play of American society. Technology is the great equalizer for persons with disabilities. Technology is available but not always financially accessible. Wallace (1994) more than a decade ago noted that ". . . the funding of assistive technology continues to be the area of greatest need identified through consumer surveys across the country" (p. 79). Recently, Professor Peter Blanck (2005), in testimony before the U. S. House of Representative's Sub-Committee on Human Rights and Wellness, noted that assistive technology and universally designed products for those persons who need such technology to live, work, and recreate in their communities is often too expensive (based on Blanck's preliminary analysis of the 2004 National Organization on Disability/Harris Survey of Americans with Disabilities). Blanck noted that the major source of knowledge about assistive technology came from physicians (49%) and then from other health care and rehabilitation professionals (22%). Blanck suggests one major implication of this finding is that more needs to be known about health care and rehabilitation professionals' awareness and knowledge of assistive technology. It would seem that all healthcare and rehabilitation professionals should possess an in-depth awareness, knowledge, and ability to access assistive technology/universally designed products, as well as payment or forgiveness options for clients or consumers.

The Americans with Disabilities Act

In 1986, the National Council on Disability issued its report *Toward Independence,* which set the stage for the development of the ADA. Frank Bowe (1992) credits the enactment of the ADA to the efforts of Justin W. Dart, Jr., and noted that

> . . . for three years . . . Dart chaired a private sector body created by Rep. Major R. Owens (D-NY), chairman of the Select Education Subcommittee in the House. Dart's U.S. House of Representatives' Task Force on the Human Rights and Empowerment of Americans with Disabilities brought several hundred thousand adults and children with disabilities from all 50 states into the ADA 'movement'. The Task Force was an entirely voluntary effort: no one was paid nor was any expenses covered by Congress. Dart himself traveled to every one of the states, at his own expense, holding hearings to solicit the input of people with disabilities, parents, employers, educators, and local government officials. (p. 3)

Senator Tom Harkins, an early legislative leader and supporter for the passage of the ADA thought the potential impact of ADA meant:

> . . . inclusion, integration, and empowerment. For business, it means more customers, increased profits and additional qualified workers. For labor, it means greater protection from arbitrary action for members. And for government, it means more taxpayers and fewer persons on welfare, social security, and other social programs. (p. 939)

Dart (1995) has noted that the substantive requirements of the ADA were based on Section 504 of the 1973 Rehabilitation Act and that the procedural requirements were based on Title VII of the 1964 Civil Rights Act. The ADA, as envisioned by Dart (National Council on Disability and its staff and consultants), observed that Sections 501, 503, and 504 of the 1973 Rehabilitation Act were useful but did not extend to the vast private sector of the American economy (Bowe, 1992). The creation of the ADA's five titles was developed with this perspective:

Title I. Employment   Prohibits discrimination on the basis of disability with regard to job application procedures, hiring, advancement, discharge, compensation, training, and other privileges of employment.

Title II. Public Services   Prohibits discrimination on the basis of disability with regard to services and programs of local and state government including accessibility of such activities and programs. Public transient systems (operated by governmental agencies) accessibility is covered by this title.

Title III. Public Accommodations   Prohibits discrimination on the basis of disability with regard to accessibility of public transportation services operated by the private sector. Cover restaurants, banks, hotels, and others regarding accessibility or exclusion. Set standards for the accessibility in existing and new buildings.

Title IV. Telecommunications   Prohibits discrimination on the basis of disability with regard to persons with speech and hearing impediments and requires the establishment of twenty-four-hour relay services.

Title V. Miscellaneous   Prohibits retaliation.

The effectiveness of the ADA has been the basis for many television news reports and has been studied by the various constituents who have been affected by its provisions. Professor Blanck (1994), in a comprehensive empirical study of the impact of the ADA, investigated 1,100 persons with mental retardation in Oklahoma over a period of three years (1990–1993) regarding Title I of the act. Blanck's findings revealed modest gains in integrated employment, wages, and independent living. Senator Bob Dole, an ardent supporter of the ADA, commented that Blanck's study focused on the correct issues for assessing progress; that is, employment and economic well-being, but if employment was the major goal sought, then the results were not that encouraging. Dole (1994), speaking from a national perspective noted "(u)nfortunately, the news isn't so good. In 1986, 33% of disabled [*sic*] Americans worked; in 1994, this figure is 31%" (p. 928). The 1998 Lou Harris Poll revealed that this percentage had declined to 29 percent. The 2004 Harris Poll notes that this percentage has increased to 35 percent, an increase of 6 percent from the 1998 survey but an increase of only 2 percent from the 1986 Harris Survey, prior to the passage and implementation of the ADA. This most recent finding reveals an employment gap of 43 percent when compared to persons without disabilities. While there has been a gain, it is, however, minimal.

West (1994) reported in The Milbank Memorial Fund's report, *Federal Implementation of the Americans with Disabilities Act, 1991–1994,* that no federal agency had plans to survey consumers regarding changes brought about as a result of the ADA; that only minimal funding for evaluation studies to determine effectiveness had been allocated; and that neither studies nor data collection activities to determine effectiveness of ADA-related tax code provisions had been planned. Nevertheless, this report did recommend that Congress:

1. Retain the current statute without amendment.
2. Establish minimal enforcement standards, including timeliness for complaint processing and closure. Adequate resources should be allocated to EEOC, DOJ, and DOT to enable them to comply with these standards.
3. Appropriate funds to the Civil Rights Division of DOJ for a comprehensive ADA public awareness/education campaign. This campaign should be developed and coordinated with EEOC, DOT, FCC, Access Board, NIDRR, NCD, PCEPD, and other relevant agencies.
4. Designate an internal ADA coordinator for each body and provide for an independent assessment of progress. (pp. x–xi)

In assessing the public accessibility titles of the ADA, McMahon noted that ". . . implementation has been more successful." Moreover, "architectural and especially communication barriers are being torn down on or ahead of schedule, access to goods and services through technology is greater, complaint and litigation levels are well below predicted levels, and compliance is high because competitive American businesses are eager to tap into the purchasing power of 54 million Americans with disabilities" (personal communication, 1998).

The National Organization on Disability (NOD) through its Harris Survey of Americans with Disabilities (2004) has documented progress in ten areas of access or participation in life activities: (a) employment, (b) income, (c) education, (d) political participation, (e) transportation, (f) social life, (g) religion, (h) general life satisfaction and optimism, (i) health care, and (j) assistive technology. The 2005 survey revealed the following quantitative measures comparing the lives of people with and without disabilities:

- *Employment:* Only 35 percent of people with disabilities aged eighteen to sixty-four are working, compared to 78 percent of people without disabilities—a gap of 43 percentage points.
- *Life satisfaction:* Just 34 percent of people with disabilities are very satisfied with their lives, compared to 61 percent of people without disabilities—a gap of 27 percentage points.
- *Transportation:* Inadequate transportation is a problem for 30 percent of people with disabilities, compared to only 9 percent of people without disabilities—a gap of 21 percentage points.
- *Income:* 26 percent of people with disabilities have household incomes of $15,000 or less, compared to only 9 percent of people without disabilities—a gap of 17 percentage points.
- *Eating in restaurants:* 57 percent compared to 73 percent report eating out at least twice a month—a 16-point gap.
- *Education:* 21 percent of people with disabilities have not graduated from high school compared to only 11 percent of people without disabilities—a 10-point gap.
- *Health care:* 18 percent of people with disabilities did not receive needed care in the past year, compared to only 7 percent of people without disabilities—an 11-point gap. (p. 4)

Collectively, these data indicate that significant advances and an over-all positive impact on American society are occurring. The National Council on Disability (2005) has recently noted in its forthcoming ADA Impact Study ". . . that significant strides have been made in such areas as transportation and accessible public facilities, including restaurants, theaters, stores, and museums" (p. 2):

- Telephone relay services are being used at high levels, and changes in technology are making usage easier.
- Public transit systems in the United States have made dramatic progress in becoming more accessible, especially to wheelchair users.
- The percentage of Americans with disabilities voting in 2004 increased dramatically.
- The education gap between people with disabilities and people without disabilities is shrinking and people with disabilities are attending postsecondary institutions in record numbers.
- People with disabilities are experiencing less discrimination in employment. (p. 2)

It is obvious that more success has been achieved in the area of pub-lic accessibility than employment for persons with disabilities. From a historical perspective, the overall effectiveness of the ADA has been somewhat mixed; however, only a brief moment of time has elapsed since the enactment of this most significant and compelling legislation.

1992 Amendments to the 1973 Rehabilitation Act

The 1992 amendments to the 1973 Rehabilitation Act continued the strong emphasis toward provision of services to persons with severe disabilities, even introducing a new category of "most severe disabili-ty"; a continuing emphasis on employment outcomes introducing a career perspective; increased consumer choice and control in the reha-bilitation process; broadened eligibility to denote that a consumer needs only to "benefit" from provision of services; and increased con-sumer control through the establishment of statewide rehabilitation advisory councils and statewide independent living councils. The declaratory statement for vocational rehabilitation services contained in the 1992 amendments stressed the importance of work and of its centrality in American society and recounted the barriers to achievement of this goal.

Eligibility criteria for receipt of vocational rehabilitation services changed as noted next:

An individual is eligible for vocational rehabilitation services when:

1. He or she has a physical or mental impairment that constitutes or results in a substantial impediment to employment,
2. The individual can benefit in terms of an employment outcome from VR services, and
3. The individual requires vocational rehabilitation services to prepare for, enter, engage in, or retain employment.

This broadened definition of eligibility allowed for increased flexibility in working with clients or customers with severe and most severe disabilities since it incorporated the qualifier "benefit" although the interpretation of this word often did not mean the same thing for a person with a disability as it did for the vocational rehabilitation (VR) agency. This definition of eligibility also allowed counselors to work with persons in a preventive manner regarding retention of employment. Other provisions related to the establishment of time limits for the determination of eligibility (sixty-day limit); however, some consumers complained that they were put in a waiting status before being allowed to apply for rehabilitation services. Use of existing data, particularly from educational agencies, as well as from the person with a disability and his or her family, was encouraged. The VR agency was mandated to conduct an extended evaluation if a person's disability was considered too severe to serve. In this same vein, the agency was required to specify the reasons for a determination of ineligibility and concurrently advise the person of the availability of services through the client assistance program.

The Individual Written Rehabilitation Program (IWRP) continued to emphasize the importance of the planning process between the client or customer and the counselor. The IWRP was to be jointly developed and reflect the unique strengths, resources, abilities, and concerns of the person with a disability in terms of the vocational objective selected. The vocational objective was to have a career focus with job placement in an integrated setting. A statement of specific services to be provided and the data and duration of such services were to be specified. An assessment of the need for post employment services was, as well, to be included in the IWRP. Each client or customer was to receive a copy of the IWRP and, in case of a disagreement regarding the plan or anticipated services, the person was to be informed of the availability of the client assistance program (as well as how to access these services). The IWRP was to be reviewed at least annually allowing for changes and the development of revisions or amendments to the IWRP.

The 1992 amendments also provided that federal support of the VR program be increased from 75 to 78.7 percent beginning in 1993. An emphasis on minority recruitment to the field of rehabilitation was to be developed through supports to college and university programs that had minority enrollments of 50 percent or greater (Rubin & Roessler, 2001).

The 1998 Amendments to the 1973 Rehabilitation Act

The Rehabilitation Act amendments of 1998 were signed into law by President William Jefferson Clinton on August 7, 1998, as a part of the Workforce Investment Act of 1998. The 1998 amendments continued and expanded emphasis on consumer involvement and choice. Fredric K. Schroeder, then commissioner of the Rehabilitation Services Administration, released an information memorandum which detailed the following areas of emphasis contained in these amendments (1998):

- Expanding the exercise of informed choice by individuals with disabilities;
- Streamlining administrative procedures to improve program efficiency and access to services;
- Increasing opportunities for high quality employment outcomes; ensuring due process; and
- Linking the VR program to a State's workforce investment system. (p. 2)

State VR agencies and the state rehabilitation councils (formally the statewide rehabilitation advisory councils) were to develop policies and procedures that would insure informed choice regarding eligibility determination, selection of vocational or employment goals, and the selection of services and service providers. The IWRP was renamed the Individualized Plan for Employment (IPE) to emphasize the expanded role of the person with a disability relative to informed choice. The IPE continued the existent requirement for comparable benefits, postemployment services, and due process procedures.

Administratively, the amendments eliminated the strategic plan requirements and supported the expansion of VR services to persons with the most significant disabilities (a change in terminology from the qualifier "severe" to "significant"). Presumptively, persons receiving Social Security Disability Insurance (SSDI) and Supplemental Security Insurance (SSI) benefits who desire an employment outcome are eligible to receive VR services without going through an eligibility process. Employment outcomes characterized as "high quality," meaning the expansion of job opportunities in such areas as telecommuting and self-employment including small business operation, are emphasized in the development of the IPE. The requirement for extended evaluation (when or if ineligibility is being assessed for persons with the most significant disabilities) was replaced with a requirement of trial work experience.

Due process requirements were enhanced for persons with disabilities who disagreed with decisions regarding eligibility, services, or case closure. Mediation is an option that is to be offered a client; the outcome, however, is not binding and cannot be used to delay or deny an impartial hearing. Decisions of the impartial hearing officer, as a result of these new due process provisions, will no longer be reviewed by the state VR director.

Linkages to the state workforce investment system (a consolidation of employment and training programs into a unified statewide system) were contemplated to lead to better coordination and cooperation among the various agencies regarding job opportunities for persons with disabilities.

Future Directions

The disability movement, as witnessed by the historic events of the preceding three decades, has come a long way toward the ideal of rehabilitation as expressed by the National Council on Rehabilitation in 1942, to the passage of the 1973 Rehabilitation Act to the passage of

Americans with Disabilities Act in 1990. Yet, in reality, we have only come a small distance when persons with disabilities are still not enjoying the benefits of American life—employment, education, transportation, health care, and recreational and social opportunities. The effects of institutionalization of persons with the most significant disabilities continue to be an issue because our society cannot or will not expend money for community options even in the light of economic gain. It costs less to provide services in the community than it does in an institutional setting. The legislative agenda for persons with disabilities has increasingly become more consumer or client centered and directed and less process oriented. This is a most positive trend that holds great promise for the future, not only for people with disabilities, but for all people.

The National Council on Disability in its report *Achieving Independence: The Challenge for the 21st Century* assessed disability policy of the recent past and concluded:

- Disability policy has made steady progress in the last decade in empowering people with disabilities; however, this progress is threatened, compromised, and often undermined by lack of understanding and support in the U.S. Congress and among particular segments of society.
- Most public policy affecting people with disabilities does not yet promote the goals of ADA—equality of opportunity, full participation, independent living, and economic self-sufficiency.
- Most Americans with disabilities remain outside the economic and social mainstream of American life. (pp. 3–4)

The National Council on Disability also offered these recommendations:

1. Existing laws should be more vigorously enforced.
2. People with disabilities should direct policy and decision making when they are affected by the outcome.
3. Outreach and awareness campaigns must be launched to educate the public about the human and societal benefits of achieving independence for people with disabilities and the important role that civil rights and community-based supports play in promoting independence.

4. Incentives for the inclusion of people with disabilities in all aspects of society must be further developed and implemented.
5. Principles of universal design should be universally applied.
6. Systems, services, and supports for people with disabilities must be further developed as a part of the mainstream of community life.
7. Accurate data about people with disabilities should be regularly collected, analyzed, and reported. (pp. 5–6)

In a recent report issued by the United States Government Accountability Office (GAO) (2005) regarding the performance of the state-federal vocational rehabilitation program, the GAO noted that the Department of Education's oversight of its eighty plus state vocational rehabilitation agencies resulted in the following findings:

- Education's performance measures are not comprehensive, and its monitoring of state VR agencies has not resulted in timely feedback.
- Education does not comprehensively measure the performance of certain key populations such as students transitioning from school to work, and tracks only the individuals who exit the program, not those still receiving services.
- Education's performance measures do not take into consideration all the variations among the state VR agencies or allow for comparisons with other workforce programs.
- Education's monitoring reports, which are its primary means of providing feedback to state VR agencies, are frequently late and based on data that are more than two years old. Consequently, state VR agencies do not receive the timely feedback needed to improve the efficiency and effectiveness of their programs.
- Education also does not manage the performance of the VR programs . . . censure poorly performing state VR agencies, reward strong performance, or take full advantage of opportunities to disseminate best practices. (pp. 30–36)

The GAO's findings documented that of the more than 650,000 persons who exited the state VR programs in fiscal year 2003, a third (217,557) were successfully employed for the requisite ninety days following receipt of substantial VR services. The remaining two-thirds were closed before obtaining employment for the following major reasons:

- Failure to cooperate (46%),
- Could not be located (24%),
- Other (22%) (institutionalization, transfer to another VR agency, death, transportation problems, unavailability of extended services, extended employment, or nondefined problems), no disabling condition, impediment to employment or need for VR services (6%),
- Disability too significant (3%)

These statistics regarding closure, particularly such a large number in the "failure to cooperate" and "could not be located categories" (approximately 260,000 persons) seem rather large given the universe of persons who want and need VR services to achieve the American Dream.

Despite these events, present-day trends in rehabilitation indicate that programs have become much larger and more complex. Because of the increasing size, recognition of other professionals in the delivery of rehabilitation-related services, and most significantly, the emerging importance of a strong alliance between the client or consumer and the rehabilitation counselor or other professional personnel, the rehabilitation movement demonstrates a positive growth during the past four decades.

While the Independent Living program is in need of additional financial assistance from the federal government, this movement and its pioneering program development have the potential of becoming the comprehensive rehabilitation program for the future. Centers for Independent Living now provide services of increased scope ranging from assistance with housing to food preparation to vocational training and placement.

Despite the phenomenal growth in the independent living field, thousands of people remain unnecessarily institutionalized and overprotected. Many of these individuals have not chosen the style of life they lead; they are awaiting the opportunity to acquire information and skills that they need in order to become independent; they are awaiting resources in their communities such as accessible housing, transportation, and attendant care; they are awaiting the continued growth of the independent living movement and new independent living programs that this growth will bring.

With this comparatively new awareness of persons with significant disabilities as capable of living independently and with the recognition of accompanying advantages of increased quality of life, frequently with economic benefit, emphasis on independent living in rehabilitation settings is on the increase. Professionals providing services focusing on skills for living independently are practicing from various disciplines: rehabilitation counseling, occupational therapy, therapeutic recreation, social work, psychology, rehabilitation nursing, special education, and others. With the firm establishment of the Independent Living movement and the new and increasing emphasis on support, encouragement, and skill development for living independently, it is expected that rehabilitation professionals of the future will have a heavy investment in the area of independent living.

REFERENCES

Americans with Disabilities Act of 1990. Public Law 101–336.

Batshaw, M. L. (Ed.). (1997). *Children with disabilities* (4th Ed.). Baltimore: Paul Brooks.

Berkowitz, E. D. (1987). *Disabled policy: America's programs for the handicapped.* New York: Twentieth Century Fund Report.

Blanck, P. (2004). *Disability civil rights law and policy.* St. Paul, MN: Thomson West.

Blanck, P. (2004). Testimony of Professor Peter Blanck before the U.S. House of Representatives, Committee on Governmental Reform, Subcommittee on Human Rights and Wellness. Retrieved November 22, 2005 from http://www.nod.org

Blanck, P. (1994). Employment integration, economic opportunity and the Americans with disabilities act: Empirical study from 1990–1993. *Iowa Law Review, 79*(4), 853–923.

Board of Education of the Henrick Hudson Central School District v. Rowley. 458 U.S. 76, Sup. Ct. 3034, 1982.

Bowe, F. F. (1992). Development of the ADA. In N. Hablutzel & B. T. McMahon (Eds.), *The Americans with disabilities act: Access and accommodations.* Orlando: Paul M. Deutsch.

Braddock, D., Hemp, R., Parish, S., & Westrich, J. (1998). *The state of the states on developmental disabilities.* Washington, DC: American Association on Mental Retardation.

Dart, J., & West, J. (1995). Americans with disabilities act. In A. E. Dell Orto & R. P. Marinelli (Eds.), *Encyclopedia of disability and rehabilitation.* New York: Simon & Schuster Macmillan.

Davis v. Southeastern Community College. 442 U.S. 397, 1979.

DeJong, G. (1979). *Report of the National Conference on Independent Living Service Rehabilitation per P.L. 95-602, March 7-8, 1979.* Boston: Medical Rehabilitation and Research Training Center No. 7, Tufts-New England Medical Center.

Developmental Disabilities Services and Facilities Construction Act. Public Law 91–517.

Dole, R. (1994). Are we keeping America's promises to people with disabilities? Commentary on Blanck. *Iowa Law Review, 79*(4), 925–939.

Education for All Handicapped Children Act of 1975. Public Law 94–142.

Government Accountability Office. (2005). *Vocational rehabilitation: Better measures and monitoring could improve the performance of the VR program.* Washington, DC: Author.

Hablutzel, N., & McMahon, B. T. (Eds.). (1992). *The Americans with disabilities act: Access and accommodations.* Orlando, FL: Paul M. Deutsch.

Harkin, T. (1994). The Americans with disabilities act: Four years later–Commentary on Blanck. *Iowa Law Review, 79*(4), 935–939.

Kiernan, W. E., & Schalock (1995). Developmental disabilities. In A. E. Dell Orto & R.P. Marinelli (Eds.). *Encyclopedia of disability and rehabilitation* (pp. 249–257). New York: Simon & Schuster McMillan.

Kurtz, L. A., & Harryman, S. E. (1997). Rehabilitation interventions: Physical therapy and occupational therapy. In M. L. Batshaw (Ed.), *Children with disabilities* (4th Ed.). Baltimore: Paul Brooks.

Lou Harris and Associates. (2004). *NOD/Harris survey of Americans with disabilities.* New York: Author.

Lou Harris and Associates. (2000). *NOD/Harris survey of Americans with disabilities.* New York: Author.

Lou Harris and Associates. (1998). *NOD/Harris survey of Americans with disabilities.* New York: Author.

Lou Harris and Associates. (1994). *NOD/Harris survey of Americans with disabilities.* New York: Author.

Lou Harris and Associates. (1995). *NOD/Harris survey on employment of people with disabilities.* New York: Author.

Lou Harris and Associates. (1986). *Harris survey on employment of people with disabilities.* New York: Author.

Lou Harris and Associates. (1986). *ICD survey of Americans with disabilities.* New York: Author.

Mills v. Board of Education of the District of Columbia. 348 F. Supp. 866, 1972.

National Council on Disability. (2005). NCD and the Americans with disabilities act: 15 years of progress. Retrieved November 22, 2005, from http://www.ncd.gov/newsroom/publications/2005/15yearprogress.htm

National Council on Disability. (2005). *A mission in action: 2004 annual report.* Washington, DC: Author.

National Council on Disability. (1996). *Achieving independence: The challenge for the 21st century.* Washington, DC: Author.

National Council on Disability. (1986). *Toward independence: An assessment of federal laws and programs affecting people with disabilities–With legislative recommendations.* Washington, DC: Author.

New York State Association for Retarded Children v. Rockefeller. 357 F. Supp. 752, 1973.

Pennsylvania Association of Retarded Children v. Commonwealth of Pennsylvania. 334 F. Supp. 1257, 1971.

Percy, S. L. (1989). *Disability, civil rights, and public policy.* Tuscaloosa, AL: The University of Alabama Press.

President's Committee on Employment of People with Disabilities (1990). ADA: A special issue. *Worklife, 3*(3), 1–48.

Rehabilitation Act of 1973. Public Law 93–112.

Rehabilitation Act Amendments of 1974. Public Law 93–651.

Rehabilitation Act Amendments of 1978. Public Law 95–602.

Rehabilitation Act Amendments of 1984. Public Law 98–221.

Rehabilitation Act Amendments of 1986. Public Law 99–506.

Rehabilitation Act Amendments of 1992. Public Law 102–569.

Rehabilitation Act Amendments of 1993. Public Law 103–73.

Rubin, S. E., & Roessler, R. T. (2001). *Foundations of the vocational rehabilitation process* (5th Ed.). Austin: PRO-ED.

Schroeder, F. K. (1998). The rehabilitation act amendments of 1998. *Information Memorandum,*

RSA-IM-98-20. Washington, DC: Rehabilitation Services Administration, United Stated Department of Education.

Scotch, R. K. (1984). *From good will to civil rights: Transforming federal disability policy.* Philadelphia: Temple University Press.

The Technology-Related Assistance Act for Individuals with Disabilities Act of 1988. Public Law 100–407.

Tucker, B. P., & Goldstein, B. A. (1992). *Legal rights of persons with disabilities: An analysis of federal law* (Volumes I & II ed.). Horsham, PA: LRP Publications.

Wallace, J. F. (1994). *A policy analysis of national loan financing practices: Strategies for the development for the loan programs for the acquisition of assistive technology.* Unpublished doctoral dissertation, Virginia Commonwealth University.

West, J. (1994). *Federal implementation of the Americans with disability act, 1991–1994.* New York: The Milbank Memorial Fund.

Wyatt v. Stickney, 344F. Supp. 752, 1973.

Chapter 2

PARTNERS IN THE TRANSITION PROCESS: SPECIAL EDUCATION AND VOCATIONAL REHABILITATION

Karen Rabren and Rebecca S. Curtis

Emerging adult roles gain importance as youth enter and progress through their adolescent years. This transition in role development occurs at a time filled with many trials and tribulations as teenagers learn more about themselves and the world around them. Arguably, some adolescents are better prepared than others to enter the next threshold of life. Why do some youth seemingly move smoothly from this stage of life to the next, while others have great difficulty?

For individuals with disabilities, this time of transition from adolescence to adulthood can be especially challenging. As youth begin developing their own sense of self, they engage in decision-making about their futures. Yet, teens with disabilities have often been considered incapable of making informed choices and decisions. According to Wehmeyer (1998), however, the professional literature does not support the contention that students with disabilities are incapable of making competent decisions. Although, he does assert that students may not have had opportunities to make decisions and are in need of support to gain more experience in this area. When given opportunity, practice, and support, students with disabilities can become engaged decision-makers and more involved in their futures.

As they move toward adulthood, teenagers also begin to learn and interact more with the world around them. Lichtenstein (1998) identifies work as one of several important ecological influences on adolescence. First, jobs forge lasting memories about the workplace and help develop lifelong work behaviors. During first jobs, youth learn that praise and monetary compensation are rewards for good work. They also learn how to accept constructive criticism and how to modify and monitor their own behaviors. However, when compared to their peers without disabilities, too many students with disabilities have difficulty gaining and maintaining employment.

The employment status of former special education students was one of many post-school outcomes examined in the 1987 *National Longitudinal Transition Study of Special Education Students* (NLTS). The NLTS included a national representative sample of 8,000 youth, thirteen to twenty-one, enrolled in special education in secondary school during the 1985–1986 school years (Wagner, 1989). Data were collected about the outcomes of these young people in 1987 and 1990. Results indicated that 46 percent of the former students who received special education services were competitively working in 1987 and 57 percent of this same group were employed three years later. Although these figures indicate an increase of 11 percent in three years, this improvement appears limited when the employment status of these young people is compared to their peers without disabilities.

The discrepancy between students with and without disabilities was reported by Blackorby and Wagner (1996) who contrasted employment rates of former students in the NTLS with a group of former students without disabilities. They found that 46 percent of those with disabilities and 59 percent of those without disabilities were employed in 1987. They also found that these comparative figures were 57 and 69 percent in 1990. This finding suggests that while the employment rates improved almost equally for both groups during these years, the employment rate for those with disabilities continued to lag 12 to 13 percentage points behind those without disabilities.

The second National Longitudinal Transition Study (NLTS2) was initiated in 2001 and examines a national sample of students with disabilities who were 13 to 16 years of age in 2000. When comparing the results of the NLTS and NLTS2, 55 percent of the 1987 cohort group compared to 70 percent of the 2003 cohort group worked for pay during their first few years after high school. This 15 percent increase is encouraging, but again is somewhat diminished when compared to the employment figures for youth without disabilities. The NTLS2, for example, found former students with disabilities had a significantly lower employment rate (41%) when compared to their same-age peers in the general population (68%) (Cameto & Levine, 2004). Although improvements were seen in the employment rate between cohort 1 in NLTS and cohort 2 in NLTS2, it is still disheartening to see the continued and even increased discrepancy in employment rates between youth and young adults with and without disabilities.

The low employment rate for former students with disabilities is one of many reasons why there has been a continued need for transition services. In fact, transition became a national movement in the 1980s with the goal and purpose of providing young people with disabilities the support and services needed to become, to the greatest extent of their capabilities, independent and contributing members of society. These supports and services require an interagency effort to meet both the educational and vocational needs of these youth. As described by Benz, Johnson, Mikkelsen, and Lindstrom (1995), "effective collaboration between schools and vocational rehabilitation (VR) agencies will be imperative as schools and VR seek to implement their respective transition-related responsibilities. . ." (p. 133). The purpose of this chapter is to focus on VR and its role in the transition process. To begin, an introduction to the historical and legislative foundation of transition services and definitions will be presented, followed by an overview of transition education practices and services. Finally, recommendations and a discussion of issues associated with transition services will be presented.

Historical and Legislative Foundation

The transition movement has been driven by the need to provide services for youth and young adults to improve their postschool outcomes. This movement was spearheaded by the advocacy and self-advocacy efforts of many who saw the need to provide assistance to these young people as they make the transition from adolescence to adulthood. The movement was also supported and strengthened by key legislation and litigation that provided the foundation for transition services. Although there is now legislation in place to support transition services, this has not always been the case. First, a broader protection of disability rights had to be established, and the attainment of these rights included years of struggle and perseverance.

Access to education for persons with disabilities has been a particularly hard fought battle. Differences among children were not tolerated in early American classrooms. For example, in *Watson v. City of Cambridge 1893,* the Massachusetts Supreme Judicial Court upheld the exclusion of a child from school based on his inability to care for himself. Although there were compulsory education laws in this country in the early 1900s, not all children were allowed, and certainly not compelled, to attend America's schools. The practice of excluding children with disabilities from public schools continued for another half-century.

Through the mid-1950s, an environment of segregation was perpetuated by separating students according to differences. Race, for example, served as a rationale to deny some children access to public schools. In 1954, however, this segregation in the schools based on race was finally found to be unconstitutional in *Brown v. Board of Education* when the U.S. Supreme Court ruled in favor of the plaintiffs. The "separate but equal" doctrine which was used to support segregation was found to violate African-American children's rights as protected by the Fourteenth Amendment. The Brown decision made a major contribution to the civil rights movement of the 1960s.

This movement provided the rationale and legal precedent for the protection of the rights of students with disabilities. Specifically, the disability rights movement was supported by the same legal principles protecting the rights of individuals who are poor, or who are in a minority due to language or race (Osborne, 1996). A decade later, during the 1970s, the protection of the rights of persons with disabilities gained national attention, resulting in a significant reaction in public policy. The disability rights movement was well launched through the advocacy and self-advocacy activities initiated during that decade. In fact, beginning in the 1970s and during the following thirty years, the majority of disability rights organizations were established in this country (Stroman, 2003). The actions of these organizations and other advocates and self-advocates brought to the attention of the public, and eventually, the lawmakers the discriminatory practices against persons with disabilities.

Fueled by legislation of the early to mid-1970s, the rights of all persons with disabilities were soon to be protected. Section 504 of the Rehabilitation Act of 1973 (P.L. 93–112) was the first civil rights legislation that protected the rights of persons with disabilities from discrimination by any recipient of federal funds in the provision of services or employment. Two years later, the Education for All Handicapped Children Act of 1975 (EAHCA) (P.L. 94–142) was signed into law and protected the rights of students with disabilities to a public education. These two legislative acts helped to "open the doors" of public education for children and youth with disabilities in the United States.

The Education for All Handicapped Children Act (EAHCA) mandated that all children with disabilities, ages three through eighteen, receive a free and appropriate public education. This law also ensured due process rights and the use of Individualized Education Programs (IEPs) for annually planning and implementing the education of students with disabilities. It also required that these students be educated in the least restrictive environment (LRE). This means they are to be educated with their peers without disabilities unless the nature or severity of their disability would not allow for a satisfactory education in the general education classroom even after the use of supplementary aids and services. By September 1980, the EAHCA service eligibility age was extended to twenty-one for students with disabilities (Yell, 1998). This was one of the early legislative actions to address the transition years of students with disabilities.

The amendments to the Education for All Handicapped Children Act in 1983 (P.L. 98–199) and the Rehabilitation Act in 1986 (P.L. 99–506) continued to support the development of transition services. EAHCA (P.L. 98–199) of 1975, for example, included Secondary Education and Transitional Services for Handicapped Youth (Section 626). The purpose of this section was to provide financial incentives for transition programming through model demonstration projects, research projects, and personnel preparation programs. Through this funding, 266 model demonstration projects were developed and initiated throughout the United States (Rusch, Chadsey-Rusch, & Szymanski, 1992). Three years later, the amendments to the Rehabilitation Act (P.L. 99–506) defined supported employment and provided a comprehensive plan for rehabilitation services regardless of the severity of the individual's disability. The establishment of supported employment provided another possible outcome option for high school students with more significant disabilities.

Other 1980s legislation supporting transition services included the Job Training Partnership Act (JTPA) (1982) and the Carl D. Perkins

Vocational Education Act (1984). The JTPA provided federal funds to establish employment training programs for youth and adults who were economically disadvantaged and for those facing serious barriers to employment. The Carl Perkins Act provided federal funds to support vocational education programs. The main goals of this act were to address our country's need to have a skilled labor force and to provide equal opportunities for all individuals in vocational education. Both the JTPA and the Carl Perkins Acts emphasized vocational preparation and funded programs that promoted and provided vocational services to those most in need of them, including individuals with disabilities.

During the 1990s, new legislation was passed and existing legislation was amended and restructured to further define and extend the rights of persons with disabilities. In 1990, one of the most comprehensive pieces of legislation designed to protect the civil rights of persons with disabilities, the Americans with Disabilities Act (ADA) (P.L. 101–336), was enacted into law. The ADA provides people with disabilities equal protection and opportunity in specific areas of public life such as employment, public accommodations, transportation, state and local government services, and telecommunications. Also during 1990, the amendments to the EAHCA included a change in the name of the act to the Individuals with Disabilities Education Act (IDEA) (P.L. 101–476). This name change not only reflected a move toward people-first language, it also acknowledged that the legislation covered young children as well as older adolescents. Although the 1983 amendments of this act had provided financial incentives, the 1990 amendments provided even more support for transition services. The IDEA of 1990, for example, provided a definition of transition, and for the first time, mandated that these services be provided to youth with disabilities. Legislation of the early 1990s reflected the need and provided the federal structure for assisting youth as they transition to adulthood and become contributing members of communities throughout the United States.

During the later half of the 1990s, major changes in the structure of workforce development programs occurred. The Workforce Investment Act (WIA) of 1998 (P.L. 105–22) was passed and replaced the JTPA. The purpose of the WIA was to "consolidate, coordinate, and improve employment, training, literacy, and vocational rehabilitation programs in the United States" (Neubert, 2006, p. 58). As part of the restructuring, The Rehabilitation Act Amendments of 1998 were also placed in this act. Services and programs under the WIA were to be consolidated and delivered through one-stop centers. This Act essentially sought to provide a legislative and administrative structure for a seamless delivery of workforce development programs.

The twenty-first century brought with it even more changes to services and programs, especially in education. The education pendulum that had swung toward supporting the use of vocational preparation programs and functional curriculum in the 1980s and 1990s took a hard swing back to a more academically focused curriculum with higher standards in the early 2000s. In 2001, the Elementary and Secondary Education Act was changed to the No Child Left Behind Act (NCLB) (P.L. 107–110) and with that change, as the name implies, focused on providing a quality education to *all* children. The NCLB includes increased emphasis on accountability standards to measure the progress of children and a focus on teacher quality. This act also requires that school systems become involved in research-based reforms to improve the annual yearly progress of students' academic performance. However, if improvement does not occur in school systems, parents have the option to remove their children from low performing schools and place them in a successful public school. A few years after the passage of NCLB, the IDEA was reauthorized. The Individuals with Disabilities Education Improvement Act of 2004 (P.L. 108–446) was amended and more closely aligned with NCLB. As a result, the emphasis on results-oriented outcomes was also made applicable for students with disabilities.

Legislation, litigation, and historical developments of the past two centuries have laid a foundation for the rights of persons with disabilities to become fully contributing members of society. This is quite a contrast to the exclusionary practices that dominated the 1800s and early 1900s. As previously mentioned, it was not until the mid-1970s that significant legislation was passed protecting the rights of students with disabilities to receive a free appropriate public education. Adults with disabilities had to wait until the 1990 passage of the ADA to have their civil rights protected. Shortly thereafter, during the last decade of the twentieth century, a full range of legislative changes was made. This is exemplified through the passage of the ADA of 1990 and WIA of 1998. These two pieces of legislation had significant yet different implications for persons with disabilities. The ADA broadened the spectrum vis-à-vis the rights of persons with disabilities are to be protected, whereas the WIA sought to streamline and consolidate services and programs. Later, as we entered the twenty-first century, even more changes were to occur. The NCLB of 2001 and the reauthorized IDEA of 2004 brought the focus of education toward accountability and results. These developments are the latest of a trend toward consolidating and focusing the legislative base for all government-supported programs. The full implications of these actions are yet to be determined as the practices supported by this legislation are implemented.

Among other things, legislation defines our practices and expectations by providing professionals and persons with disabilities definitions of programs and services. Transition, for example, was defined in the early 1980s and has been continually refined throughout the various amendments. Definitions are important to both the professionals who provide services and the recipients of those services because they provide guidelines of what is to be expected.

Transition Definitions

In the early 1980s, one of the first definitions of transition was advanced by Madeleine Will, then Assistant Secretary of the Office of Special Education and Rehabilitative Services (OSERS), United States Department of Education. During this time period, youth and young adults with disabilities became the focus of federal initiatives, and as a result, financial incentives to direct services and programs for them were made available to the states. In addition, transition concepts and policies were formulated. Will's definition and model were established to guide efforts for improving the transition from school-to-work for all individuals with disabilities. Transition, as defined by Will, was described as:

> . . . an outcome oriented process encompassing a broad array of services and experiences that lead to employment. Transition is a period that includes high school, the point of graduation, additional post secondary education or adult services, and the initial years of employment. Transition is a bridge between the security and structure offered by the school and the risks of life. (1984, p. 1)

Will's transition service delivery model, also known as the *Bridges Model,* includes different levels or means of crossing *bridges* from school to adulthood. These three levels, or *bridges,* include (a) no special services, (b) time-limited services, and (c) ongoing services. Each *bridge* focuses on what the individual with a disability might need in order to obtain his or her desired employment outcome. The first *bridge,* or level, indicates the person with a disability would not be in need of any special services to successfully reach their outcome of employment. The next level of Will's model identifies time-limited services as a service delivery option that may be needed by some youth as they work toward the attainment of employment (e.g., vocational rehabilitation services). The most service-oriented level of the model suggests that more intensive, ongoing services may be needed to obtain a successful employment outcome (e.g., supported employment).

Will's definition and model provided a structure for the development and implementation of the early transition programs. The focus of Will's *Bridges Model* was employment, which is one of the more important adult outcomes for independence and self-sufficiency. However, some professionals in the field considered the single outcome of employment to be too narrow. In the mid-1980s, Andrew Halpern offered another definition and model of transition that broadened the desired outcome options. Halpern's *Community Adjustment Model* included services to address successful attainment of a residential environment, social and interpersonal relationships, as well as employment (Halpern, 1985). The introduction of Halpern's model and definition gave transition professionals a broader scope of what was required for successful transition and community adjustment for youth and young adults with disabilities. Subsequently, this more comprehensive approach was adopted in 1994 by the Council for Exceptional Children (CEC), Division of Career Development and Transition (DCDT):

> Transition refers to a change in status from behaving primarily as a student to assuming emergent adult roles in the community. These roles include employment, participating in postsecondary education, maintaining a home, becoming appropriately involved in the community, and experiencing satisfactory personal and social relationships. The process of enhancing transition involves the participation and coordination of school programs, adult agency services, and natural supports

within the community. The foundations for transition should be laid during the elementary and middle school years, guided by the broad concept of career development. Transition planning should begin no later than age 14, and students should be encouraged, to the full extent of their capabilities, to assume a maximum amount of responsibility for such planning. (Halpern, 1994, p. 117)

In 1990, transition became a requirement in IDEA (P.L. 101–476). This first legislative mandate that defined transition was described as:

. . . a coordinated set of activities for a student, designed within an out-come-oriented process, which promotes movement from school to post-school activities, including post-secondary education, vocational train-ing, integrated employment (including supported employment), contin-uing and adult education, adult services, independent living and com-munity participation. The coordinated set of activities shall take into account the student's preferences and interests, and shall include instruction, community experiences, the development of employment and other post-school adult living objectives, and when appropriate, acquisition of daily living skills and functional vocational evaluation. [IDEA, P.L. 101–476, 20 U.S.C. Chapter 33, § 140 (a) (19)]

This legislative definition provided specific requirements as to the types of services that should be considered in developing a transition program for youth with disabilities (e.g., community experiences and functional vocational evaluation).

The transition definition developed by Halpern (1994) and adopted by the CEC, DCDT, extends beyond basic federal mandates and broadens the outcomes of transition. In contrast, the IDEA 1997 defi-nition provides transition professionals a set of federal requirements and, to some degree, parameters by which transition services are to be delivered. There are many similarities between IDEA's and DCDT's definitions, but there are also two distinct differences: the extent of stu-dents' input *and* the nature of the transition process.

The IDEA and DCDT definitions both address students' input in the transition process. The IDEA definition requires transition profes-sionals to take into account students' *preferences and interests.* The DCDT definition also addresses students' input but in a more descrip-tive and prescriptive manner. The DCDT definition, for example, states that students should be *encouraged, to the fullest extent of their capa-*

bilities, to assume a maximum amount of responsibility for such [transition] *planning.* The manner in which the students' input are described in these two definitions represents a conceptual difference in the interpretation of *students' input.* It also indicated a difference in the level of significance placed upon the students' involvement in the transition process.

The IDEA definition refers to transition as a process that *promotes movement from school to postschool activities* [IDEA, P.L. 101–476, 20 U.S.C. Chapter 33, § 140 (a) (19)]. The transition process in this definition refers to an outward change from one environment (i.e., school) to another environment that addresses different activities (i.e., postschool activities). The nature of the transition process in the DCDT definition is quite different. The DCDT definition refers to the transitions as a *change in status from behaving primarily as a student to assuming emergent adult roles* (Halpern, 1994, p. 117). The transition process in this definition is internal occurring within the individual.

Despite the differences in these two definitions, both address issues critical to the success of young people with disabilities. The guidance provided by both of these definitions gives transition providers direction as they provide services to youth and young adults with disabilities. The language of the federal transition legislation provides an overall description of transition services, whereas the DCDT definition provides a description as to how these services might be accomplished. In summary, IDEA's definition might be considered the *letter of the law,* whereas DCDT's definition reflects the *spirit of the law.*

The definition of transition services remained the same between the 1990 and 1997 amendments to IDEA. However, in 2004, the IDEA was amended and the legislative definition of transition was further delineated. These changes were made, in part, to bring IDEA closer aligned with the NCLBA. Some of the changes in the transition definition from the IDEA of 1997 amendments to those of the 2004 amendments are found in bold print in Table 2-1.

A significant change in terminology between the 1997 and 2004 definitions is the change from *outcome-oriented process* to *results-oriented process.* The 2004 definition also provides more clarification as to what is expected as the focus of the transition process (i.e., *improving the academic and functional achievement of the child with a disability*). Another change occurred with the replacement of *vocational training with voca-*

Table 2-1. A COMPARISON OF THE IDEA 1997 AND IDEA 2004.

Individuals with Disabilities Education Act of 1997 P.L. 105–17	*Individuals with Disabilities Education Improvement Act of 2004 P.L. 108–446*
Transition services—The term 'transition services' means a coordinated set of activities for a **student with a disability** that—	Transition services—term "transition services" means a coordinated set of activities for a **child** with a disability that—
(A) are designed within an **outcome**-oriented process, which **promotes** movement from school to post-school activities, including postsecondary education, vocational **training**, integrated employment (including supported employment), continuing and adult education, adult services, independent living, or community participation;	(A) are designed to be within a **results-oriented process, that is focused on improving the academic and functional achievement of the child with a disability to facilitate the child's** movement from school to post-school activities, including postsecondary education, vocational **education**, integrated employment (including supported employment), continuing and adult education, adult services, independent living, or community participation;
(B) are based upon the individual student's needs, taking into account the student's preferences and interests; and	(B) are based on the individual child's needs, taking into account the **child's strengths**, preferences, and interests; and
(C) include instruction, related services, community experiences, the development of employment and other post-school adult living objectives, and, when appropriate, acquisition of daily living skills and functional vocational evaluation.	(C) include instruction, related services, community experiences, the development of employment and other post-school adult living objectives, and when appropriate, acquisition of daily living skills and functional vocational evaluation.
[IDEA, P.L. 105–17, 20 U.S.C. Chapter 33, § 633 (a) (25)]	[IDEA, P.L. 108–446, 20 U.S.C. Chapter 34, § 602 (a) (34)]

tional education. As of this writing, the regulations for IDEA 2004 have yet to be released. By examining the changes in the 1997 and 2004 definitions at a surface level only, it seems that the definition has become more specific in terms of the transition process and that this process should have results. It also appears to include more of an emphasis on academics. The interpretations of these changes, however, must wait until regulations are provided.

An understanding of the definition of transition is important because it sets the parameters for policy development, program implementation, and evaluation standards. The elements of the transition definition set specific requirements that must be implemented in transition programs, e.g., postsecondary education, vocational education, integrated employment. In addition, transition professionals need to have a shared definition and vision of transition so they can collaboratively work toward the successful transition of the young people with disabilities they serve. Although obtaining a shared understanding of transition is one of the first steps in delivering effective transition services, it is also necessary to develop an understanding of the nature and purpose of agencies that provide transition services. Special education services is an entitlement, whereas one must be eligible to receive VR services. Confusion between the requirements of these two programs can lead to misunderstanding, poor relations, and worse yet, lack of services to young people with disabilities.

Transition: Education and Services

Entitlement versus Eligibility

Educational and vocational services are provided through transition programs that are primarily rendered through the service delivery systems of special education and VR. In the area of transition, these service systems have an opportunity to combine their efforts to produce best practices along with successful outcomes for youth and young adults with disabilities. As in most cases, however, there are barriers that impede this movement. These barriers, or "traffic jams," in the movement toward successful transition can be identified as barriers that stem from potential differences in the systems; their respective goals, philosophies, and practices.

One such basic difference found between the systems of special education and VR begins with the initial question of who receives services and how that decision is made. Special education is considered an *entitlement* program, whereas VR services are provided to those who meet certain *eligibility* criteria. In the special education system, "entitlement" refers to the concept that all children (specifically including those with disabilities) have the right to a free and appropriate public education in the least restrictive environment along with the guarantee of due process procedures (1975, Education for All Handicapped

Children Act, P.L. 94–142). This lies in sharp contrast to VR services, where there is no guarantee or right to services, but rather becoming a recipient of such services is contingent upon an individual meeting eligibility requirements. Basic eligibility is determined upon the following areas of inquiry which reflect language used in federal laws such as the 1973 Rehabilitation Act and subsequent amendments. This inquiry includes the following reasoning: (1) Does the individual have a disability? (2) Does the individual have functional limitations as a result of the disability that significantly interfere with their ability to obtain or maintain gainful employment? (3) Is there a reasonable expectation that vocational rehabilitation services can be provided that will lead to employment? (Brabham, Mandeville, & Koch, 1998).

Of significance is the fact that VR services are targeted toward serving individuals who are considered those with the most significant disabilities. When considering degree or level of disability, some students who have benefited from special education may not be considered to meet the criterion of "most significant disability" to be eligible for VR services. Students with what may be considered by some to be milder forms of disabilities (learning disabilities, attention deficit disorder) may be able to navigate their transition from school to work successfully without the benefit or need of VR services even though the presence of a disability is recognized. Alternatively, upon initial intake and assessment, other students may be considered to meet the eligibility criteria although potential for gainful employment (and consequently the provision of VR services) would be problematic.

Differences seen in the systems include definitions that drive practices for both. An example of this difference is seen in the nature of services provided via each system. In special education, services are available for students based upon the need for these services. In fact, the need for services guarantees their provision in order to meet federal legislation ensuring children with disabilities an appropriate education in the least restrictive environment. Therefore, as long as a need exists, the service will be made available. By comparison, in the VR system, upon a favorable eligibility determination, services are provided that are time-limited. In comparison to special education, in VR there is no guarantee that as long as there is a need, the provision of specific services will be extended. Inherent in the VR system is the goal of gainful employment for each individual and the provision of services is used as a tool to meet this goal. Once an individual has completed the course of a time-limited service, they are not entitled to remain indefinitely in services or programs such as vocational evaluation, job training, or work adjustment. Typically, individuals receive a series of necessary services that are needed to meet one's overall goal of employment. Often parents of children with the most significant disabilities receiving special education services are delighted with services received in VR programs but are dismayed when they realize that such programs or services have a "shelf-life" and usually will not be ongoing throughout their son's or daughter's life.

The difference between systems as exemplified in those seen in the governing philosophies of *entitlement* versus *eligibility* often creates confusion and may result in a lack of provision of services for some youth with disabilities. For example, students with physical disabilities may not qualify for special education but may be determined eligible for VR services (Szymanski, Hanley-Maxwell, & Asselin, 1992). Alternatively, students may be characterized as having behavioral or disciplinary problems that interfere with learning and one's typical educational progression. This, in turn, may lead to the use of potential resources offered through special education services. When these youth prepare to leave secondary education, additional assistance and resources may be sought through VR in order to arrive at a successful transition to adult life. While an identified disability may provide an opportunity for an intake interview, and possibly a vocational evaluation in the VR system, it does not automatically guarantee the provision of services through that system. If the student, with an identified disability, does not meet the above-noted eligibility criteria, vocational services may not be forthcoming. In many situations, students, parents, teachers, and others may not understand the difference in the philosophical orientation of systems but only see the systems as potential sources of hope and help. When services are denied from VR after a student has received services from special education in some fashion throughout their primary and/or secondary school years, it is easy to understand why students, parents, and others react with indignation and hostility to a system they feel is refusing to offer needed help. Misunderstanding abounds because systems are based on differing philosophies and service criteria, yet they are linked in their directives to assist in the successful transition of youth with disabilities.

Transition Planning and Service Delivery

Collaboration: Special Education and Rehabilitation

Inherent in the definition of "transition" is the concept of collaboration. As stated in the Individuals with Disabilities Education Act (IDEA), transition is referred to as "a coordinated set of activities for a student. . ." (IDEA, P.L. 101–476). For activities to be coordinated and lead to the outcomes identified, it is apparent that more than one individual or one agency will be working toward a common goal. Indeed, in order to produce quality interventions for transition students, various disciplines must collaborate and function on a team basis in order to coordinate transition activities and services (Browning, 1997). As service providers attempt to meet their goals and carry out their individual agency's missions, the process of collaborating and teaming do not always meet with success. Due to differing philosophies (entitlement versus eligibility) and service delivery needs and processes, a teaming spirit can easily be compromised by an "us versus them" mentality.

Issues that tend to produce "speed bumps" in the path toward meaningful collaboration and teaming are commonly found in specific process areas. These include the Individualized Educational Plan (IEP) and Individualized Plan for Employment (IPE), documents produced by each system that should help to establish student-identified goals, the *referral process,* where students with disabilities in need of transition services may be overlooked altogether, and *assessment,* an area where confusion and mismatched goals abound. In addition, individuals comprising the two systems may not coordinate their timing or agree upon the priority or delivery methods of such services, thereby affecting the successful completion of identified goals. Finally, *service delivery* is an area where best practices can be highlighted, especially those that point toward successful collaboration.

Individualized Education Program

The purpose of an Individualized Education Program (IEP) is to identify the student's educational needs and to develop a plan to address those needs through special education and related services. In order to properly address a student's needs, the IEP must include a statement of his or her present levels of academic and functional performance. This information is helpful in identifying annual goals that will address the student's needs and the progress to be achieved within one year. If the student has significant disabilities, the IEP will also include objectives or benchmarks to provide periodic measurements toward the attainment of annual goals. In order to monitor the student's progress throughout the year, the IEP must also identify when periodic progress reports on the student's attainment of his or her annual IEP goals will be provided. These progress reports must be provided periodically and at least as often as reports are provided to students without disabilities

The IEP must also address how the student's disability affects his or her "involvement and progress in the general education curriculum" [IDEA, P.L. 108–446, 20 U.S.C. 1401, § 612 (a) (14)]. Specifically, the extent to which the student is educated and participates with other children without disabilities must be described in an IEP. A student's participation in extracurricular or other nonacademic activities must also be included. In addition, a rationale must be provided if the student is not to participate and be included with students without disabilities. With regard to participation in districtwide assessments, the IEP must identify any appropriate accommodations that might be necessary for the individual student so that his or her academic and functional performance can be measured. Also, the IEP should indicate if the students shall take an alternate assessment or the regular statewide or districtwide assessment used to measure student achievement.

An IEP for transition must be in effect when a student is sixteen years of age and updated annually until he or she exits high school. This IEP must include a statement of transition services that addresses the student's course of study. This should include the consideration of a college preparatory or a vocational education high school program. The identification of the type of program the student will participate consequently will involve the decision regarding what type of exit document the student will be working towards during his or her high school years, i.e., diploma or nondiploma course of study. Requirements for a regular high school diploma are set by state and/or local education agencies. Criteria for high school diplomas may include "(1) completing certain courses, (2) accumulating a certain number of credits, (3) passing a test that may be known as a proficiency, graduation, or exit exam" (Garfinkel, 2000, p. 4:4). Alternative exit documents to a high school diploma include certificates of completion or attendance and alternative diploma options (e.g., occupational diploma). The statement of transition services should be based on transition assessments that measure the student's need for training, education, employment and, as appropriate, independent living skills.

The IEP is a plan developed by a team of persons who meet annually to review the student's progress and develop goals to be accomplished during the upcoming academic year. This team must include the parents of the student, at least one general education and one special education teacher for the student, a representative of the local education agency, someone to interpret evaluation results, other individuals with knowledge or special expertise of the student, and the student, whenever appropriate. As the student becomes transition age, the appropriateness of the attendance of other agency representatives and the student become more evident.

Students should be a part of their transition IEP meetings because it is their future that is being planned at the meeting. The importance of student involvement in IEP transition planning has been recognized by professional organizations such as the CEC's DCDT. According to the DCDT position statement on self-determination, the benefits of student involvement in IEP meetings include the opportunity for them to learn ". . . self-advocacy, decision-making, self-evaluation, and goal attainment skills" (Field, Martin, Miller, Ward, & Wehmeyer, 1998, p. 120). The development of these skills will provide students with disabilities the tools needed to become empowered adults who can make their own decisions and who are in control of their lives. The development of self-determination does not occur, however, by happenstance. Professionals who work with these students must value the importance of self-determination and provide opportunities and guidance for its development. Student involvement or, better yet, student-led IEPs provide an appropriate and logical opportunity for students to practice and improve their self-determination, self-advocacy, and decision-making skills.

VR counselors should be included in IEP team meetings for students preparing for transition, since they are individuals who would be considered as having special expertise and/or personnel who would provide a related service. Their attendance at the IEP meeting is especially important when VR services are being considered and/or when the student is in need of VR services to obtain the postschool outcome of employment or VR services are needed to obtain a college degree that will lead to employment. The legislative definition of transition requires a "coordinated set of services" to meet the transition needs of students with disabilities. As such, school and VR personnel must collaboratively work together in order to prevent parents and students from becoming "confused," "intimidated," "frustrated," and "overwhelmed" (Benz et al., 1995, p. 143).

The IEP for transition should be a team process resulting in planning that addresses the students' needs and reflects their interests and preferences. Postschool outcome goals should be identified and appropriate curricula planning and necessary transition services should be provided to reach those goals. The collaboration between school and VR professionals is needed to provide students with disabilities a smooth transition from the entitlement programs of the schools to the eligibility programs of adult services agencies such as VR and/or community mental health/mental retardation. The IEP serves as a working document that provides the structure for developing coordinated services while the student is in high school. For those who qualify for VR, they will also have an IPE that outlines the plan and services needed for the person to obtain employment.

Individualized Plan for Employment

Upon determination of eligibility for services, the VR needs of each individual are assessed. The written plan that results from this process forms the IPE, a jointly formulated plan that specifies the vocational goal and details the ways and means of achieving the specified employment goal. For youth receiving transition services, the IPE is accomplished after the rehabilitation counselor becomes involved in their case, typically originating through attendance and participation in the student's IEP meeting. The IPE should be formulated in a timely manner once all necessary assessments have been completed. This results in two documents that serve as guides for the student. The IEP is the document of record for the school system, while the IPE is the document of record for the VR agency. Both documents should work in tandem to bring about a successful transition process.

The IPE is provided in writing to the person who is the recipient of VR services, or their representative (usually a family member or guardian). The IPE must be developed and provided to the individual in a written format, but also in a format that constitutes an appropriate mode of communication for persons whose reading ability is compromised by disability. While the IPE is primarily a planning document that outlines VR's role and responsibilities, it also specifies the role and responsibilities of the client as well as the rights and remedies available to the client if a dispute arises during the rehabilitation process. Information regarding due process, the availability of client assistance program services and support in obtaining such services must be explained when the IPE is signed and at other points during the rehabilitation process.

The IPE document contains several component parts. Of major importance in the formulation of the IPE is the role that informed choice plays. Informed choice implies that each individual is given sufficient and specific information regarding potential choices in order to make decisions that reflect their individual needs, preferences, and goals. The component parts of this plan include (a) the client's identification and selection of an employment outcome (or goal), (b) identification and selection of specific VR services that will be provided to achieve the employment outcome, (c) the entity and the setting in which the VR services will be provided, (d) the employment setting, and (e) the methods used to procure the services. Of necessity, goals and services are set within a timeline for completion based on the overall employability goal of the individual. The written document itself is agreed to and signed by the consumer (or their representative) and the rehabilitation counselor.

Of additional importance, found within the IPE document, criteria are identified that help to evaluate the progress and movement each individual is making toward their overall employment goal. As such, IPEs are reviewed based on timelines established for short-term and long-term goals. This must occur, at a minimum, on an annual basis and this review is conducted by the rehabilitation counselor and the client. When appropriate and needed, substantive changes must be agreed to, resulting in an amendment to the IPE, and acknowledged by signature of both the client and rehabilitation counselor.

For students who are in transition programs, the IPE usually becomes part of the IEP meeting in its formulation, planning, implementation, and evaluation. As students are assessed for their IEPs in conjunction with needs for training, education, and employment, the IPE becomes a vehicle by which additional services can be brought to the table and specific plans that speak to the employment issues of youth with disabilities are implemented. With this in mind, the necessity of making sure that collaboration exists between the VR and special education systems becomes apparent. Without agreed-upon collaborative measures, the two systems may not produce the appropriate services needed for successful transition.

VR Referral Process

The referral process can be described best as the manner in which students receiving special education services become involved with VR and its transition services. In other words, how do most students who are involved in special education access VR services and, in turn, become involved with services that assist in their movement to postsecondary outcomes and adult life?

Referrals to VR occur in several ways. In a scenario where best practices in transition occur, the referral to VR is a process agreed upon by the local school system and the VR agency. Typically, there is a memorandum of understanding (MOU) between service systems to establish procedures, roles, and lines of communication. For instance, each school year when planning IEP meetings for students receiving special education services, students and parents are given information regarding service agencies from who they may receive assistance. When communication lines are open and activities are coordinated between the two systems, referrals are made to a local VR counselor whose caseload is in the area of transition. The special education program provides the VR counselor with names of potential students who may be eligible based on their involvement in special educational services due to a disability. This referral to VR is often followed by an eligibility determination. After the determination of eligibility and before the IEP meeting for transition is held, students and their parents have the right to request that a VR counselor be involved in the IEP meeting. In this instance, the VR counselor along with the student, family, and IEP team helps to identify postsecondary goals and needed services, set timelines, and coordinate activities that encompass both educational goals and planning for employment. In fact, this is where the IPE comes into being and, along with the IEP, is considered the contract which guides service provision for transition.

In the best case scenario, communication between the two systems is a coordinated, seamless event where activities are put into action based on students' goals and dreams which are established in writing in the IEP and IPE documents. Utilizing best practices may indicate that a VR counselor with a transition caseload be housed in a secondary school setting on either a full-time or part-time basis. Referrals are made routinely along with team meetings being held where various service providers review and re-evaluate IEP and IPE documents in terms of timelines, goals, and needed services. In such a situation, the VR counselor is considered a team member at each student's IEP meeting unless it is indicated by the student and/or parents that the counselor's services are not required.

When a best case scenario does not exist, referrals to VR can and do occur; however, such referrals typically may take place at a later point for the student. Referrals to VR can be made through involvement with agencies such as mental retardation and developmental disabilities (MR/DD) programs, WIA programs, mental health programs, community rehabilitation programs, youth services programs, or employment agencies (Baer, 2005). Finally, self-referral is always an option for students and families. Upon referral, an intake interview is usually scheduled to begin the process of determining eligibility.

Assessment

Assessment is "a systematic approach to gathering information about individuals" and is conducted for some specific purpose (U.S. Department of Labor, 1999, p. 1–1). In transition, assessments occur at several junctures for varying reasons. While each assessment continues to gather information about an individual, the specific purpose and end goal of that assessment indicate a different point in the transition process. Because of differing philosophies and roles, assessment is an additional area where confusion may exist between special education and VR. Although assessment needs may mirror one another to some degree in each system, questions about the purpose and the exact nature of assessments used may leave students and families wondering why so many and to what end.

All students are quite familiar with assessment from the standpoint of academics. In relationship to academics, assessment is used to determine knowledge, ability, ranking, skills, and achievement. Assessment is part and parcel of the school experience. It is expected and planned whether preparing for a quiz on lessons learned each week or for high school exit exams or SAT scores. Students with disabilities who are involved in special education are quite familiar with being assessed as well. Additionally, these students are assessed relative to their need for services dependent upon the nature of the disability as well as how a disability may impede ability to learn and successfully maneuver through the schooling process. Assessment then is used to determine if students are meeting short-term and long-term goals. Consequently, assessment results may be used to assist teachers and students in the development of remediation plans, the identification of successful learning and behavioral strategies, and the formulation of a written IEP document.

In rehabilitation, the focus of assessment typically takes a more global perspective and academics are considered as one segment in the overall picture of life related to employability. Of necessity, and based on priorities of the VR system, the primary focus of assessment centers on eligibility for services and the determination of vocational functioning regarding the goals of an individual consumer. The same misunderstandings concerning entitlement versus eligibility are encountered when students with disabilities are assessed, yet again, as to the type, nature, and scope of disability and potential for impact in meeting postsecondary goals specifically leading to employment. Resulting feelings from parents or students regarding what often seems to be redundant may not always be positive, although from the perspective of the VR agency, this may or may not be the case.

When individuals apply for VR services and eligibility determinations are made, the rehabilitation counselor can use existing current information regarding the applicant. This may include information that is available from other programs and providers such as educational settings and other agencies, e.g., Social Security Administration. If the existing information is unavailable or insufficient, the rehabilitation counselor may order other assessments to determine eligibility. The need for specific types of information center on the criteria VR employs to determine eligibility: (a) the applicant has a physical or mental impairment, (b) the physical or mental impairment constitutes or results in a substantial impediment to employment, (c) the applicant can benefit in terms of an employment outcome from the provision of services from VR, and (d) a determination that the applicant requires VR services to prepare for, secure, retain, or regain employment.

Further, when there are questions regarding the person's ability to benefit from VR services leading to employment, the rehabilitation counselor must explore the individual's abilities, capabilities, and capacity to perform in a work situation through the use of a trial work experience.

Identification of the presence of a disability is usually not a question or concern; however, school documents may be incomplete or insufficient for VR's purposes when considering the diagnosis of a disability for a particular student. If documentation of the disability does not exist in case records provided by the school or other agencies, then a medical or psychiatric/psychological assessment regarding a diagnosis may be considered a priority from the rehabilitation counselor's perspective. This requires an assessment from a third party who may or may not be a part of the individual student's school system. If a statement or diagnosis of disability does exist, there are provisions relative to the timeliness of previous diagnoses. A statement of disability must be made within a time frame that is considered current by state and federal regulations. Parents may feel that continued assessment is one more hurdle when the school system has already indicated the need for special education services based on observed impediments. Parents may legitimately wonder about the VR agency's need for additional documentation if the school system has already indicated it has such information or documentation. Educating parents, students, and service providers about the differences in systems helps those seeking services from the VR agency to realize that diagnosis can be an important issue in the determination of eligibility and continued assessment is not always redundant.

Greater congruence between the systems is being sought and reinforced through federal legislative changes (WIA Act of 1998). In a determination for eligibility, if appropriate evidence is given that indicates the applicant is eligible for Social Security benefits and the individual can benefit in terms of an employment outcome from VR services, a presumption of eligibility may be made for the applicant. This presumption of eligibility helps to speed timeliness that individuals can move from system to system and receive appropriate services and supports. For students in transition programs, presumed eligibility also decreases the risk of losing students with disabilities based on poor referral methods and lack of interagency collaboration.

Following the determination of eligibility, vocational assessment becomes important as the rehabilitation counselor and student work together to formulate employment goals. Federal legislation for VR services indicates that employment goals should be based on an individual's strengths, resources, priorities, concerns, abilities, capabilities, and interests. From this perspective, it is imperative that a dynamic and ecological evaluation be employed. Havranek, Field, and Grimes (2001) describe dynamic assessments as a process referring:

> . . . to the collection of information about the performance of an individual in several community settings and under several naturally occurring conditions. Situational tests require the person to perform a task in a situation similar to that for which the person is being evaluated. Situational tests often prove to be beneficial in predicting performance in a situation similar to that of the test. (p. 62)

Further, ecological evaluations are performed where students live, work, and attend school or training; in general, in naturally occurring environments for that student. Academic performance is not the priority and is considered just one aspect of an individual's overall life. Ecological evaluation is considered a comprehensive way to analyze skills and behaviors of individuals in their natural environments. This approach helps to focus on strengths and lets the student, along with the rehabilitation counselor, determine "whether their weaknesses can be accommodated with adaptive equipment or alternative methods, such as job restructuring, or remediation through training or skill acquisition" (Havranek, Field, & Grimes, 2001, p. 65).

Finally, the most important aspect of assessment, from either system's perspective, is that results are summarized, synthesized, and integrated into meaningful and relevant information that is used for the benefit of the student. Assessment results provide the foundation for planning, identification of needed services, implementation of strategies leading to success in the areas of behavior, academics, and employment (or postsecondary outcomes), and, finally, form the basis for the development of formative and summative evaluation criteria (assessment without a clear purpose and goal is meaningless and yields little meaningful information).

Best Practices in Service Delivery:
Special Education and Rehabilitation

Self-Determination

Finding ways in which to foster self-determination in transition service delivery is considered a best practice because it goes to the very heart of the values and philosophy that support the rehabilitation system (Curtis, 1998). The values of choice and independence are closely related to self-determination and all are considered to exist within the rubric of empowerment (Szymanski, 1994). By fostering self-determination in youth who are in transition, we mean creating an understanding that youth with disabilities have the *right* and the *ability* to make choices. More importantly, this often means helping one to experience what it *feels* like and how one *acts* when they are truly self-determined and empowered.

Self-determination and empowerment are key indicators that point to quality of life issues for most individuals with disabilities. Learning how to act upon these rights, privileges, and responsibilities, unfortunately, may be lost to many youth in transition. Negative factors that may impede this process include paternalistic attitudes and behaviors of service providers or parents. For example, when it comes to youth with disabilities, how many of us have heard the following, or some variation?

- "I'm the professional here. I know what's best and I'll make the final decision. After all, it's the agency's money and I want to make sure it's well spent."
- "I can't let her make this decision alone. Her IQ is just too low and she just doesn't understand."
- "He can't go to work there. They'll take advantage of him or they might even make fun of him and he'll get hurt in the process."

While these fears and feelings may have their basis in actual life experiences, they tend to move the individual with a disability into a passive stance of learned helplessness and dependence which may be accompanied by a sense of powerlessness and inadequacy. At the very least, one loses his or her willingness to risk and learns that compliance results in the delivery of resources that may not fulfill one's dreams or personal goals.

For most adolescents, and specifically for adolescents with disabilities, learning to be self-determined entails learning quality decision-making skills so that choices are made that are consistent within one's framework of goals, abilities, skills, and dreams for the future. This means that we teach decision-making skills by working through lists of potential consequences and benefits based on differing scenarios, allow adolescents to make their decisions, and then analyze the outcomes of those decisions in a psychoeducational learning paradigm.

What does self-determination look like? Indicators of self-determination have been described by Martin and Marshall (1996), who identified seven constructs of self-determination. These include (a) self-awareness, (b) self-advocacy, (c) self-efficacy, (d) decision making, (e) independent performance, (f) self-evaluation, and (g) adjustment. Strategies that foster self-determination skills have been identified by West, Barcus, Brooke, and Rayfield (1995, p. 363). These include:

- Enhancing students goal-setting and decision-making skills;
- Instructing students in their legal rights and self-advocacy skills;
- Building students' confidence and self-esteem through positive experiences with choice and control;
- Allowing students with disabilities opportunities to participate in educational transition planning and rewarding their participation;
- Reinforcing students' inner strengths such as persistence, motivation, creativity, and responsibility;
- Facilitating informed choice through direct exposure to vocational, social, and independent living options.

Based on these strategies, it is clear that self-determination involves a skill-building element, not just a philosophical orientation towards the delivery of services. Both special education and VR can include measures that allow students to learn how to make decisions and gain an understanding of what self-determination feels and looks like. Most importantly, self-determination means that students with disabilities get the opportunity to experience success on their terms.

Family Involvement

Families help define who, as people, we are and to understand our potential as well as our limits. Families act as the boundaries that constitute our world until we are ready emotionally, physically, and mentally to venture beyond those boundaries. As adults, when life becomes uncertain, we may seek to return to the confines of those same boundaries where we hope to find love, acceptance, and security.

For youth with disabilities, family involvement has the potential for influencing the transition process. For all of us, families provide a sense of continuity that goes beyond our individual self. The family acts as a placeholder in time and gives context to life. We are in relationships in families. For youth with disabilities, this may be especially important when there is a sense of being different or not fitting in across one or several environments. The security and familiarity of home may help to yield the assurance needed for individuals to take risks, engage in new behaviors, and form new relationships. The sense of willingness and degree of trust exhibited by an individual often stem from the nature and depth of relationships experienced in the family and home environment.

As young people progress through transition programs and services, they will meet many new and different people. The majority of these individuals may be service providers who are involved with the student for varying lengths of time and to varying degrees of closeness. While service providers have the opportunity to impact the lives of such youth, most service providers remain on a peripheral level that is not at the same level as family members. Service providers will come and go, and may or may not impact the student's life; however, family members and the home context will continue to influence the student and serve as a base from which the student responds to the world (including transition programs and service providers). Therefore, the quality and nature of family environments greatly impact the amount of support and the nature of support a student with disabilities can count on as he or she progresses through transition. Inherent in the concept of supporting the student in transition is the ability of the family to promote independence for their child and the expertise that family members can provide as transition professionals seek ways to enhance postsecondary outcomes (Browning, 1997).

Of significance to the VR professional are data related to employment and youth with disabilities. Hasazi et al. (1985) reported, in their study, that 83 percent of youth with disabilities found jobs through a network of family and friends, whereas 17 percent were assisted in finding jobs by a variety of services. Sitlington, Frank, and Cooper (1989) studied 648 graduates with learning disabilities who were out of school for one year and employed. Their findings indicated that 43 percent of the students studied had found jobs by themselves and 40 percent found jobs through the involvement of family members. Additionally, Bissonnette (2002) indicates that most employers go about filling a job opening using the following steps: (a) hiring someone the supervisor knows, (b) hiring someone a co-worker knows, (c) hiring someone who has already been interviewed by human resources, (d) using private employment agencies and/or nonprofit employment programs, and (e) advertising the job opening in the newspaper. She further indicates that 80 to 90 percent of all jobs are filled using the first three elements listed above.

In light of this information, the role and significance of family involvement are further enhanced when discussing postsecondary outcomes for students, especially employment outcomes. Family members provide a source of information and serve as a network for youth with disabilities regarding employment concerns. The importance of ensuring that families are *actively* involved in IEP and IPE teams is emphasized when there is an understanding of what families can add with their involvement in these activities. Transition service providers must first understand the potential role that families can play in supporting independence, providing information, and utilizing their connections in conjunction with students with disabilities. Transition service providers then can assist families in understanding the role both parties can play as they seek to partner together to provide successful transition outcomes.

Postsecondary Education and Training

A recognized positive postschool outcome for students with disabilities is their participation in postsecondary education and training (Sitlington & Clark, 2006; Test, Aspel, & Everson, 2006; Webster, Clary, & Griffith, 2005). Although this is considered to be a desired outcome, there are differences in postsecondary participation between students with and without disabilities. According to the National Longitudinal Transition Study–2 report, of the former students surveyed, only 19 percent were attending postsecondary education compared to

40 percent of their peers without disabilities (Newman, 2005). There are also differences between the types of institutions students with and without disabilities attend. According to Horn and Berktold (1999), students with disabilities were less likely than their peers without disabilities to enroll in public four-year institutions and more likely to be enrolled in sub-baccalaureate institutions, i.e., public two-year colleges. For those students who do attend four-year institutions, of the 9 percent of undergraduates who reported having disabilities in 1999–2000, 22 percent of them reported not receiving needed services or accommodations. In addition to their difficulty attaining services, students with disabilities are unfortunately less likely to be academically qualified for admission and less prepared for college-level courses than their peers without disabilities (National Center on Educational Statistics, 1999).

Transition planning that addresses postsecondary options and includes the necessary coursework and experiences can help prepare students for their transition to postsecondary education settings. Students with disabilities who plan to attend college go through the same processes as those without disabilities experience, but they must also address additional challenges (Sitlington, 2003). In order to address these challenges, transition planning should include the development of the students' (a) knowledge of disability, (b) knowledge of legislation, (c) knowledge of postsecondary supports, and (d) ability to self advocate (Milsom & Hartley, 2005). Students must be able to locate support services for students with disabilities on the campuses of postsecondary institutions and then seek supports that are needed for them to be successful. Having access to educational accommodations, supports, and services is an essential factor in the success of students with disabilities who pursue a postsecondary education (Tagayuna, Stodden, Zeleznik, & Whelley, 2005). However, students must first fully understand their disability and describe to others the supports they need.

Prior to entering college, students with disabilities are protected under IDEA. After they exit the public schools, students must be responsible for the services they may need to be successful (Flexer, et al., 2005). They also need to know about legislation and their rights. Armed with the knowledge of how and under what laws they are protected, students will be able to recognize when their rights are being violated. Finally, students need to have self-advocacy skills because as students exit from their high school programs, they must be able to advocate on their own behalf and not depend upon their parents or teachers.

Employment and Community Rehabilitation Services

Employment is one component of the multifaceted prism of life that helps to reflect meaning and structure for an individual. Employment obviously yields a salary, but it also provides intangibles that point to quality of life indicators for people. Some examples include the status of having a job, satisfaction in knowing that you can perform a job in a quality manner, security in the sense that one is a contributing member of society and "fits" into society because you are employed, and the benefits of friendships and supports formed in relationship to one's job. For students with disabilities, transition programs include employment as a priority because for many youth, employment is the primary postschool outcome sought. In this sense, employment, specifically located within one's community of choice, is considered a best practice in transition because it helps to establish and provide a context for an individual's life. Employment is part of the "ebb and flow" of life. Our jobs support us in monetary and emotional ways, and we in turn support other individuals, jobs, and places of employment through our lives and resources.

Employment and community rehabilitation services are employment services that primarily take place within natural community environments. Specific vocational goals and objectives that have been identified in the student's IPE are implemented through the community rehabilitation experience. These experiences typically have a broad range and are developmental in nature. Initial rehabilitation services can serve the function of helping youth to understand the world of work and establish a healthy understanding of working requirements and a positive work ethic. More intense rehabilitation services may include temporary and trial employment experiences, job clubs and mentoring projects, and planning for supported employment. Within the context of employment and community rehabilitation services are two overriding concerns: (a) ensuring that employment outcomes occur in integrated settings for youth with disabilities to the fullest extent possible and (b) ensuring that personal choice is reflected in employment outcomes. Strategies used within a community rehabilitation context are described below.

SITUATIONAL ASSESSMENT AND JOB ANALYSES. "The primary purpose of a situational assessment is to observe, record, and interpret a student's general work behavior and adaptation in a specific work or community setting" (Flexer & Luft, 2005, pp. 128–131). This type of assessment provides the service provider an opportunity to examine the student's performance in a specific environment by looking for behaviors or work skills that apply to that environment. Situational assessments can be used in a variety of settings with simulated job tasks or environments or as a means to examine specific portions of jobs that may be problematic. Job analyses can be used as a tool to identify the component parts of jobs or tasks to ensure that no critical steps are left undone and that the task is completed in an efficient manner. Once the necessary steps are identified to complete a task, the student can be cued using visual images, verbal instructions, gestures, or other memory tools for overall successful completion of the task or job.

JOB TRYOUT. Job tryouts include the concept of a mobile work crew or enclave. In this situation, a group of usually less than eight students provides services that are contractual in nature, i.e., janitorial, landscaping. The crew and/or enclave members are supervised by an employment specialist (usually called a job coach) as they perform their jobs in an integrated work setting. Job tryouts may include simulated job sites and environments as well.

JOB-SITE TRAINING/PAID WORK TRIALS. On-the-job training is systematic instruction of job tasks and related behavioral skills that are appropriate in a specified employment setting. Related behavioral skills may include appropriate professional communication, on-task behavior, and proper use of meal and break times. The student is typically oriented to the job, including the physical working environment and natural supports found in co-workers who are willing to assist when necessary. In this situation, individuals are paid for their work and for the time needed to orient and train them to the job.

JOB COACHING. A job coach is an employment specialist who accompanies a student with a disability to the worksite and guides them in understanding the requirements and tasks involved in a job (usually in a competitive employment setting). A job coach may be used extensively as an individual begins his or her training or starts to learn the job tasks required in the work setting. As the worker makes progress and requires less coaching, the job coach fades his or her instructional cues and prompts, eventually fading his or her presence from the work area and then the job site.

SUPPORTED EMPLOYMENT. Supported employment is useful for individuals who are considered to have the most significant disabilities. Employment goals include integrated work setting opportunities as well as the opportunity to earn equitable wages and benefits for individuals with significant disabilities. Positive outcomes associated with supported employment include the development of new skills, enhanced self-esteem, and increased community participation. Types of supported employment services used depends on the needs of individual consumers and the severity of disability involved. Supported employment services may include the use of a job coach for long-term follow-along and individual support in the work setting. Long-term supports are a significant aspect of supported employment services and, in addition to a job coach, may include the use of family and friends, community organizations or service groups, and co-workers and supervisors who provide natural supports in the workplace. Supported employment is a viable option for students with significant disabilities but is not always available depending upon the local school system and resources found within the local community rehabilitation service programs for the state.

Current Issues Impacting Future Service Provisions

There have been over forty years of focused efforts to provide persons with disabilities the rights and opportunities to access integrated environments. These efforts include service goals and priorities in both special education and VR. Positive examples of successful outcomes of the disability movement include deinstitutionalization, integrated classrooms and workplaces, and community integration. Although there have been many changes in philosophy, service delivery, and societal attitudes toward persons with disabilities, there continues to be issues that need to be addressed.

Changes in Legislation

One of the most overriding issues in the delivery of transition services is related to legislation that mandates services for students with disabilities. For example, there continues to be changes in the amendments to the Rehabilitation Act and the IDEA on a regular basis. Although there have been positive outcomes such as the agreed upon definition of transition in both the Rehabilitation and IDEA Acts, there also have been issues associated with changes in mandates that adversely affect service delivery and transition goals. For instance, the focus of IDEA has become more academically oriented in an effort to become more aligned with the No Child Left Behind Act. Concerns of VR may center on deficits in states' budgets that lead to services being provided by order of selection. Although VR services are potentially available to all individuals with disabilities who qualify, legislation requires that individuals with the most significant disabilities be provided services before those with less significant disabilities–hence the term "order of selection." Issues such as these illustrate how legislation can change goals, outcomes, and service delivery.

Collaboration

Although the definition of *transition* indicates that it should be a "coordinated set of activities," there continues to be issues surrounding collaborative efforts between special education and VR. These issues include the need for (a) communication for the coordinated planning of both IEP/IPE meetings, (b) agreement among professionals regarding the nature of appropriate assessments and services, (c) establishing procedures for sharing assessment results across agencies, and (d) developing an understanding of professional roles for each discipline. These are examples of why collaboration continues to be such an important issue in transition and how systems must actively work to provide avenues for collaborative practices and procedures.

Personnel Shortage

There has been an increased shortage of trained personnel in both the special education and VR systems. Reasons for this shortage include the aging out of veteran service providers and problems with recruiting and retaining personnel. In VR, for example, the Comprehensive System for Professional Development has increased the educational requirements needed for new personnel entering the field as well as for current VR counselors. This has resulted in a number of veteran workers who are choosing to exit the field as opposed to obtaining higher education requirements. Although individuals are obtaining graduate degrees, the pay scale for VR professionals has not significantly increased accordingly. Therefore, retaining qualified professionals has been difficult because opportunities that maximize earning potential are available in related fields.

The field of special education has similar issues regarding the recruitment and retention of qualified personnel. For example, educational requirements are continuing to be elevated and redefined, which makes it more difficult to recruit personnel. Also, there is a high level of recidivism in special education. Many first-year special educators, for example, leave teaching within their first five years (Singer, 1992). These shared problems of both special education and VR professions will ultimately impact services for individuals with disabilities.

Conclusion

In conclusion, as the definition of transition indicates, the process requires a "coordinated set of activities." This coordination must involve, at a minimum, the systems of special education and VR to meet the individual educational needs and postschool outcomes for students with disabilities. As service providers, we must continue efforts to maximize best practices and successful outcomes in transition. People with disabilities are at a point in American history where they have the right and should expect no less for their voices to be heard. Recognizing the ability to speak for one's self should result in his or her active involvement in the planning of his or her lives from multiple perspectives (i.e., setting educational and vocational goals). In the process of gaining control of their lives and planning their futures, students with disabilities are becoming advocates for themselves for integration into society.

As seen from previous legislative amendments and priorities, laws will continue to change and shape practices. However, a shared vision among all stakeholders in transition should result in positive postschool outcomes for youth being served. This can be accomplished through shared best practices that are agreed upon and implemented by both systems. This includes a shared understanding of planning procedures for IEP/IPE meetings and enhanced collaboration between the two systems. An understanding of the purpose and role of each system should lead to a further understanding of procedures used by both such as assessment, eligibility versus entitlement, best practices in self-determination, family involvement, and employment practices. These are best practices that have the potential to positively impact post-school outcomes of youth with disabilities.

REFERENCES

Americans with Disabilities Act of 1990, Public Law 101–336, § 2, 104 Stat. 328 (1991).

Baer, R. (2005). Transition planning. In R. W. Flexer, T. J. Simmons, P. Luft, & R. M. Baer (Eds.) *Transition planning for secondary students with disabilities* (2nd Ed., pp. 305–335). Upper Saddle River, NJ: Pearson/Merrill Prentice Hall.

Benz, M. R., Johnson, D. H., Mikkelsen, K. S., & Lindstrom, L. E. (1995). Improving collaboration between schools and vocational rehabilitation: Stakeholder identified barriers and strategies. *Career Development for Exceptional Individuals, 18*(2), 133–144.

Bissonnette, D. (2002). *Beyond traditional job development: The art of creating opportunity.* Chatsworth, CA: Milt Wright & Associates, Inc.

Blackorby, J., & Wagner, M. (1996). Longitudinal post-school outcomes of youth with disabilities: Findings from the National Longitudinal Transition Study. *Exceptional Children, 62*(5), 399–413.

Brabham, R., Mandeville, K., & Koch, L. (1998). The state-federal vocational rehabilitation program. In R. M. Parker & E. M. Szymanski (Eds.), *Rehabilitation counseling; Basics and beyond* (3rd Ed., pp. 41–70). Austin, TX: Pro-Ed.

Brown v. Board of Education, 347 U.S. 483 (1954).

Browning, P. (1997). *Transition-in-action for youth and young adults with disabilities.* Montgomery, AL: Wells Printing.

Cameto, R., & Levine, P. (2004). Changes in employment status and job characteristics of out-of-school youth with disabilities. In M. Wagner, L., Newman, R. Cameto, & P. Levine (Eds.), *Changes over time in the early post-school outcomes of youth with disabilities: A report of findings from the National Longitudinal Transition Study (NLTS) and the National Longitudinal Transition Study-2* (NLTS–2). Retrieved October 21, 2005 from http://www.nlts2.org/pdfs/str6_ch5_emp.pdf

Carl D. Perkins Vocational Education Act. (1984). P.L. 98–524, 98, Stat. 2435.

Curtis, R. S. (1998). Values and valuing in rehabilitation. *Journal of Rehabilitation, 64*(1), 42–47.

Education for All Handicapped Children Act of 1975, Public Law 94–142, § 3, 89 Stat. 773 (1975).

Education for All Handicapped Children Act of 1975, Public Law 98–199, § 1, 97 Stat. 1357 (1983).

Flexer, R. W., & Luft, P. (2005). Transition assessment and post-school outcomes. In R. W. Flexer, T. J. Simmons, P. Luft, & R. M. Baer (Eds.), *Transition planning for secondary students with disabilities* (2nd Ed., pp. 110–140). Upper Saddle River, NJ: Pearson/Merrill Prentice Hall.

Hasazi, S., Gordon, L., Roe, C., Finck, J., Hull, M., & Salembier, G. (1985). A statewide follow-up on post high school employment and residential status of students labeled 'mentally retarded.' *Education and Training of the Mentally Retarded, 20,* 222–234.

Havranek, J., Field, T., & Grimes, J. W. (2001). *Vocational assessment: Evaluating employment potential.* Athens, GA: Elliott & Fitzpatrick, Inc.

Horn, L., & Berktold, J. (1999). Students with disabilities in postsecondary education: A profile of preparation, participation, and outcomes. *Educational Statistics Quarterly, 1*(3), retrieved November 12, 2005, from http://nces.ed.gov/programs/quarterly/vol_1/1_3/4-esq13-a.asp

Individuals with Disabilities Education Act of 1997, P.L. 101–476, § 202, 104 Stat. 1111, 1144 (1990).

Individuals with Disabilities Education Act Amendments of 1997, Public Law 105–17, § 101, 111 Stat. 42 (1997).

Individuals with Disabilities Education Improvement Act, Public Law 108–446, 118, Stat. 2647.

Job Training Partnership Act of 1982, Public Law 97–300, 29, U.S.C. §1501.

Lichtenstein, S. (1998). Characteristics of youth and young adults. In F. R. Rusch & J. G. Chadsey (Eds.), *Beyond high school: Transition from school to work* (pp. 3–35). New York: Wadsworth.

Martin, J. E., & Huber Marshall, L. H. (1996). Choice Maker: Infusing self-determination instruction into the IEP and transition process. In D. J. Sands & M. L. Wehmeyer (Eds.), *Self-determination across the life span* (pp. 215–236). Baltimore: Paul H. Brookes.

Milsom, A., & Hartley, M. T. (2005). Assisting students with learning disabilities transitioning to college: What school counselors should know. *Professional School Counseling, 85,* 436–441.

National Center on Educational Statistics. (1999). *Students with disabilities in postsecondary education: A profile of preparation, participation, and outcomes.* Washington, DC: U.S. Department of Education.

Neubert, D. A. (2006). Legislation and guidelines for secondary special education. In P.L. Sitlington & G. M. Clark (Eds.), *Transition education and services* (4th Ed., pp. 35–70). Boston: Pearson.

Newman, L. (2005). Postsecondary education participation of youth with disabilities. In Wagner, M., Newman, L., Cameto, R., Garza, N., & Levine, P. (2005). *After high school: A first look at the post-school experiences of youth with disabilities.* A report from the national longitudinal transition study-2 (NLTS2). Menlo Park, CA: SRI International. Retrieved November 7, 2005, from www.nlts2.org/pdfs/afterhighschool_chp4.pdf

No Child Left Behind Act of 2001, Public Law 107–110, 20 U.S.C. § 6301 (2002).

Osborne, A. G. (1996). *Special education law: An introduction. Legal issues in special education.* Needham Heights, MA: Allyn & Bacon.

Rehabilitation Act of 1973, Public Law 93–112, 29 U.S.C. § 793.

Rehabilitation Act of 1986, Public Law 99–506, 29 U.S.C. § 16.

Rusch, F. R., Chadsey-Rusch, J., & Szymanski, E. (1992). The emerging field of transition services. In F. R. Rusch & J. G. Chadsey (Eds.), *Transition from school to adult life* (pp. 4–15). Sycamore, IL: Sycamore.

Singer, J. D. (1992). Are special educators' career paths special? Results from a 13-year longitudinal study. *Exceptional Children, 59,* 262–279.

Sitlington, P. L., Frank, A. R., & Cooper, L. (1989). *Iowa statewide follow-up study: Adult adjustment of individuals with learning disabilities one year after leaving school.* Des Moines, IA: Iowa Department of Education.

Sitlington, P. L. (2003). Postsecondary education: The other transition. *Exceptionality, 11*(2), 103–113.

Sitlington, P. L., & Clark, G. M. (2006). *Transition to postsecondary education. Transition Education and Services* (4th Ed., pp. 204–231). Boston, MA: Pearson.

Szymanski, E. M. (1994). Transitions: Life-span and life-space considerations for empowerment. *Exceptional Children, 60,* 402–410.

Szymanski, E. M., Hanley-Maxwell, C., & Asselin, S. B. (1992). Systems interface: Vocational rehabilitation, special education, and vocational evaluation. In F. R. Rusch, L. Destefano,

J. Chadsey-Rusch, L. A. Phelps, & E. M. Szymanski (Eds.), *Transition from school to adult life: Models, linkages, issues* (pp. 153–171). Sycamore, IL: Sycamore.

Tagayuna, A., Stodden, R. A., Chang, C., Zleeznick, M. E., & Whelley, T. A. (2005). A two-year comparison of support provision for persons with disabilities in postsecondary education. *Journal of Vocational Rehabilitation, 22,* 13–21.

Test, D. W., Aspel, N. P., & Everson J. M. (2006). *Transition methods for youth with disabilities* (pp. 170–217). Upper Saddle River, NJ: Pearson.

The Rehabilitation Act Amendments of 1998, 29 U.S.C. § 794.

U.S. Department of Labor. (1999). *Testing and assessment: An employer's guide to good practices.* Washington, DC: Employment and Training Administration.

Watson v. City of Cambridge, 32 NE 864 (Mass. 1893).

Wagner, M. (1989). *Youth with disabilities during transition: An overview of descriptive findings from the national longitudinal transition study.* Menlo Park, CA: SRI International.

Webster, D. D., Clary, G., & Griffith, P. L. (2005). Postsecondary education and career paths. In R. W. Flexer, T. J. Simmons, P. Luft, and R. M. Baer (Eds.), *Transition planning for secondary students* (2nd Ed., pp. 388–423). Upper Saddle River, NJ: Pearson.

Wehmeyer, M. L. (1998). Involving students in the educational process. In M. L. Wehmeyer & D. J. Sands (Eds.), *Making it happen: Student involvement in education planning, decision making and instruction* (pp. 3–24). Baltimore, MD: Paul H. Brookes.

West, M. D., Barcus, J. M., Brooke, V., & Rayfield, R. G. (1995). An exploratory analysis of self-determination of persons with disabilities. *Journal of Vocational Rehabilitation, 5,* 357–364.

Will, M. (1984). *OSERS programming for the transition of youth with disabilities: Bridges from school to working life.* Washington, DC: Office of Special Education and Rehabilitative Services, U.S. Office of Education.

Workforce Investment Act, Public Law 105–22, 112 Stat. 936.

Yell, M. L. (1998). *The history of the law and children with disabilities. The law and special education.* Upper Saddle River, NJ: Prentice-Hall.

Chapter 3

ADAPTATION TO DISABILITY: PERSPECTIVES OF PERSONS WITH DISABILITIES

E. Davis Martin, Jr.

Adaptation to disability is a highly individualized process. Severity of disability, on the surface, would seem to be a crucial factor. However, severity of disability or the perception of severity varies from person to person. Persons who have significant disabilities (e.g., blindness, cerebral palsy, mental retardation, paraplegia) will vary in his or her reaction(s) to the disability. The perception of severity among others (for instance, parents, siblings, loved ones, friends, work and school mates) will, as well, vary considerably. The effect of paraplegia for one person, for example, may be completely devastating and for another be relatively insignificant. These two extremes certainly do not characterize all persons who have a paralysis disability. The majority of persons with disabilities' reaction will probably fall somewhere between these two extremes.

Personal Reactions to Disability

John Hockenberry's (1995) memoir, *Moving Violations,* is a superb reaction and analysis of Hockenberry's adaptation to his disability. This book was written from the perspective of an ordinary human being confronted with the obstacles we all face in life plus the added frustrations of environmental and attitudinal barriers unique to persons who have a paralysis disability and who use a wheelchair for

71

mobility. Similarly, books such as *Flying Without Wings: Personal Reflections on Being Disabled* [sic] (1989) and *A Graceful Passage* (1990) by Arnold Beisser; *If You Could Hear What I See* (2001) by Kathy Buckley; *A Special Kind of Hero* (1991) by Chris Burke and Jo Beth McDaniel; *On the Edge of Darkness* (1994) by Kathy Cronkite; *Thinking in Pictures and Other Reports from My Life with Autism* (1995) by Temple Grandin; *An Unquiet Mind* (1995) by Kay Redfield Jamison; *Undercurrents: A Life Beneath the Surface* (1994) by Martha Manning; *Waist High in the World* (1996) by Nancy Mairs; *The Body Silent* (1987) by Robert Murphy; *A Whole New Life* (1982) by Reynolds Price; *Still Me* (1998) by Christopher Reeve; *The Beast: A Reckoning with Depression* (1995) by Tracey Thompson; *I Raise My Eyes to Say Yes* (1989) by Ruth Sienkiewicz-Mercer and Steven Kaplan; *Darkness Visible* (1992) by William Styron; *Prozac Nation* (1994) and *More, Now, Again: A Memoir of Addiction* (2002) by Elizabeth Wurtzel; and *Nobody, Nowhere* (1992) by Donna Williams, among many others. In each of these memoirs and the memoirs contained in *Significant Disability* (Martin, 2001), the reader is led to a truth that is revealed in Harold Kushner's widely read *When Bad Things Happen to Good People* (1981); that is, the counterproductive effects of focusing on the *why* questions that are often asked when disability occurs. Justin Rybacki (2001), a person with multiple sclerosis, best expressed the resolution of this often characteristic behavior when he suggests that:

> . . . in the final analysis, it is not the question of why bad things happen that is relevant, it is how we will respond now that it has happened. Our process of adaptation must lead us to that ultimate end when we do not question, do not blame God nor ourselves. It has happened and we need to move on, not saying what we can no longer do, but instead, saying what we can still do, enjoy, and participate in. (p. 188)

Disability, it should not be assumed, will always result in psychological turmoil. Disability will present frustration, inconvenience, and grief to the person with a disability but the disability may, as well, present the person with a ". . . potentially powerful stimulant to psychological growth" (Vash & Crewe, 2004, p. 151).

> I have been disabled [sic] since I was sixteen, yet hardly a week goes by, nearly thirty years later, that I don't make some discovery or improve-

ment that in one way or another makes my disability less handicapping. Since I hope that happy process never stops, I have to say that I hope I am never fully 'rehabilitated.' My physical abilities are still increasing. When, with age, they begin to decrease, I fully expect to continue or accelerate in the psychological and spiritual discoveries that make my disability not only less handicapping, but a matter of trivia compared with the nonphysical realms of discovery and improvement I am experiencing. Each in its own age, but all part of my own human growth . . . or psychological development . . . or rehabilitation . . . or whatever you prefer to call it. Sometimes I'm not sure what my disability is. Is it being paralyzed, or does that add a laughably small increment to the primordial handicap of being mortal human? The core of psychological development is realistic acceptance of one's limitations—be they physical, intellectual, spiritual, or of some other realm. We are not perfect; we are never what we would wish to be—however beautiful, good, gifted, serene, or strong we appear. These imperfections must be accepted without rancor before we can get on with the real and simple business of psychological development—doing the best we can with whatever we've got. (Vash, 1976, pp. 2–3; Vash, 1981, p. 130; Vash & Crewe, 2004, pp. 152–153)

Vash (1994) also suggests that reframing attitudes and enlarging perspectives regarding the perception of adversity can be a very positive factor in adjustment:

The common social view is that lacks, losses, pain, and suffering are adverse and undesirable; and that anyone who thinks differently is a masochist or some other kind of nut. To be about 80% paralyzed is generally considered to be a tragic catastrophe. I shared this view before I became 80% paralyzed. The cultural evaluation fell apart afterward in the face of persistent refutation. Paralysis and all, I kept having fun, successes, and general feelings of life satisfaction that belied expectations. Adverse experience changed my attitudes and three decades' work as a rehabilitation psychologist, plus conscious dedication to evolving a communicable philosophy of life, helped me formalize the process. (pp. 201–202)

Michael Payne (2001), in commenting on his disability and the significance of adaptation for himself and for his family, notes:

Chronic pain is an invisible impairment that affects the entire family. I have three sons that I have not been able to take fishing, to play golf or simply toss a baseball around with. My wife understands, but does not understand. As a consequence, a short separation occurred while the family adapted. Family and individual counseling was essential for our adaptation. . . . Adaptation is a lifelong process. (p. 172)

Similarly, those persons who share in the life of a person with a disability may also experience difficulty in coping or relating to the person with a disability. This arises, not so much from the reality of the disability, but more likely because the disability has introduced a new element into the relationship; it has, in essence, changed the relationship. The ability to cope with the changes brought about as a result of the disability then portends the future relationship. Beatrice Wright (1983) long ago noted that

> . . . the burden in interpersonal relations will be borne by the person who has the disability. Although the pathology may lie with the group, the person with the disability is the one who is annoyed or hurt most directly. It is he or she who has to "take it", who has to handle the ineptitudes of others in the ordinary affairs of getting along. (p. 335)

In the final analysis, it is the person with the disability who must help those persons who are close to him or her and, as well, those persons who are strangers deal with and adjust to his or her disability. While this may seem to be an overwhelming or at least an unfair responsibility that has been placed upon the person with a disability, it is, nevertheless, a reality that must be faced.

Reynolds Price (1994) reveals in his excellent memoir, *A Whole New Life,* that the advent of disability and its consequences for him and, by extension, to others led him to the following *facts* regarding adaptation:

1. You're in your present calamity alone, far as this life goes. If you want a way out, then dig it yourself, if there turns out to be any trace of a way. Nobody—least of all a doctor—can rescue you now, not once they've stitched your gaping wound.
2. Generous people—true practical saints, some of them as boring as root canals—are waiting to give you everything on Earth but your main want, which is simply the *person you used to be.*
3. But you're not that person now. Who'll you be tomorrow? And

who do you propose to be from here to the grave, which may be hours or decades down the road? (p. 182)

Moreover, he noted that these first two facts take care of themselves (acceptance of reality) but it is the third fact that a person may exert a measure of control over; that is, the ability to adapt to a new way of accomplishing tasks and a new way of living. Price's advice is to "grieve for a decent limited time over whatever parts of your old self you know you'll miss" (p. 183) . . . and by implication get on with the business of life—living, growing, and becoming.

Persons with developmental disabilities pose a similar yet somewhat different situation. The effect of a child's disability on the family varies in terms of adaptation, not only for the child but for the whole family. The achievement or nonachievement of typical developmental milestones has the capacity to produce additional stress within the family unit. A common reaction initially is to stop communicating, removing one's self emotionally from the attitudinal and physical impediments (e.g., reactions of others to the child in terms of participation in school, transportation, recreational or leisure pursuits) and sometimes physically resulting in separation, desertion or divorce. However, this does not have to occur. Parents, such as Pat and Dewey Brown (2001), have noted:

> We have learned that raising a person with a disability is a partnership effort between the individual with the disability, therapists, other family members, the schools, community agencies, medical staff, friends, family, neighbors and colleagues. (p. 137)

Pat and Dewey Brown (2001) offer the following advice:

> All people belong together. We need to empower and help people to move toward a goal or dream, to help people make choices, and to act on those choices. A friend once reminded us that we, like Native Americans, need to be dream catchers. We need to capture wonderful dreams and let the bad dreams escape. She said, "together we can make things happen but alone the task is impossible." (p. 138)

Siblings, as well, demonstrate great insight regarding the needs of their siblings: Witness, for instance, Christopher Brown's thoughts about his brother Patrick:

People need to be taught how to act with others who are different from them. We need to teach others that people with disabilities are good people, too. If each of us would just show one other person that people with disabilities have many abilities, what a great world this could be. (Brown, C., 1995; Brown & Brown, 2001, p. 137)

Michele Martin Murmer (2001), similarly, shares these thoughts about her brother, Richard:

Richard, like a lot of people, has a disability; it is a part of who he is, not what he is. . . . I hate to hear people say that someone is retarded and use it to mean stupid. My brother is not stupid. My brother is a very special person who just happens to need more time to learn. There is nothing stupid about that. (pp. 167–168)

Centrality of Work and Vocational Rehabilitation

The centrality and significance of work in our lives must not be underestimated. Recent legislation, as noted elsewhere herein, supports the basic thesis that meaningful work presents the mechanism and means to be a part of the community. Opportunities for persons with disabilities to access the American Dream are provided through the 1973 Rehabilitation Act and subsequent amendments, the IDEA and subsequent amendments, the 1990 Americans with Disabilities Act, and the Ticket to Work and Work Incentives Improvement Act. John Coates (2001), a high school English and history teacher, who is a person with Charcot-Marie-Tooth disease, illustrates the importance of this point:

For the student or worker with a disability, though, life is different. The range of jobs available to him or her is intrinsically smaller because the physical (or cognitive, sensory, mental) requirements simply exceed the person's capabilities. Many jobs now theoretically open because of the Americans with Disabilities Act (ADA) still may be beyond the person's reach if approached in the same passive and thoughtless way as many applicants. The person with a disability needs to generate interest and enthusiasm in the would-be employer by coming to the job interview with goals: "How can I set things up to accommodate my needs with a minimum of fuss for others?' Once I am hired, how can I consistently meet or exceed my job's requirements?" (p. 140)

Coates continues:

> Success follows focused understanding that is enthusiastically lived. But understanding of what? How many people discover a task worthy of their best efforts and throw themselves into it, only to lose interest or become discouraged when the hill looks too steep to climb or the slight too humiliating to be set aside? Yet perseverance, the magic quality, can be nurtured even among those to whom it does not come naturally. The first step is to set appropriate goals. (p. 140)

The setting of achievable goals is a hallmark of the counselor-client relationship. The mutual formulation of the Individualized Plan for Employment (IPE) is no less than the blueprint for the client's successful rehabilitation. On the subject of vocational rehabilitation, Charles Wakefield (2001), a special education teacher and a person with rheumatoid arthritis, speaks of the value of vocational rehabilitation and suggests that rehabilitation is a difficult undertaking in which many factors have the capacity to impede success:

> Where would I be now if I had been unable to receive the excellent help that was afforded to me? Financially I would not have been able to achieve the necessary education and training had not I applied for and been granted Social Security Disability benefits. I would be worst off physically, because I would not have been able to manage my severe arthritis without medical assistance. Other factors such as transportation, housing, recreation, and social activities would have been problematic to say the least. All of these factors have affected my life and must be considered in any realistic rehabilitation effort. I have been lucky enough to view the rehabilitation effort from both sides, as a professional and as a client, and I can sincerely relate that you have chosen a difficult profession in which to perform; however, good can develop out of a bad situation. Believe me, my life can attest to the fact that change has been hard. Going back to school is difficult as you approach middle age, especially with significant physical and emotional stressors. Any form of rehabilitation is not easy. Thank God for people like you, who help make the journey just a little more tolerable. (p. 194)

Advocacy

Advocacy is more than just an activity to support a position or viewpoint. Advocacy is a commitment to advance and protect the rights of one or others. In terms of the disability movement, it is to advance the independence, productivity, and inclusion of all persons with disabilities into the fabric of American society. Advocacy represents the need to be recognized as contributing members of society, as ordinary human beings who aspire to live, work, and play within his or her community of choice. As a part of this commitment, the vocational rehabilitation (VR) program in the United States of America was created to bring to fruition the ideal of equality of opportunity. Through the provision of VR services to eligible persons, the VR agency strives to lessen or ameliorate the impediments of disability so persons with disabilities may participate and compete in work activity on the basis of equality and, by implication, to access the American Dream. Robin Hoerber (2001), a disability rights advocate and a person who is blind, in expressing her advocacy, notes that services provided by rehabilitation agencies:

> . . . need to take more of a holistic perspective; that is, we as clients, customers, consumers (all labels which I do not particularly care for—person with a disability is preferable when a label is needed) are not something that needs to be fixed. We need a hand up, not a hand out. (p. 153)

Hoerber (2001) suggests that the ideal of living, working, and recreating in the community requires that the following factors must be incorporated into the various organizations and agencies that provide services to people with disabilities:

- Technology is the great equalizer for persons who are blind, but this technology needs to be available both at a work site and in one's home.
- Transportation that is available, accessible, and dependable is a must for people who have visual impairments or who are blind.
- Recreational opportunities need to be more inclusive, that is, be a regular part of the community and not just available on an exception basis.
- There is a great need for mentors and more employer awareness regarding the abilities of persons with disabilities.
- Policies that relate to the receipt of Social Security disability benefits and the amount of money that may be earned must be real-

istic and provide incentives, not disincentives, to working. It is
better to pay some taxes than not to pay any taxes.
• Finally, the general public needs to be educated about disability.
Stereotypical thinking that is based on limiting characteristics of a
particular medical condition results in false myths. We need to
make people more aware of the ability that resides in disability;
that is, what people can do, not what they cannot do. (pp. 153–154)

Ann Durden (2001), a rehabilitation counselor in the public non-
profit sector and a person with a disability, comments on the importance of the relationship that is established between the person with a
disability and the professional. She suggests that the responsibility of
the professional must go beyond merely providing this or that service.
She admonishes professionals to take a holistic perspective:

> I believe that it is vital that professionals approach a client not simply
> as a problem, but as a person. Professionals must determine what moti-
> vates a person through the eyes of that person in order to foster stabili-
> ty. Stability facilitates growth and development that allows the person
> the opportunity to build a meaningful life. (p. 149)

To facilitate change and to empower persons with disabilities, we–
persons with disabilities, family members, loved ones, and rehabilitation counselors–must become effective advocates. To make a difference in the lives of those that we work with, within ourselves, or those
persons we may not know personally but, nevertheless, advocate on
their behalf for change, we need to become actively involved in the
political process in the communities we live in and beyond. Change in
a democracy comes about through the actions of an enlighten citizen-
ry. Advocacy is the first step in bringing about change. And, in the
words of Jim Rothrock (2001), currently commissioner of the Virginia
Department of Rehabilitative Services and a person who has a paralysis disability, suggests that:

> . . . sustained advocacy in the streets, at the state and national capitals,
> within the legislative halls is the essential ingredient to realizing the
> promise of the ADA and subsequently finding Americans with signifi-
> cant disabilities fully integrated into the mainstream of American life.
> (p. 184)

The VR agency, in particular, but also other rehabilitative organizations and educational systems, must, through their counselors and teachers, offer meaningful educational and training opportunities that facilitate entry into careers that are in the primary labor market. This is particularly relevant for youth with disabilities as suggested by John Oehler (2001), former dean of education at Virginia Commonwealth University:

> Our schools must continue to develop inclusive models that afford the best possible opportunities for children and youth to become a part of American society. Separation and stereotypical thinking . . . leads to a parallel existence of shadow within the larger community after exiting a school experience of separation. (p. xi)

Ruth and Dave Martin (2001), in commenting on their experiences with their son, Richard, provide the following advice for rehabilitation counselors, teachers, and other human service workers:

> . . . know and understand that your actions can and will have a tremendous impact on the lives of those you interact with, counsel, provide services to or teach. The nature of that impact may be subtle and, perhaps, imperceptible to you at any specific point in time. Nevertheless, you can choose to be positive or negative, growth enhancing or retarding, encouraging or discouraging, or ego building or deflating. Choose wisely the nature of your impact—it is life altering! (p. 165)

Conclusion

The process of coping with the effects of disability affects not only the person with a disability but those who share in the life of that person as well. Adaptation to disability is not a lock-step process but is highly individualized and is not related to severity of disability. Impediments associated with a disability result not only from the disability, but from societal attitudes as well. These latter misperceptions are often more limiting than the disability itself.

Parents and siblings of persons with disabilities often find themselves limited by their attitudes and a myriad of feelings and emotions regarding the son, daughter, brother or sister who has a disability. Within families where positive attitudes are the norm, effective adaptation and interaction within the family and community is the result, and where ambivalent or negative attitudes are present, physical and emotional withdrawal is often the outcome. Parents and siblings of persons with developmental disabilities, in particular, will come into contact with many human service workers throughout their lifetime. Because disability is a dynamic phenomenon, it is essential that rehabilitation counselors, teachers, and other human service workers know and understand their own attitudes, both positive and negative, and work toward the elimination of stereotypical responses to persons with disabilities and to family members as well. Attitudes are subtle and difficult to determine; we do not carry a three-by-five card listing of our attitudes or values in our pocketbook or wallet. To be an effective rehabilitation counselor, a person must know, understand, and appreciate the value systems or philosophies that rehabilitation rests upon and those of the client or client's family. To do so allows the rehabilitation counselor to empower persons with disabilities and, similarly, to empower others who share in the life of the person with a disability.

Rehabilitation counselors must be cognizant of the dynamic nature of disability and must be willing and able to provide an environment that is conducive to success for the person with a disability and for those close to that person. The rehabilitation counselor must assist not only the person with a disability but also those whose lives are intertwined with that person to move from a perspective that is dominated by a comparative status value orientation to that of an asset value orientation.

REFERENCES

Beisser, A. E. (1990). *Flying without wings.* New York: Bantam.

Beisser, A. R. (1990). *A graceful passage.* New York: Bantam.

Brown, J. D., & Brown, P. J. (2001). Patrick's metamorphosis. In E. D. Martin, Jr. (Ed.), *Significant disability: Issues affecting people with disabilities from a historical, policy, leadership and systems perspective* (pp. 125–138). Springfield, IL: Charles C Thomas.

Brown, C. (December, 1995). My brother. *The Exceptional Parent.*

Buckley, K., & Padwa, L. (2001). *If you could hear what I see: Lessons about life luck, and the choices we make.* New York: Dutton.

Burke, C., & McDaniel, J. B. (1991). *A special kind of hero.* New York: Dell.

Coates, J. P. (2001). How I got here. In E. D. Martin, Jr. (Ed.), *Significant disability: Issues affecting people with disabilities from a historical, policy, leadership and systems perspective* (pp. 139–143). Springfield, IL: Charles C Thomas.

Cronkite, K. (1994). *On the edge of darkness.* New York: Delta.

Durden, A. T. (2001). A voice to heed. In E. D. Martin, Jr. (Ed.), *Significant disability: Issues affecting people with disabilities from a historical, policy, leadership and systems perspective* (pp. 144–149). Springfield, IL: Charles C Thomas.

Grandin, T. (1995). *Thinking in pictures and other reports from my life with autism.* New York: Doubleday.

Hockenberry, J. (1995). *Moving violations: War zones, wheelchairs, and declarations of independence.* New York: Hyperion.

Hoerber, R. F. (2001). I'm blind: What about it? In E. D. Martin, Jr. (Ed.), *Significant disability: Issues affecting people with disabilities from a historical, policy, leadership and systems perspective* (pp. 150–154). Springfield, IL: Charles C Thomas.

Jamison, K R. (1995). *An unquiet mind.* New York: Vintage Books.

Kushner, H. S. (1981). *When bad things happen to good people.* New York: Avon.

Mairs, N. (1996). *Waist-high in the world: A life among the non-disabled.* Boston: Beacon Press.

Manning, M. (1994). *Undercurrents: A life beneath the surface.* San Francisco: Harper.

Martin, E. D., Jr. (Ed.). (2001). *Significant disability: Issues affecting people with disabilities from a historical, policy, leadership and systems perspective.* Springfield, IL: Charles C Thomas.

Martin, R. M., & Martin, E. D., Jr. (2001). Richard's journey. In E. D. Martin, Jr. (Ed.), *Significant disability: Issues affecting people with disabilities from a historical, policy, leadership and systems perspective* (pp. 155–165). Springfield, IL: Charles C Thomas.

Murmer, M. M. (2001). My big brother. In E. D. Martin, Jr. (Ed.), *Significant disability: Issues affecting people with disabilities from a historical, policy, leadership and systems perspective* (pp. 166–168). Springfield, IL: Charles C Thomas.

Oehler, J. S. (2001). Foreword. In E. D. Martin, Jr. (Ed.), *Significant disability: Issues affecting people with disabilities from a historical, policy, leadership and systems perspective* (pp. xi–xii). Springfield, IL: Charles C Thomas.

Murphy, R. (1987). *The body silent.* New York: W. W. Norton

Payne, M. C. (2001). My invisible disability: Chronic pain. In E. D. Martin, Jr. (Ed.), *Significant disability: Issues affecting people with disabilities from a historical, policy, leadership and systems perspective* (pp. 169–174). Springfield, IL: Charles C Thomas.

Price, R. (1982). *A whole new life.* New York: Atheneum.

Reeve, C. (1998). *Still me.* New York: Random House.

Rothrock, J. A. (2001). Leadership and advocacy: A political primer. In E. D. Martin, Jr. (Ed.), *Significant disability: Issues affecting people with disabilities from a historical, policy, leadership and systems perspective* (pp. 175–185). Springfield, IL: Charles C Thomas.

Rybacki, J. S. (2001). Adaptation to disability. In E. D. Martin, Jr. (Ed.), *Significant disability: Issues affecting people with disabilities from a historical, policy, leadership and systems perspective* (pp. 186–188). Springfield, IL: Charles C Thomas.

Sienkiewicz-Mercer, R., & Kaplan, S. B. (1989). *I raise my eyes to say yes.* West Hartford, CT: Whole Health Books.

Styron, W. (1992). *Darkness visible.* New York: Random House.

Thompson, T. (1995). *The beast: A reckoning with depression.* New York: G. P. Putnam's Sons.

Vash, C. L. (1981). *The psychology of disability.* New York: Springer.

Vash, C. L. (1994). *Personality and adversity: Psychospiritual aspects of rehabilitation.* New York: Springer.

Vash, C. L., & Crewe, N. M. (2004). *The psychology of disability.* New York: Springer.

Wakefield, C. C., Jr. (2001). To make a difference. In E. D. Martin, Jr. (Ed.), *Significant disability: Issues affecting people with disabilities from a historical, policy, leadership and systems perspective* (pp. 189–194). Springfield, IL: Charles C Thomas.

Williams, D. (1992). *Nobody, nowhere.* New York: Times Books.

Wurtzel, E. (1994). *Prozac nation: Young and depressed in America.* Boston: Houghton Mifflin.

PART 2

REHABILITATION APPROACHES

Chapter 4

THE REHABILITATION PROCESS: THE PURPOSE AND FUNCTION OF THE REHABILITATION COUNSELOR

E. DAVIS MARTIN, JR. AND KEITH C. WRIGHT

D isability is a dynamic phenomenon affected by interactions with others and with the environment. As such, it is essential that rehabilitation counselors know and understand their own values and attitudes toward persons with disabilities, both positive and negative, and work toward the elimination of stereotypical responses that may be displayed during the rehabilitation process by other professionals, prospective employers, and others including family members. Values and attitudes are subtle and difficult to articulate, yet behavioral actions often belie the reality of thoughts and feelings that run counter to the notions of independence and empowerment. The expectations for a person with a significant disability involved in a training situation or program, for instance, may be lower and consequently the person may be exempted from a project or activity because the teacher or leader is unaware of assistive technology that would lessen or eliminate an impediment thought to compromise the person's ability to successfully participate. Or, it may simply be that the unconscious thought is, "You can't do this, so go sit down, I don't want to embarrass you."

To the credit of people with disabilities, rehabilitation professionals, and other advocates, over the course of the past three decades, we have tried to develop educational and vocational programs that foster independence, productivity, and inclusion. These same programs designed to build self-esteem and provide opportunities for meaningful work, however, continue to be constrained by the following stereotypes (Gerry & Mirsky, 1992):

- **The medical/pathological stereotype**, in which persons with severe disabilities are viewed as sick or unmotivated individuals who it is proper to regard as burdens of charity who should passively accept permanent social and economic dependence.
- **The economic worth stereotype**, in which people with disabilities are discounted as economically worthless and excluded from the workforce on the basis of their perceived congenital unproductiveness.
- **The needed professional stereotype**, in which the continued dependence of people with severe disabilities is assured by career structures of the helping professionals whose very jobs depend on retaining the power to distribute scarce resources to their *de facto* wards.
- **The bureaucratic stereotype**, in which disability is characterized as a set of administrative problems to be solved by administrators rather than as a label signaling the restrictions on personal dignity and social freedom. (p. 342)

Regardless of the severity of a particular impairment, the impact may be slight or overwhelming, insignificant or devastating to the person who has a disability as well as to all those persons–family members and significant others–who share in that person's life. Society is, likewise, affected by the effects of disability through lost productivity as a result of the impediment(s) imposed by a medical impairment(s) but more often from the attitudinal barriers imposed by society. Throughout the relatively short history of the state-federal program of vocational rehabilitation (VR), professionals and advocates have sought to ameliorate the effects of disability, especially through the development of employment opportunities. Much of the legislation that has been passed during the latter third of the twentieth century, and continuing to the present, has been directed toward an ideal of equality of opportunity and, in particular, to the creation of employment opportunities for persons with disabilities.

Employment, it is thought, is the vehicle that will provide passage to the American Dream. This is true if employment is secured in the primary labor market. Primary labor market jobs are characterized as employment that pays or has the capacity to pay beyond the minimum wage, and has benefits and a career path; while jobs in the secondary labor market may be characterized as employment that pays low wages, and has minimal benefits and little, if any, opportunity for career advancement (Hagner, 2000). Moreover, Hagner (Gilbride & Hagner, 2005)

> . . . asserted that the distinction between primary and secondary labor markets has significant implications for rehabilitation counselors. Overwhelmingly, supported employment consumers, as well as a significant percentage of all people with disabilities, are placed in secondary sector positions. Hagner suggested that too often rehabilitation providers place consumers in what are called 'food' and 'filth' occupations. A common justification for such placements is a belief in the generic value of work experience that will allow the consumer the opportunity for advancement over time. The results of research on dual labor markets, along with outcome studies of the long-term effectiveness of vocational rehabilitation, suggest that 'quick and dirty' placements may have significant detrimental effects that are often unrecognized by rehabilitation counselors. (p. 286)

Again, the values and beliefs that we hold toward persons with disabilities affect in subtle ways what we believe a person *can* and *cannot* do. Consequently, as suggested by Hagner, the overrepresentation of persons with disabilities in the secondary labor market, and perhaps a diminishment of training opportunities because of lower expectations, are a result manifested by these same values and beliefs. Unfortunately, it is what a person cannot do more often than what a person can do that is in the forefront of our actions. This attitude obviously impacts employment and career opportunities. If one holds to a *cannot do* perspective, employment in the secondary labor market is more likely to occur, limiting the creativity of the counselor and client in the development of the Individualized Plan for Employment (IPE).

To be an effective rehabilitation practitioner and advocate for an individual with a disability, a rehabilitation counselor must know, understand, and appreciate the value systems that rehabilitation rests upon and those of the client and his or her family. To do so allows the rehabilitation counselor to empower persons with disabilities and, similarly, to empower others who share in the life of the person with a disability. Rehabilitation counselors must be cognizant of the dynamic nature of disability and must be willing and able to provide an environment that is conducive to success for the person with a disability and for those close to that person. Rehabilitation counselors should assist clients to seek excellence in all they do and to focus on what they can do, not on what they cannot do.

The Role of the Rehabilitation Counselor

The role of the rehabilitation counselor, regardless of employment setting consists of the following duties and responsibilities (Jenkins, Patterson, & Szymanski, 1992):

- Rehabilitation counselors assess client needs.
- Rehabilitation counselors, in concert with the client, develop goals and individualized plans to meet identified needs.
- Rehabilitation counselors provide or arrange for the therapeutic services and interventions (e.g., medical, psychological, social, behavioral) needed by clients including job placement and follow-up services.

Counseling skills are considered an essential component of all of these activities.

Research conducted by Leahy, Szymanski and Linkowski (1993) indicated that the following ten knowledge domains represent the core competency requirements of rehabilitation counselors:

- Vocational counseling and consultation services
- Medical and psychological aspects of disability
- Individual and group counseling
- Program evaluation and research
- Case management and service coordination
- Family, gender, and multicultural issues
- Foundations of rehabilitation
- Workers' Compensation
- Environmental and attitudinal barriers
- Assessment

Typically, rehabilitation counselors in the public sector are employed in the state-federal program of VR, yet a growing number of rehabilitation counselors in the public sector are employed in employee assistance programs, school-based transition programs, university services for students with disabilities, medical centers and clinics, and community mental health programs. Opportunities in the private sector exist in the areas of workers' compensation, insurance rehabilitation, forensic rehabilitation, and disability management programs within employer settings to name a few. Rehabilitation counselors work with clients who have physical, sensory, mental, cognitive, and addiction disabilities dependent on the employment setting in which they practice.

Scope of Practice for Rehabilitation Counseling

The Foundation for Rehabilitation Education and Research (author, Scope of Practice insert, n.d.) has defined rehabilitation counseling ". . . as a systematic process which assists persons with physical, mental, developmental, cognitive, and emotional disabilities to achieve their personal, career, and independent living goals in the most integrated setting possible through the application of the counseling process." It is through the counseling relationship that a solid foundation for the rehabilitation process is developed. The rehabilitation process provides, in a sense, a platform for the client's transformation. The rehabilitation process may be likened to a journey that has the capacity to transform a person from a *cannot do* perspective to a *can do* perspective. The tools employed by the rehabilitation counselor in this transformation process include the following skills and abilities, commonly known as the scope of practice for rehabilitation counseling (The Foundation for Rehabilitation Education and Research, Scope of Practice insert, n.d.):

- Assessment and appraisal
- Diagnosis and treatment planning
- Career (vocational) counseling
- Individual and group counseling treatment interventions focused on facilitating adjustments to the medical and psychosocial impact of disability
- Case management, referral, and service coordination
- Program evaluation and research
- Interventions to remove environmental, employment, and attitu-

dinal barriers
- Consultation services among multiple parties and regulatory systems
- Job analysis, job development, and placement services, including assistance with employment and job accommodations
- The provision of consultation about and access to rehabilitation technology

While each rehabilitation counselor may have been exposed to each of the above noted areas of knowledge, he or she will have an individual scope of practice based on the particular knowledge, skills, and abilities gained through educational attainment, experience, and subsequent certification as a certified rehabilitation counselor (CRC). No rehabilitation counselor shall practice beyond his or her individual scope of practice. To do so would constitute an ethical transgression as noted in the *Code of Professional Ethics for Rehabilitation Counselors.*

Unique Characteristics of the Rehabilitation Process

The rehabilitation process is individualized, flexible, sequential, comprehensive, and goal oriented. It is not an assembly line of delivered services based on the type of the disability. The rehabilitation counselor is a highly trained professional who coordinates an interagency, interdisciplinary method of service delivery requiring knowledge of the community and its resources–public, private, and voluntary. Steps in this process provide a structure and management system that promote efficiency and allow for effectiveness to be measured on an individual basis. The steps in this process are:

- Case-finding (including application and referral)
- Diagnostic and case study procedures
- Development of the IPE
- Provision and coordination of services
- Placement and follow-along

Prior to the discussion of each of these steps in the rehabilitation process, let us examine the uniqueness of this process.

Continuity of the Client-Counselor Relationship

The continuity of the client-counselor relationship throughout the rehabilitation process constitutes a unique professional role. In most rehabilitation-related professions, the professional is involved with his or her client or patient at a very select point in time (e.g., physician, psychologist, and other related or specialized medical personnel) or involved for the delivery of a specific service over a period of time (e.g., occupational therapist, physical therapist, special education teachers and staff, vocational evaluator). The rehabilitation counselor's relationship with the client is from the beginning of this process until the case is closed. Accordingly, a major concern for the rehabilitation counselor is to give meaning to the role and purpose of all professional and other contributors to the development of the client's IPE. Thus, the rehabilitation counselor functions as a focal point for the client throughout the process. It is the rehabilitation counselor to whom the client turns for interpretation of medical, psychological, vocational, social, educational, and economic information so that informed choices or decisions may be made. Similarly, the rehabilitation counselor provides clarity to the relationships in service delivery and the coordination of such services. It is the rehabilitation counselor who has a holistic perspective of the client's impairment(s), and together the client and the counselor develop a mutually formulated plan for eliminating or ameliorating the effects of the resulting impediment(s). The continuity of the client-counselor relationship is, indeed, a unique and essential aspect of the rehabilitation counselor's role as case manager, coordinator of services, and most importantly as a counselor during the client's journey through the rehabilitation process.

Comprehensiveness of the Diagnostic and Case Study Procedure

More often than not, disability is not a discrete event. The effects of a particular disability often have multiple impacts on related areas of a person's life and that of his or her family or significant others. Medical, psychological, social, educational, economic, and vocational aspects of a person's life are impacted by the resulting impediment(s) of impairment. From a holistic perspective, then, the rehabilitation counselor must assist the client in gaining a perspective regarding the impact on each of these aspects of the person's life. Holism applied to people refers to the notion that the totality of a person has a reality that is unique and a reality that is dependent upon the various attributes of that person. A person can be artificially divided into a physical part, a mental part, a psychological part, an educational part, an economic part, and a vocational part and certain conclusions may be made that relate to each aspect separately. However, such a perspective yields little information about the individual or that individual's family or significant others until then these aspects of a person's life are viewed collectively, then a unique picture of that person emerges. Much like the uniqueness of a person's fingerprints, so too, are the life patterns as revealed by the infinite combinations of a person's medical, psychological, educational, economic, and vocational characteristics. The relationship of these differing aspects of a person's life has a dramatic impact in terms of vocational choice and ultimately entry into the labor market. A major concern of the rehabilitation counselor is to assist the client in gaining a perspective of his or her strengths (uniqueness) in the exploration of occupations and the process of occupational choice.

Functional Emphasis in Diagnostic and Case Study Procedure

Rehabilitation has been defined as a series of services packaged within a restorative or corrective context (Parker & Szymanski, 1998). Rehabilitation is, indeed, that and more. Each service that is requested for a client should adhere to a principle of functionality; that is, the emphasis must be on functional ability—a *can do* rather than a *cannot do* perspective. The rehabilitation counselor is interested in what the client can do. For instance, if a psychological evaluation is ordered for a client with a cognitive disability who wants to undergo a particular job training program, the emphasis in the report should not be on the client's deficits but on the client's strengths or how best the client learns in a new situation. If a psychological evaluation is requested and no questions are asked other than for a standard evaluation, do not be surprised if the report focuses on the client's deficits. It is the rehabilitation counselor's task to provide the service provider with sufficient background information as well as prospective information regarding vocational choice. In a situation such as this, the most important question to ask very well may be "How best does this person acquire new information and skills?" "With proper supports and accommodations, can this person undertake this training program and be successful?" "What are those supports and accommodations and are they transferable to a vocational setting?" Similarly, in each area of evaluation, the emphasis is on functional ability.

Diagnosis of disability is the first step in the diagnostic and case study procedure; it is used primarily for eligibility determination, but it should also be used in a prospective or preplanning manner, clarifying the impact of the resultant impediment(s) upon vocational choice. The challenge to the rehabilitation counselor is to assist the client in the interpretation of these data relative to informed choice and decision-making in the development of the IPE.

Utilization and Coordination of Services

A fourth characteristic of the process impacting a counselor's role is the utilization and coordination of services outside the agency structure, that is, locating and utilizing the community and its resources for the benefit of the client. The counselor identifies, coordinates, and supplements these services. Management and coordination skills requirements have given special emphasis to the counseling function. It is the counselor's ability to coordinate and provide access to multiple services in a seamless way that the client is able to move forward in his or her individualized rehabilitation process with a minimum of delay. Cassell, Mulkey, and Engen (1997, p. 214) have observed that the ". . . practice of rehabilitation counseling rests on the confluence of two professional resources: counseling and management." Moreover, they noted ". . . no single professional force can be said to predominate, as synergy is only established through concepts and practice surrounding a 'balance' principle." In other words, rehabilitation is, ". . . a multispecialty-oriented program requiring the coordination of many disciplines to meet the needs of people with severe disabilities" (Rubin & Roessler, 1995, p. 222).

The process is a highly individualized, coordinated, interagency, and interdisciplinary method of service requiring knowledge of the community and its many resources—public, private, and voluntary. Accountability in rehabilitation has been much too superficial, usually related to numbers of referrals, numbers of persons served and/or rehabilitated. Annual reports often make reference to cooperative interagency agreements, but place little emphasis on rehabilitation's role of putting the community together for their clients. This coordinating and unifying role of rehabilitation, if well done, could very well provide for a qualitative and budgetary accountability not yet attained.

Case-Finding

Case-finding is a necessary first step to begin the rehabilitation process. It might be defined as the activity of locating persons who may be in need of and potentially eligible for vocational rehabilitation services. Case-finding includes the interpretation of objectives and services of the vocational rehabilitation agency to (a) persons with disabilities, (b) interested public, private, and volunteer agencies, and (c) to the general public through personal contacts with groups and organizations and through the public information media (electronic and print media). Case-finding, as well, includes the development and continued maintenance of communication with referral sources and early agency attention to those referred, for example, transition age students with disabilities.

It is known, for instance, that the present VR program reaches only a fraction of the total number of persons in need of rehabilitation services. It is also known that many persons are unaware of VR services, or are unsure of how to access such services. Because VR is an eligibility program, an application is a necessary first step for the potential client. As such, it is very important that other helping agencies and those professionals serving clientele who may have disabilities understand the eligibility criteria for receipt of VR services.

Eligibility criteria, as well as VR resources, continue to expand. The strong emphasis existent today on serving persons with significant disabilities has made it possible to serve persons who were previously denied service because of the severity of his or her disability. Advances in medical knowledge and treatment, and the availability and utilization of rehabilitation engineering and assistive technology, have increased the ability of persons with the most significant disabilities to secure employment. These factors have placed a continuing emphasis on case-finding. The Rehabilitation Act amendments of 1992 state that an individual is eligible for VR services when:

- He or she has a physical or mental impairment that constitutes or results in a substantial impediment to employment.
- The individual can benefit in terms of an employment outcome from VR services.
- The individual requires VR services to prepare for, enter, engage in, or retain employment.

This broadened definition of eligibility allowed for increased flexibility in working with clients with severe and most severe disabilities (later changed to read *significant* and *most significant* by the 1998 Rehabilitation Act amendments) since it incorporated the qualifier *benefit,* although the interpretation of this word often did not mean the same thing for a person with a disability as it did for the state-federal vocational rehabilitation agency. This definition of eligibility also allowed rehabilitation counselors to work with persons in a preventative manner regarding retention of employment. Other provisions related to the establishment of time limits for the determination of eligibility (sixty-day limit); however, some persons complained that they were put into a waiting status before being allowed to apply for services. Use of existing data from the person with a disability or from family members or educational institutions (public secondary schools) was encouraged. The Rehabilitation Act amendments of 1998 replaced the requirement for extended evaluation (when or if ineligibility was being assessed for persons with the most significant disabilities) with a requirement of trial work experience. Due process requirements were further enhanced by the 1998 amendments for persons who disagreed with decisions regarding eligibility. Mediation was an option to be offered by the vocational rehabilitation agency; however, the outcome was not binding and could not be used to deny or delay an impartial hearing if so requested. The impact of these changes for case-finding is extremely important, in particular, for referral sources.

In sum, then, characteristics of an adequate case-finding program include:

- Referrals should occur early.
- Referrals should be representative of the population of persons with disabilities.
- Referral should come from all potential sources.
- There should be a close coordination and exchange of services by all agencies and organizations serving persons with disabilities.
- There must be a mutual respect, courtesy, and reporting back to referral sources.
- Good casework.

Good case-finding requires a continuing emphasis on communication with public, private, and volunteer organizations. Professionals and others who are employed by these organizations must understand the purpose of the state-federal vocational rehabilitation agency and, in particular, the eligibility criteria for receipt of services.

Diagnostic and Case Study Procedures

One of the unique characteristics of the rehabilitation process is the comprehensiveness of the diagnostic and case study procedures. For the rehabilitation counselor to understand the potential client as a unique individual from a holistic perspective, a comprehensive assessment from six major vantage points is necessary: (a) medical, (b) psychological, (c) social, (d) educational, (e) economic, and (f) vocational.

Medical

A medical evaluation is required of all applicants for VR services for several major reasons. The counselor must establish the nature and extent of the disability as well as appraise the total health of the applicant to determine capacities and functional limitations. These two factors allow the rehabilitation counselor to determine and certify the existing medical impairment and the resulting impediments that exist because of the disability. The counselor must ascertain if physical and /or mental restoration services could remove, correct, or minimize the effects of the resultant impediments. The medical evaluation is also utilized to contribute a sound medical basis for selection of a vocational objective, and it contributes significant information for use in counseling.

Medical re-evaluation may also be provided. This might be indicated for some of the following reasons:

- Periodically for health maintenance purposes in long-term training cases.
- When extensive or lengthy physical and or mental restoration services have been initiated.
- Situations where medical impairments may involve acute episodes such as rheumatic heart disease, epilepsy, diabetes, etc.
- Instances of otherwise unexplained failure in vocational training or other rehabilitation activities.
- Appraisal of the individual's medical status prior to placement.

Psychological

A rehabilitation counselor orders a psychological evaluation for a variety of reasons. Disability may cause psychological problems in terms of adaptation to the disability, or it may be requested because the nature and extent of the psychological aspects of a particular mental or cognitive disability is not fully known, or it may be to determine appropriate accommodations or learning strategies that will enhance vocational success. This evaluation, as well, may be accomplished by a thorough review of existing psychological reports and/or observations. All potential clients or current clients should not be required to undergo psychological testing or evaluation, particularly if current psychological information or reports are available that fulfill the needs of the rehabilitation counselor.

Psychological evaluation, however, may be provided to help the rehabilitation counselor in terms of a plan of counseling to better assist the clients understanding of the psychological aspects of adaptation as well as to facilitate planning and decision-making. Psychological evaluation may also aid clients in identifying problems and understanding their relative strengths and weaknesses. This evaluation is often necessary to provide information or confirmation of a client's abilities, aptitudes, achievements, interests, and personality. Psychological evaluation is important when data on the client's capacities and abilities are lacking or are ambiguous or contradictory. Psychological testing or evaluation is mandated when the potential client is referred because of mental retardation, mental disability, behavioral or adjustment disorder, learning disability, and a disability diagnosis for eligibility must be affirmed.

Social

The social evaluation is a major source of information that the rehabilitation counselor must be concerned with as the development of an individualized plan for employment is mutually formulated by the client and rehabilitation counselor. Rehabilitation counselors and other helping professionals have not always acknowledged the importance of social and cultural influences vis-à-vis the rehabilitation process. An unwillingness or hesitation to acknowledge and understand the beliefs, value systems, and traditions of clients may become further complicated because of the presence of disability, physical environment (architectural barriers), attitudinal barriers, and family influences in addition to cultural differences.

Rehabilitation counselors do not necessarily have the most influence on the client. Family relationships are very important. Rehabilitation is essentially a family concern, and VR programs that do not take this factor into consideration may not be successful because we have not incorporated the attitudes and support of family members and significant others. The attitudes and relationships of family and friends have often conditioned the motivation and behavior of the person with a disability and must be considered when developing a rehabilitation program. Home visits can be very important as well as counseling sessions with other persons directly involved with the client.

Economic

Economic evaluation is for the purpose of determining what investment clients can make toward their own rehabilitation. This evaluation is directly related to a long-standing rehabilitation concept that we as counselors should not do for clients those things that they can and should do for themselves. This concept also recognizes that most clients do better when they have an investment in their own program. Generally speaking, as far as economic need is concerned, rehabilitation services are basically intended to supplement and complement the resources of the person.

The existing resources of clients are often in the form of entitlements. These are referred to as *comparable benefits* and should be incorporated into the individualized plan for employment as appropriate. In certain cases, the VR agency is prohibited from spending its own funds for services prior to a maximum effort to seek alternative funding for the similar service. This prevents duplication, aids cooperative programming, and establishes appropriate linkages in the human services network. Rehabilitation, since its inception, has not operated in a vacuum, and its success has been dependent on the condition of public and private resources in the community (Hardy & Wright, 1973).

Educational

Educational evaluation provides the rehabilitation counselor with important information for rehabilitation planning. It is important to know how the client performed in the educational setting; that is, in what subject areas did he or she do well or excel or enjoy the most and in what subjects did he or she have trouble or was limited by the impediments resulting from his or her impairment. These data often provide valuable insights into the client's learning style, ability to accept instruction, and ability to get along with others. The rehabilitation counselor can build on these educational experiences and attainments in the mutual formulation of the IPE. Contact with former teachers, principals, guidance counselors, or school social workers or other related personnel may often result in information that could be helpful in the consideration and implementation of the IPE.

Vocational

Vocational evaluation can be defined as the gathering, interpreting, and then synthesizing of all the vocationally significant data regarding the client and relating this information to occupational requirements and opportunities. The concept of vocational evaluation is much more than the mere collection of a work history for an individual. In essence, the vocational evaluation is a process in itself, where all of the assessments (medical, psychological, social, educational, economic, and vocational) are synthesized toward a meaningful vocational or occupational choice for the client.

Following evaluations in the six above-mentioned categories, the rehabilitation counselor and his or her client can then proceed to the next step in the rehabilitation process, the development of the IPE.

Individualized Plan for Employment

The Rehabilitation Act amendments of 1998 modified the former provision related to the Individualized Written Rehabilitation Program [101(a) (9)], by changing the name to the IPE and adding a provision that the IPE is to be accomplished (developed and implemented) in a timely fashion. Significantly, the provisions related to the IPE also (Schroeder, 1998):

- Expand the role of the eligible individual as a collaborating partner with a qualified rehabilitation counselor in the development, monitoring, implementation, and evaluation of the IPE.
- Individuals (or their representative) now have the option to

develop their own IPEs or request the technical assistance of a qualified rehabilitation counselor in developing their IPEs.

- Incorporate current regulatory language with respect to the exercise of informed choice in the selection of the IPE's employment goal, services, service providers, and procurement methods.
- Requirement that assessment services and services under an IPE must be provided in the most integrated setting that both is appropriate to the service being provided and also reflects the informed choice of the individual. (p. 3)

The IPE, like the Individual Written Rehabilitation Program (IWRP), remains a statement of the ways and means by which the client is to overcome the impediment(s) created by disability and regain or acquire the capacity for work and/or independent living. It is a comprehensive, businesslike, organized statement of the obstacles preventing success and the resources and methods for resolving these barriers to employment. The IPE may be jointly developed by the counselor and client or by the client with or without the assistance of the counselor (hopefully with the assistance of a qualified rehabilitation counselor) and is based on a sound rehabilitation diagnosis involving individualized, coordinated, and discriminating use of varied resources. The IPE is an integral aspect of consumerism.

The philosophy prominent in rehabilitation counseling, and particularly supported by the mandates for the IPE, is the belief that the client should be an active participant in the rehabilitation process. As rehabilitation counselors we must keep in mind that we do not really rehabilitate anyone; we assist persons to rehabilitate themselves. The IPE helps to insure that clients understand the agency's services and procedures as well as their own responsibility toward rehabilitation.

Client rights and appeal procedures, if dissatisfaction occurs, are provided at this stage of the process for eligible clients. For applicants deemed ineligible, the rights and appeal procedure accompanies the statement of ineligibility. All applicants must receive a statement in writing of their eligibility or ineligibility to receive vocational rehabilitation services. Clients must also receive a copy of their IPE.

Counseling pervades the entire rehabilitation process. It should be emphasized, however, that at this stage of the process:

- The counseling relationship is critical.

- All assessment or evaluative areas are synthesized in a meaningful manner.
- The interpretation of these assessments or evaluations will affect the planning process and becomes essential to the successful implementation of the IPE.
- It is at this point in the rehabilitation process that the counselor and the client reason together in a problem-solving effort to determine the ways and means by which the client will accommodate his or her impediments.
- It is at this point in the process that the client will be counseled as to the services that will be received, by whom, and in what order.
- It is at this stage that the responsibilities of both client and counselor are determined.

Provision and Coordination of Services

The issue of counselor versus coordinator has been discussed in many sources over the years, originally by C. H. Patterson in 1957. Whitehouse (1975) suggested that the rehabilitation counselor was more than just a counselor or coordinator; that the counselor (Rubin & Roessler, 2001) was ". . . a professional whose skills include those of therapist, guidance counselor, case manager, case coordinator, psychometrician, clinical life reviewer, vocational evaluator, educator, team member, social and family relator, placement counselor, community and client advocate, life engagement counselor, long-term conservator, and clinician" (p. 252).

Hershenson (1990), as well, stressed a mediation role for the rehabilitation counselor:

> Through their counseling function, rehabilitation counselors enable people with disabilities to reexamine and reconstitute their self-concepts and personal goals. Coordinator skills are needed by the rehabilitation counselor to select and monitor the wide variety of physical, social, and vocational services that clients require to achieve their rehabilitation goals. Finally, through their consulting function, rehabilitation counselors work with the client's family, friends, and employers to redesign the environment in order to maximize access and opportunity for people with disabilities. (Rubin & Roessler, 2001, p. 253)

The rehabilitation counselor, as the focal point in the rehabilitation process, must assure that the agreed-upon services are delivered in a timely manner so a continuity of services exists, and it is the rehabilitation counselor who coordinates this process.

The rehabilitation counselor may provide and/or arrange for any goods and/or services necessary to render an eligible individual fit to engage in a gainful occupation. In addition to evaluation, counseling and guidance, and placement services, the counselor can, when indicated, arrange and provide for physical and/or mental restoration services, training, books and training materials (including tools), maintenance during provision of other services, equipment, initial stocks and supplies, transportation, business and occupational licenses, services to family members, and other goods and services. This wide array of possibilities gives the rehabilitation counselor and the client the opportunity to effectively develop an IPE specifically suited to the client's particular set of skills and abilities. It also requires that the rehabilitation counselor be community-oriented as well as client-oriented.

Physical restoration services can be defined as medical or medically related services necessary to correct or substantially modify, within a reasonable period of time, a physical or mental condition that is stable (static) or slowly progressive. In this instance, we would include psychiatric treatment and psychotherapy under this definition. Physical restoration services would include medical and surgical treatment, dentistry, nursing, hospitalization, convalescent care, drugs and supplies, prosthetic devices, physical therapy, occupational therapy, and other medically related rehabilitation services such as speech and hearing therapy.

Rehabilitation training services can be defined as any type of training that may be necessary in order to facilitate the rehabilitation of a person with a disability. This would include prevocational, personal adjustment, vocational, and other training that contributes to the individual's vocational adjustment. The rehabilitation counselor can provide or arrange for several types of training in various settings, for instance, institutional training such as at a college or university, business or trade school, residential rehabilitation facility, or community rehabilitation program. The counselor may also utilize employment or on-the-job training, supported employment, as well as correspondence training and tutorial training.

Prevocational training would include any form of academic or basic training given for the acquisition of background knowledge or skills. That is, prerequisite or preparatory to vocational training or to employment where the primary occupational knowledge and skills are learned on the job. Personal adjustment training could be provided for a variety of reasons, such as (a) to assist the individual to function more effectively, (b) to assist in developing an increase in work tolerance, (c) to assist in the development of good work habits, (d) to assist in the provision of compensatory skills or techniques, and (e) to learn advocacy skills.

The rehabilitation counselor must advise each person at the beginning of a training program what is expected. The counselor must require periodic progress reports and promptly call the client's attention to evidence of unsatisfactory progress or attendance before such conditions become detrimental to the success of the IPE. The counselor must provide encouragement to the client with due commendation for effective efforts. During the training or educational program, the counselor must continue and maintain a close counseling relationship with appropriate supervision of the training or educational program.

Placement and Follow Along

The final step in the rehabilitation process is placement and follow-along. This involves assisting a person to find suitable work in a remunerative occupation and following up entrance into employment to ensure that vocational rehabilitation has been achieved. This activity depends on much more than a referral to potential employers. It is at this stage in the process that the counselor reassesses the client in relation to the vocational objective. The counselor must determine whether or not the client is ready for work. The counselor must also ascertain that all necessary services identified in the IPE have been provided and that the client has sufficient work tolerance. Clients must understand his or her occupational skills, abilities, and limitations in terms of their disability while also knowing the job objective in terms of performance standards, usual wages and benefits, working conditions, and opportunities for advancement. The counselor must also be assured that the client has the skills and knowledge required for the vocational objective and the attitude of a desirable employee.

In arriving at an evaluation of job readiness, the counselor must consider such factors as physical readiness, psychological readiness, occupational readiness, and placement readiness. The counselor might prepare the client for employment interviews, arrange for training in job-seeking skills, refer the client to a one-stop center or to the agency's employment specialist, or accompany the client to the employer for direct placement.

Several purposes for follow along become evident. For instance, follow-along can provide the occasion for the giving of emotional support to the client when needed. It also provides the opportunity to make needed adjustments and often forestalls the client's quitting without attempts at such adjustment. It indicates the counselor's continuing interest in the client and affords the counselor the opportunity to determine if further counseling or training is necessary or desirable. Follow-along is necessary to determine if a revised or amended plan is needed. It allows for ventilation of client feelings.

Not only is follow-along concerned with the client, but it also provides evidence of interest in the employer's welfare. It provides the counselor an opportunity to determine the employer's satisfaction with the client and with information concerning the possibility of future consultations and placements. It will also help to acquaint the employer with rehabilitation services. It is at this point that the counselor determines if employment is suitable, if the work might aggravate the client's disability, and if additional training or other rehabilitation services are needed.

Prior to closing the case record, the counselor must consider at least three basic criteria. If these are determined as satisfactory, closure is appropriate. These criteria are that (a) the program of rehabilitation services has been completed, (b) substantial rehabilitation services have been rendered by the counselor, and (c) the client is suitably employed, preferably in the primary labor market or in instances where this is not feasible, approximation to the primary labor market is attempted (and achieved in part or whole).

Due Process and the Receipt
of Vocational Rehabilitation Services

Regulatory Authority

The 1973 Rehabilitation Act recognized the sometimes difficult position of applicants and clients in understanding reasons for the denial of eligibility to receive VR services or to be actively involved in decision-making for the formulation and implementation of the rehabilitation plan. As a consequence of this situation, the 1973 Rehabilitation Act authorized a limited number of pilot projects called client assistance projects (CAPs) to develop a model that could provide assistance to clients in the resolution of problems or to facilitate communication between clients and the state vocational rehabilitation agency (Parker, Szymanski, & Patterson, 2005; Rubin & Roessler, 2001). Ultimately, the 1984 amendments to the Rehabilitation Act made the CAPs a permanent program, requiring each state to establish such programs. Subsequent amendments to the Rehabilitation Act strengthened and enhanced the due process rights of persons with disabilities who disagreed with VR agency decisions regarding eligibility, selection or provision of services, or case closure. The 1998 amendments offered mediation as an option, hopefully to resolve disputes although the outcome of such would not be binding; that is, mediation could not be used to delay or deny an impartial hearing. Significantly, the decision of the impartial hearing officer, as a result of the new due process provisions contained in the 1998 amendments, would no longer be reviewed by the VR director.

Fair Hearing Process

When disputes cannot be resolved by the mutual actions and good faith of the rehabilitation counselor, the supervisor and the applicant/client or through the efforts of mediation, the complainant in the process has a right to a fair hearing before an impartial hearing officer. The role of the rehabilitation counselor in the process is awkward. The complaint in many instances is directed toward the counselor but may center on the agency's policies and procedures. The counselor is thrust into the role of an adversary, defending polices, procedures, or decisions that may run counter to his or her values and beliefs. The counselor must defend actions taken or not taken and must, as well, shepherd the client through this process. While this aspect of the rehabilitation counselor's responsibility to the client may seem contradictory, it nevertheless is his or her responsibility to assist and help the client (and agency) grow and learn from the experience.

A fair hearing is not a court process; however, to ensure that all parties are treated equitably and that all facts, laws, regulations, and policies are considered, the hearing should follow a standard format. The hearing officer is the person responsible for ensuring that the hearing is fair and impartial. The hearing officer, even though employed on a contractual basis (and approved by the state rehabilitation council), is not an employee of the VR agency, must not have participated in any decision(s) regarding the complainant, and is not bound by any previous decision(s) regarding the applicant/client's complaint or dispute with the agency. The hearing officer will render a new decision based on the documents presented and the testimony of all witnesses at the hearing. In order to ensure an accurate record of the proceedings, the hearing must be recorded and all testimony must be taken under oath.

The general procedure followed in a fair hearing should adhere to the following or similar format:

- The hearing officer begins the hearing by making an opening statement. He or she will:
  ○ State the limits of his or her authority,
  ○ State the time line for making a decision,
  ○ Identify all participants for the record,
  ○ Read the complaint into the record.
- The hearing officer will administer the oath to all persons who will testify.
- The VR agency representative presents the agency's actions, stating the policies and regulations followed in making the decision that is being disputed. The VR agency representative may call witnesses to testify. The client or his or her representative may ask questions or cross-examine any witness(es) called by the VR agency representative.
- The client or his or her representative presents the complaint and the reason(s) it is believed that the VR agency's decision(s) was not fair. The VR agency representative may ask questions or cross examine any witness(es) called by the client or his or her representative.
- The hearing office may ask questions of witnesses to clarify the facts in dispute.
- The VR agency representative will be given an opportunity to make a closing statement.

- The client or his or her representative will be given an opportunity to make a closing statement.
- The hearing officer may present a summary statement of the issues. The hearing officer does not ordinarily present his or her decision at this time. This awaits the hearing officer's review of the case file, other documentary evidence, and the testimony received at the hearing. The hearing officer's report of findings and decision is provided to all parties within a specified period of time.

If the hearing officer's decision finds in favor of the client, the hearing officer will order the VR director to undertake certain actions that resolve the dispute (e.g., reversal of ineligibility, provision of a denied service or service provider, or case closure). The decision of the hearing officer, as noted in the 1998 amendments, is no longer subject to review by the VR director but may be reviewed at a higher governmental level (e.g., attorney general or governor's office) if requested by the VR director. Within Appendix A, two case abstracts illustrate the nature of disputes that may rise to the level of a fair hearing. Questions to consider are included following each abstract that may facilitate discussion and potential remedies for resolution.

Conclusion

The role of the rehabilitation counselor is unique in the social sciences and is characterized principally by the continuity of the client-counselor relationship. The function of the rehabilitation counselor is that of a coordinator, consultant, and, most important, a counselor throughout the rehabilitation process. The counselor serves as the focal point for the client throughout this process. It is the rehabilitation counselor to whom the client looks for interpretation of the various assessments (e.g., medical, psychological, vocational, and assistive technology) regarding the impact of the medical impairment and resultant vocational impediments, the determination of eligibility and prospectively to the formulation of the individualized plan for employment, the coordination and delivery of services, job placement and follow-along, and, ultimately, case closure. The rehabilitation counselor represents hope to the client and to this person's significant others.

Appendix A

FAIR HEARING CASES

I Ms. B., a 55-year-old client of the Department of the Blind

Ms. B. has requested postemployment services (job placement closer to her home) and was refused by the regional manager (who also functioned as her counselor following the resignation of her previous rehabilitation counselor).

Ms. B. is legally blind (progressive myopia) and had, after an initial period of referral and re-referral between the Department of the Blind (DB) and the Department of Vocational Rehabilitation (general agency), been determined eligible to receive DB services (VR/RT/ ILR). After receiving training (primarily in assistive technology), she secured employment as an administrative assistant at a bank some thirty miles from her home. She chose this position over another clerical job that was closer to her home because it was very similar to the type of work she had done for the past twenty years. Initially she did not think the commute via public transportation would present impediments; she thought, after a short period of time, that she would be able to secure private transportation. This did not occur, and her myopia increased and she experienced other medical problems (diabetes, thyroid). Her rehabilitation counselor/regional manager refused to provide job placement assistance, noting that she was employed; moreover, he had advised Ms. B. not to take the bank position. He did offer her more O&M training (because he believed that she had not really accepted her blindness) that he said would reduce the problems she was encountering in her daily commute.

Questions to Consider

1. Given that the potential need for postemployment services was-anticipated and placed in the IPE by a previous counselor, did Ms. B. have a valid dispute against the manager/counselor? Of what effect is the previous counselor's action regarding postemployment services?
2. Should Ms. B.'s other medical problems (diabetes, thyroid) be

assessed and evaluated? Could this be a postemployment service? How would these services be justified?

3. Was it appropriate to decline job placement service to Ms. B. and instead offer O&M training?

4. How would you have decided this dispute? How would you justify your decision?

II Mr. P., a 22-year-old client of the Department of Vocational Rehabilitation

Mr. P., a resident student of a comprehensive rehabilitation facility, was suspended from the facility for a period of thirty days for alcohol consumption on the grounds of the facility—a clear violation of the facility's written rules. Mr. P. acknowledged the consumption of alcohol, but protested the suspension on the basis that it would be too harsh and would be disruptive of his vocational training program (in computer programming). After an administrative review and denial, Mr. P. requested a fair hearing.

Mr. P. has a paralysis disability, quadriplegia (C4), as a result of a sports injury. After undergoing physical rehabilitation, Mr. P. applied for VR services and was declared eligible. Prior to requesting VR services, Mr. P. had resided in a nursing home where his physical needs were adequately met. However, he had little to do to occupy his time other than to watch television, as most of the nursing home residents were at least sixty years old. Going to the rehabilitation facility was the great hope of his life (and for his family). The suspension would cause him to be transferred to a nursing home for the thirty days, as his parent's house was not fully accessible. At the hearing, Mr. P.'s attorney argued that:

- The suspension was inappropriate for the offense,
- The suspension would cause a "set-back" in his vocational training,
- The imposition of the thirty-day suspension and consequent transfer to a nursing home would create a situation where Mr. P. would be "unnecessarily isolated, emotionally debased, depressed, and without any ongoing rehabilitative services."

Questions to Consider

1. What harm would it do to waive the facility's rule and consequences for consuming alcoholic beverages on the grounds of the facility?
2. Should Mr. P.'s disability be a factor in the application of this rule?
3. If Mr. P. is suspended from the facility, what is the responsibility of the facility or the VR agency in terms of payment for the nursing home?
4. What would be your decision? How would you justify this decision?

REFERENCES

Berkowitz, M. (1984). The economist and rehabilitation. *Rehabilitation Literature, 45,* 354–357.

Cassell, J. L., Mulkey, S. W., & Engen, C. (1997). Systematic practice: Case and caseload management. In D. R. Maki & T. F. Riggar (Eds.), *Rehabilitation counseling: Profession and practice* (pp. 214–233). New York: Springer.

Commission on Rehabilitation Counselor Certification. (2002). *Code of profession ethics for rehabilitation counselors.* Rolling Meadows, IL: Author.

Foundation for Rehabilitation Education and Research. (n.d.). *Rehabilitation counseling: The profession and standards of practice.* Rolling Meadows, IL. Author.

Fifth Institute on Rehabilitation Issues. (1978). *Similar benefits.* Menomonie, WI: Stout Vocational Rehabilitation Institute.

Gandy, G. L., Martin, E. D. Jr., & Hardy, R. E. (Eds.) (1999): *Counseling in the rehabilitation Process: Community services for mental and physical disabilities* (2nd Ed). Springfield, IL: Charles C Thomas.

Gilbride, D., & Hagner, D. (2005). People with disabilities in the workplace. In Parker, R. M., E. M. Szymanski., & J. B. Patterson (Eds.), *Rehabilitation counseling: Basics and beyond* (4th Ed., pp. 281–305). Austin, TX: PRO-ED.

Hagner, D. (2000). Primary and secondary labor markets: Implications for vocational rehabilitation. *Rehabilitation Counseling Bulletin, 44,* 22–29.

Hardy, R. E., & Wright, K. C. (1973). Cooperative alternatives to duplication in social and rehabilitation services. In J. G. Cull & R. E. Hardy (Eds.), *The big welfare mess.* Springfield, IL: Charles C Thomas.

Hershenson, D. (1990). A theoretical model for rehabilitation counseling. *Rehabilitation Counseling Bulletin, 33,* 268–278.

Maki, D. R, & Riggar, T. F. (1997). *Rehabilitation counseling: Profession and practice.* New York: Springer.

Maki, D. R. (1986). Foundations of applied rehabilitation counseling. In T. F. Riggar, D. R. Maki, & A. Wolf (Eds.), *Applied rehabilitation counseling.* New York: Springer.

Martin, E. D. Jr. (2001). *Significant disability: Issues, affecting people with disabilities from a historical, policy, leadership, and systems perspective.* Springfield, IL: Charles C Thomas.

McGowan, J. F., & Porter, T L. (1967). *An introduction to the vocational rehabilitation process.*

Washington, DC: U.S. Department of Health, Education & Welfare.

Parker, R. M., & Hansen, C. E. (1981). *Rehabilitation counseling.* Boston: Allyn & Bacon.

Parker, R M., Szymanski, E. M., & Patterson, J. B. (2005). *Rehabilitation counseling: Basics and beyond* (4th Ed.). Austin, TX: PRO-ED.

Rubin, S. E., & Roessler, R. T. (2001). *Foundations of the vocational rehabilitation process* (5th Ed.). Austin, TX: PRO-ED.

Schroeder, F. K (1998). *The rehabilitation act amendments of 1998.* Information Memorandum, RSA–IM–98–20. Washington, DC: Rehabilitation Services Administration, United States Department of Education.

Schumacher, B. (1977). Rehabilitation counseling. In P. J. Valletutti & F. Christoplos (Eds.), *Interdisciplinary approaches to human services.* Baltimore: University Park Press.

Sixth Institute on Rehabilitation Issues (1979). *VR and the community.* Dunbar, WV: West Virginia Research and Training Center.

Sixth Institute on Rehabilitation Services. (1968). *Principles for developing cooperative programs in vocational rehabilitation.* Washington, DC: U.S. Department of Health, Education & Welfare.

Chapter 5

ASSESSMENT OF DISABILITY: CONSIDERATIONS FOR THE REHABILITATION COUNSELOR

E. DAVIS MARTIN, JR., REBECCA S. CURTIS, AND ALLISON E. SHIPP

Probably the most common notion that defines *disability* is the perception that a medical or psychological condition prevents or precludes a person's ability to engage in work activity. Perceiving one's self to be unable to work may be a starting point for the determination of disability. While this may satisfy the individual, it is not sufficient from a programmatic perspective. Definitions for disability typically arise from federal or state law. Inherent in these various definitions are eligibility criteria that must be met in order to qualify for a specific program or benefit, e.g., disability retirement benefits, receipt of Social Security benefits, Workers' Compensation benefits, medical benefits, or qualification for vocational rehabilitation (VR) services. Common to each of these various disability programs is the presence of a medical impairment. A definitive medical diagnosis of a medical condition or impairment is a necessary first step in the determination of disability.

The state-federal VR program requires considerably more input than just medical opinion stating chronic disease or the limiting effects of an injury in an individual. An estimate of the effects of a physical, mental, cognitive, or sensory impairment relative to the individual's ability to function in an occupation is essential to the qualification to receive VR services. A careful consideration of a number of other factors inclusive of age, education, prior work experience, and environmental limitation(s) in terms of the substantive impact that a disability may impose must as well be accessed regarding occupational choice and the need for VR services. This chapter examines the effect(s) of these factors regarding the determination of eligibility to receive vocational rehabilitation services. For the convenience of the reader, a *Disability Guide* has been developed (and may be located in Appendix A) that provides a concise checklist that can be used to ensure that all pertinent factors are considered in this determination. This guide may prove to be a useful adjunct when analyzing cases presented in Part 3 of the text. Additionally, Appendixes B and C provide the reader with standard definitions of working conditions and physical demands as presented in the *Dictionary of Occupational Titles (DOT)* and companion documents. Even though the *DOT* has been replaced by the Occupational Information Network (O*NET), many government units and other organizations concerned with occupational information continue to utilize the *DOT* and its concepts and operational definitions. In fact, crosswalks between the two systems are a part of O*NET. Nevertheless, O*NET is the principal occupational resource that will provide definitions and concepts for work force development efforts and a common frame of reference for job performance in the future. O*NET has been developed as a Web-based application that is easily accessible and will be the primary source of occupational information for the United States. The Department of Labor's Website for the O*NET is www.onetcenter.org.

The Medical Report

Disability denotes a medical impairment that impedes a person's ability to perform work activity or activities of daily living as a result of a disease process (e.g., diabetes), trauma (e.g., traumatic brain injury, TBI), or developmental condition (e.g., mental retardation). Impediments imposed as a result of a medical impairment may be manifested in varying degrees in one or more of the following spheres and represent the type of informed medical opinion needed to determine programmatic eligibility for disability:

- **Physical**, affecting ambulation, coordination, speech production, vision
- **Cognitive**, affecting ability to think, remember, comprehend, or

general learning ability
- **Social**, affecting ability to communicate and establish relationships with other people
- **Emotional**, affecting self-image, self-acceptance, mental health
- **Occupational**, affecting vocational performance or the performance of activities of daily living

In determining the effects of any particular medical condition, the physician is a major contributor to the establishment of programmatic eligibility, e.g., the state-federal VR program, Social Security disability, Workers' Compensation, disability retirement programs, or insurance programs. The physician's report provides the rehabilitation counselor with the following general information:

- Information on the presence and extent of the medical condition
- The remediableness of the medical condition
- The probable course of the medical condition
- Any functional limitations imposed as a result of the medical condition

A well-written medical report may serve to (a) provide medical opinion as to the presence or absence of disease or injury, (b) delineate periods and modes of treatment, and (c) provide a prognosis. While these are important elements, other aspects of the medical report, usually not as prominent, may be of greater utility in the determination future rehabilitation planning. These factors are:

- To ascertain the degree that physical or mental restoration services (and/or assistive technology) could lessen or ameliorate the effects of the resulting impediments,
- To appraise the person's overall health status, thus contributing to a sound medical basis for a vocational objective,
- To provide a holistic perspective regarding the person's overall rehabilitation goal.

The specific effects of a medical condition, trauma, or injury upon the individual's ability to function in activities of daily living and in the occupational market place are paramount in the determination of eligibility to receive VR services. In those instances where the physician concludes the person does not have the ability to perform work activity or activities of daily living, particularly without considering the utilization of assistive technology or adjunctive treatment, e.g., occupational therapy, physical therapy, working hardening, pain programs, options, the need to obtain additional medical opinion-medical reevaluation or specialist examination may be indicated.

The rehabilitation counselor must be able to recognize when there is insufficient information in the medical opinion(s) to substantiate a claim of disability and, if absent, to be able to formulate questions that will elicit from the physician, specialist, or psychologist the type of information needed to make an eligibility determination. Factors such as the effects of a psychiatric impairment on the individual's ability to perform physical activity in a work setting are equally as important. The functional overlay checklist (contained in Appendix A) serves to focus professional opinion upon the residuals of physiological, psychiatric, or other nonexertional impairments. Environmental considerations are included so that consideration may be given to those factors that impede the individual's physical or mental capacity.

Within the first two sections of this chapter, definitions for (a) age, education, (b) exertional and nonexertional considerations, (c) environmental considerations, (d) vocational adjustment, (e) work experience (skill requirements), and (f) transferability of skills are derived from the *Code of Federal Regulations, Title 20, Employees' Benefits, Chapter III, Social Security Administration, Part 404, Federal Old-Age, Survivors and Disability Insurance (1950–)* (particularly Subpart P, Determining Disability and Blindness) and from the *DOT* and companion documents to the *DOT.*

Vocational Factors

Age

The term "age" refers to chronological age and the extent to which it affects the individual's capability to engage in work in competition with others. However, the factor of age is not determinative of disability: the residual functional capacity and the education and work experience of the individual must also be considered. An individual who is unemployed because of age cannot be found incapable of engaging in work activity when the individual's impairment and other vocational considerations such as education and work experience would enable the individual to perform a significant number of jobs that exist in the national economy.

In the case of a younger individual (under age fifty), age in itself is ordinarily not considered to affect significantly the individual's ability to adapt to a new work situation.

For the individual not of advanced age but who is closely approaching advanced age (age fifty to fifty-four), the factor of age, in combination with a significant impairment and limited vocational background may substantially affect the individual's adaptability to a significant number of jobs in a competitive work environment.

"Advanced" age (age fifty-five or over) represents the point where age significantly affects the ability to engage in substantial work. Where a person with a significant disability and resultant impediments is of advanced age, such ability may be adversely affected except where the individual has skills that are readily transferable to jobs which exist in significant numbers in the national economy.

Education

The term "education" is primarily used in the sense of formal schooling or other training which contributes to the individual's ability to meet vocational requirements, such as (a) reasoning ability, (b) communication skills, and (c) arithmetical ability. Lack of formal schooling is not necessarily proof that the individual is uneducated or lacks such capabilities. Past work experience and the kinds of responsibilities assumed when working may indicate the existence of such intellectual capacities although his or her formal education is limited. Other evidence of such capabilities, for individuals without past work experience, may consist of daily activities, hobbies, or the results of testing. The significance of an individual's educational background may be materially affected by the time lapse between the completion of the individual's formal education and the onset of a medical impairment(s), and by what the individual has done with his or her education in a work context.

Formal education that was completed many years prior to onset of impairment or unused skills and knowledge that were a part of such formal education may no longer be useful or meaningful in terms of the individual's ability to work. Thus, the numerical grade level of educational attainment may not be representative of an individual's present educational competence that could be higher or lower.

"Illiteracy" refers to the inability to read or write. An individual who is able to sign his or her name, for example, but cannot read or write a simple communication (e.g., instructions, inventory lists) is considered illiterate. Generally, an illiterate individual has had little or no formal schooling. Marginal education refers to competence in reasoning, arithmetic, and language skills which are required for the performance of simple, unskilled types of jobs. Formal schooling at a grade level of sixth grade or less is considered a marginal education.

"Limited education" refers to competence in reasoning, arithmetic, and language skills that, although more than that which is generally required to carry out the duties of unskilled work, does not provide the individual with the educational qualifications necessary to perform the majority of more complex job duties involved in semiskilled or skilled jobs. A seventh grade through the eleventh grade of formal education is considered a limited education.

High school education and above refers to competence in reasoning, arithmetic, and language skills acquired through formal schooling at a level of grade twelve or above. These educational capacities qualify an individual for work at semiskilled through a skilled level of job complexity.

Exertional Considerations

For the purpose of determining exertional requirements of work in the national economy, jobs are classified as sedentary, light, medium, heavy, and very heavy. Such terms have the same meaning as they have in the *DOT,* published by the Department of Labor, and are defined as follows:

- **Sedentary work:** Sedentary work entails lifting ten pounds maximum and occasionally lifting or carrying such articles as dockets, e.g., files, ledgers, and small tools. Although a sedentary job is defined as one which involves sitting at least six hours in an eight-hour day, a certain amount of walking and standing (two to three hours per eight-hour day) is often necessary in carrying out job duties. Jobs are sedentary if walking and standing are required occasionally and other sedentary criteria are met.

• **Light work:** Light work entails occasionally lifting twenty pounds maximum with frequent lifting or carrying of objects weighing up to ten pounds. Even though the weight lifted may be only a negligible amount, a job requiring walking or standing to a significant degree or sitting most of the time with a degree of pushing and pulling of arm or leg controls is classified as light. To be considered capable of performing a wide range of light work, an individual must be capable of performing substantially all of the foregoing activities. The functional capacity to perform light work includes the functional capacity to perform sedentary work.

• **Medium work:** Medium work entails occasionally lifting fifty pounds maximum with frequent lifting or carrying of objects weighing up to twenty-five pounds and the ability to stand and work at least six hours during the work day. The functional capacity to perform medium work includes the functional capacity to perform sedentary work and light work as well.

• **Heavy work:** Heavy work entails lifting one hundred pounds maximum with frequent lifting or carrying of objects weighing up to fifty pounds and the ability to stand and walk at least six hours during the work day. The functional capacity to perform heavy work includes the functional capacity to perform work at all of the lesser exertional levels.

• **Very heavy work:** Very heavy work entails lifting objects in excess of one hundred pounds with frequent lifting or carrying of objects weighting fifty pounds or more. The functional capacity to perform very heavy work includes the functional capacity to perform work at all the lesser exertional levels.

Nonexertional Considerations

The assessment of impairments because of mental conditions includes consideration of such factors as the capacity to (a) understand and (b) carry out and remember instructions and (c) respond appropriately to supervisiors, co-workers and (d) customary work pressures in a routine work setting. Any medically determinable condition(s) resulting in nonexertional impairment such as certain mental, sensory, or skin impairments, must be considered in terms of the impediments resulting from the medical impairment. When an individual has a nonexertional impairment in addition to an exertional impairment(s), the residual functional capacity must be assessed in terms of the degree of any additional narrowing of the individual's work-related capabilities.

Environmental Considerations

Impairment may leave an individual with the capacity to meet the strength requirements of jobs. However, the physical surroundings may pose a hazard to the individual's health and therefore must be considered. Environmental restrictions are those restrictions that result in the inability to tolerate some physical features that exist in certain types of work such as an inability to tolerate dust or fumes or sudden changes in temperature.

Vocational Adjustment

An individual who is suddenly prevented from work by injury or medical impairment may have the residual functional capacity to perform some type of work; however, the person may lack the capacity to adjust and therefore be incapable of performing work. This is extremely important in those instances where injury or the medical condition prevents the individual from engaging in his or her usual occupation. One nonexertional factor to be considered is whether or not the individual can accommodate new physical surroundings, new fellow employees, and new tasks. This factor is worthy of consideration for individuals who have:

- A long work history in skilled occupations
- Exhibited poor adjustment on the job
- Received psychiatric treatment
- Experienced traumatic injury after age fifty-five

Work Experience

The term *work experience* means skills and abilities acquired through work previously performed by the individual and indicates the type of work the individual may be expected to perform. Work for which the individual has demonstrated a capability is the best indicator of the kind of work that the individual can be expected to do. Such work experience has current vocational relevance where the work and the skills acquired within the last fifteen years demonstrate the individual's ability to perform work. In our economic system, a gradual transition occurs in the job functions of most jobs so that by the time fifteen years has elapsed, it is no longer realistic to assume that skills and abilities acquired in a job performed more than fifteen years ago continue to be relevant. An individual who has no prior work experience or has worked only sporadically or for brief periods of time may be considered to have no relevant work experience. Any skills acquired through work experience are vocational assets unless they are not transferable to other skilled or semiskilled work within the individual's current capacities. An individual need not have work experience, however, to qualify for unskilled work that requires little or no judgment in the performance of simple duties that can be learned in a short period of time.

Skill Requirements

For purposes of assessing the skills reflected by an individual's work experience, and to determine the existence of work the individual is competent to do, occupations are classified as unskilled, semiskilled, and skilled. When used in making disability determinations, these terms are used in the following sense:

- **Unskilled work:** Unskilled work denotes work that requires little or no judgment in the performance of simple duties that can be learned on the job in a short period of time. Considerable strength may or may not be required. As an example, where the primary work function of occupations consists of handling, feeding and off bearing, i.e., placing or removing materials from machines that are automatic or operated by others, or machine tending, an average successful job performance can ordinarily be achieved within thirty days, such occupations are considered unskilled. Other types of jobs requiring little specific vocational preparation and little judgment are likewise unskilled. No acquired skills can be attributed to individuals who have performed only unskilled work.
- **Semiskilled work:** Semiskilled work denotes work in which some skills are involved but the more complex work functions are not required. Semiskilled jobs may require alertness and close attention to watching machine processes; or inspecting, testing, or otherwise detecting irregularities; or tending or guarding equip-

ment, property, materials, or persons against loss, damage, or injury; or other types of activities involving work functions of similar complexity. A job may be classified as semiskilled where coordination and dexterity are necessary as in the use of the hands or feet for the rapid performance of repetitive tasks.

- **Skilled work:** Skilled work requires qualifications in which the independent judgment of the individual determines the machine and manual operations to be performed in obtaining the proper form, quality, or quantity of material to be produced. The individual may be required to lay out work; to estimate quality, suitability, and needed quantities of materials; to make precise measurements; to read blueprints or other specifications; or to make necessary computations or mechanical adjustments to control or regulate processes. Other skilled jobs may require dealing with personnel, data, or abstract ideas at a high level of complexity.

Transferability of Skills

An individual is considered to have transferable skills when the skilled or semiskilled work functions that he or she has demonstrated in past work can be applied to meet the requirements of skills or semiskilled work functions of other jobs or kinds of work. Transferability depends largely on the similarity of occupationally significant work functions among jobs. Transferability is (a) most probable and meaningful among jobs in which the same or a lesser degree of skill is required; (b) the same or similar tools and machines are used; (c) and the same or similar raw materials, products, processes, or services are involved. There are degrees of transferability ranging from a close approximation of work functions involving all three factors to only remote and incidental similarities among jobs. A complete similarity of all three factors is not necessary to warrant the inference of transferability. Where an individual's work skills are so specialized or have been acquired in such a limited vocational setting that they are not readily usable in other industries, jobs and work environments, they are not transferable and the individual may be considered as if he or she is unskilled.

Vocational Evaluation

Assessing vocational considerations in relationship to disability has historically been accomplished by a vocational evaluator who collects and synthesizes data relative to the vocational experiences of an individual while taking into consideration the individual's medical, psychological, and psychoeducational profile. Practical concerns involving the vocational evaluation process must be addressed prior to the referral in order to produce a clear and valuable snapshot of each individual assessed. The individual being evaluated, the rehabilitation counselor, and the vocational evaluator each have an unique perspective and expectations for this process. For a successful evaluation to occur, one that results in information that may be used during the planning phase of the rehabilitation process, all parties must reach a common understanding regarding the purpose and goals of a vocational assessment (i.e., that clearly identifies strengths, providing viable recommendations for training, education, or direct job placement consistent with expressed job or career goals).

Practical Considerations: What Is Being Assessed?

PURPOSE. When a vocational evaluation is requested, what information is being sought? Specifically, as a rehabilitation counselor, what information do you need to know and expect to find in a vocational evaluation report? How is quality determined in a vocational evaluation report? If the majority of reports that make their way across your desk seem as though they came from the same "cookie cutter," then one could say that you are most likely *not* looking at reports that contain quality information. Quality in vocational evaluation is directly related to the purpose of conducting this assessment. Do your expectations of the report match the intended purpose of conducting the evaluation? For an assessment to be meaningful, it is extremely important that a clear understanding exists of what needs to be measured and for what purpose. The vocational evaluation process begins by asking an appropriate referral question(s) related to the purpose of the assessment.

THE REFERRAL QUESTION. A good vocational evaluation report begins with a clear, well-written referral question. A well-written referral question concentrates the attention of the evaluator on issues that are pertinent to the vocational rehabilitation of the client. The referral question is the first half of an equation that should result in recommendations and suggestions that are specific and behaviorally based.

If the assumption is made that a vocational evaluator will know what you want by simply requesting a vocational evaluation, then, more often than not, you will be disappointed. By requesting a generic or nonspecific vocational evaluation, you will most likely get generic information in the vocational report; information that is adequate but may not be very useful, client-targeted, or meaningful.

To ensure the referral question(s) is relevant; the rehabilitation counselor must spend time getting to know his or her client, usually in the form of interviewing. This approach focuses on person-centered planning methods where the client is able to explore options, desires, dreams, and vocational goals. In this process, the rehabilitation counselor may identify environmental barriers that could prove to be an impediment to vocational success. Time and discussions spent with the client are vital and should not be compressed if you are to include relevant personal information in the referring material. A good referral question may require the counselor to *synthesize* information known about the client. What clues do the client's stated goals, interests, and past experiences give you about potential career paths and job exploration that the vocational evaluator can further assess? In other words, for the evaluation process to be meaningful, it must flow from the working relationship the rehabilitation counselor initiates with the client. The evaluation process and subsequent report should be a natural outcome of this endeavor. A good vocational evaluation should be a tool that assists the counselor and the client to broaden vocational prospects, ideas, and possibilities (U.S. Department of Labor, 1999).

ISSUES RELATED TO THE PURPOSE OF CONDUCTING A VOCATIONAL ASSESSMENT. When reviewing the results of a vocational evaluation it is important to keep the overall purpose and referral question in mind. Even when the evaluation report contains quality information and responds appropriately to the referring question(s), as the reader, you may have a sense of disappointment: "But I thought an evaluation would tell me _____" (fill in the blank with any number of traits, behaviors, or personality quirks you may have questioned but did not specify in the referral).

Knowing how to ask appropriate questions for the purpose of evaluation is closely related to knowing what *not* to expect from an assessment or evaluation report. Some information may not be collected in this process, even if it is specifically requested. Some areas are extremely difficult to assess and are mercurial in nature. For some individuals, responses to specific concerns may or may not be discovered on any given day. Even when addressed in the most appropriate manner possible, it may not be possible to discern the factors or elements that this particular person's learning and developmental process have experienced. This is especially true in areas such as:

• Identifying one's level of motivation to succeed
• Identifying what "success" means to an individual
• Identifying one's work ethic (both on a short-term and long-term basis)
• Understanding the influence of family expectations on jobs and salary
• Understanding one's level of trust in the evaluation and rehabilitation process

INCLUDING ASSISTIVE TECHNOLOGY. Technology plays a significant role in the evaluation process. The rehabilitation counselor must recognize that assistive technology is a tool that can be used to help clients lessen the impact of an impediment(s) imposed as a result of disability. At times, vocational success may be based on work redesign and the incorporation of assistive technology in the workplace (note the following section for a detailed discussion of assistive technology).

Practical Considerations: Methods Used to Evaluate

Multiple types of data are produced as a result of assessing vocational issues. How one uses this information is central to the purpose of the evaluation. Specific concerns must be assessed using tools and methods that will yield the needed information. The method of assessment used will determine the type of information obtained (U.S. Department of Labor, 1999). As such, the vocational evaluator and rehabilitation counselor must have a thorough understanding of the types of assessments that may be utilized and the resulting nature of the data derived from the use of various assessment instruments. This information also needs to be communicated to the client in a manner that is straightforward and free from jargon. As a rehabilitation counselor, it is important to actively listen to what your client is telling you, and then consider what specific areas you want explored. These content areas may include behaviors, skills, endurance, or specific job trials. Below are listed the various categories of assessments:

- **Paper-and-pencil assessment**. Psychometric tests, or paper-and-pencil assessments, are commonly used to assess various aspects of an individual. They can be very specific in the trait, characteristic, or aptitude that is being assessed. Likewise, they may be more global by examining a broad spectrum of a client's interests or personality traits, indicating what areas represent above-average, average- or below-average areas. Traditional psychometric tests are typically quick to administer, score, and interpret. When norm groups are used as part of the assessment make-up, the evaluator must be careful to use the appropriate norm group for comparison. This can be especially problematic for individuals with disabilities who may not have a "norm" group to be used for comparison purposes (e.g., someone with autism). Problems that arise from not following standardized procedures generally do not favor individuals with disabilities. Using assessment instruments of this type, however, can yield significant information. Information that results from paper-and-pencil testing reveals:
  - *Handwriting ability* (Can the person write their own name? Is the handwriting legible?)
  - *Dexterity* (Does the person have the fine motor skills and dexterity needed to write?)
  - *Academic achievement* (Based on traditional achievement tests, clues can be gathered regarding academic achievement levels in specific content areas and one's equivalent grade levels)
  - *General aptitudes, interests, and clues about one's personality* (Paper-and-pencil assessments in the areas of aptitudes, interests, personality assessment, and character traits abound and give further clues about a person).
- **Work samples**. Work samples are considered a traditional form of vocational evaluation. Work samples typically involve the use of commercially developed equipment used to analyze specific skill or ability areas (e.g., eye-motor-hand coordination). These traits are then compared to jobs where such skills are used in the successful performance of the job. The use of work samples is typically based on a comparison of one's performance to a similar population (i.e., norm referenced). This comparison often leaves individuals with disabilities displaying more deficits than stren-

gths. Using instruments of this type focuses on what the client cannot do, rather that what the client can do. A more accurate assessment of what a person can do may be accomplished by employing criterion-referenced measures where one's performance is compared to an identified criterion yielding what a person can do.

- **Behavioral observations**. Behavioral observations take various formats but all involve someone witnessing an individual's behavior and noting aspects of that behavior in various settings. Behavioral observations may be extremely informal or more sophisticated in nature. For example, an evaluator may use behavior rating scales, formalized interviews, case-notes, or general work-related or task-specific observations. Using this type of assessment, information that results from behavioral observations gives clues to how someone acts in specific settings. General or specific behaviors may be targeted for an evaluator to observe. Behavioral observations are generally the most used methods of assessment. This type of assessment can lead to recommendations that enhance success by assisting the rehabilitation counselor in identifying appropriate supports, accommodations, and/or training needs.

- **Self-appraisal assessment**. Self-appraisal assessment is information that is gathered about the client by the client. In other words, how well does the client know his or her own desires, strengths, weaknesses, areas of interests, and goals? For some persons, this information is a vital component based on life experience and history. For others, this information is an as-yet-unknown aspect to be explored. Self-appraisal information is usually collected through the use of self-reports such as (a) interviews (either formal or informal), (b) stated goals of the client, (c) personal futures planning, and (d) exploration and assessment of one's work values, interests, and preferences. Because information gathered from self-assessment may be based on an unknown quality, it may represent the ideal self rather than present capabilities. The importance and usefulness of this type of assessment is that it contains an educational component. Self-assessment can be used as a way of building self-awareness. It is a quite appropriate method to use with person centered concerns in self-discovery and personal exploration.

- **Community-based assessment methods**. Community-based methods of assessment are conducted in real work settings in order to collect information about a client's functional ability and capacity. Community-based methods typically include situational assessments, job-site evaluations, or trial work experiences. An assessment of this type is based on the need to understand how a person performs in a specific setting under certain conditions. Community-based assessment should not be considered a method of work adjustment (Havranek, Field, & Grimes, 2001). Community-based assessment is one aspect of vocational evaluation that fits into the overall rehabilitation process.
- **Situational assessment**. This type of assessment investigates specific skills and behaviors for a given setting. Situational assessments typically focus on adaptive behavior. A situational assessment must be professionally organized and supervised to ensure that what one is claiming to assess is truly the object of assessment. Areas that situational assessments may best determine include: (a) endurance, (b) strength, (c) communication skills, (d) response to supervision, (e) response to co-workers, (f) job preferences, and (g) responses to varying work environments (Havranek, Field, & Grimes, 2001).
- **Job-site evaluation**. This type of assessment focuses on the environmental demands and skill requirements of a particular job or workplace. Job-site evaluation is important because it focuses on the demands of the job comparing this to the capabilities, strengths, skills, and environmental needs of the worker. In other words, what are the essential functions of the job and the functional limitations of the client? Based on this information, will this potential job-site be a satisfactory match for the client? A good job-site evaluation begins with a complete, thorough description of the job and the component parts or tasks involved. Job-site evaluation may include job analysis. Job analysis is a tool that helps to identify the key elements needed to successfully perform a job. This may include the identification of specific content areas such as (a) the type of equipment used to complete a job, (b) the demands of the physical environment associated with the job, (c) the nature of the work (sedentary versus active), (d) the specific procedures used to perform a task, (e) the materials used in performing a task, (f) the identification of routines associated with job

tasks and performance, and (g) the rules and workplace culture that often are not codified but, nonetheless, have an enormous impact on the worker's ability to fit in and "get along" with co-workers (Havranek, Field, & Grimes, 2001).

- **Trial work experience**. A trial work experience typically involves a client actually working in the community in a "real-life" work situation. The job itself may be temporary in nature, an apprenticeship position, or part-time employment. In a trial work experience, a client's performance and behaviors on the job are assessed. In this type of situation, the employer usually rates the performance of the worker. The beneficial aspect of this type of assessment is that it may help to broaden the work experience and knowledge about work requirements for novice workers.

Practical Considerations: Analysis and Synthesis of Information

SUCCESSFUL JOB MATCHING. Attempts at appropriate job matching include the synthesis of multiple sources of data that may be gathered by the rehabilitation counselor and the vocational evaluator. This information originates from the client and his or her expressed interests, goals, and choice. Included in this synthesis are issues of disability, that is, impediments, possible accommodation(s), and/or the use of assistive technology, social considerations, and any other aspects of disability that may impact the vocational potential of the client. Of major importance is an understanding of the client's vocational experiences. This includes his or her employment record—a detailed work history that includes where employed, length of employment, pay, reasons for leaving, strengths and likes/dislikes, and problem areas for each job. Other information that is pertinent to the client should be collected includes academic experience and level and background information about living conditions, family concerns, transportation issues, and other social issues.

Information that should be included in any successful job matching includes an understanding of the local labor market. For example, what is the job market in a specific geographic area for a particular occupational category? Are industrial sites available or are most jobs in a specific area in the service arena? Will the client need to relocate in order to find a job that matches his or her skills or proposed career goal? Local labor market analysis is an integral aspect of job matching that must not be ignored. To do so would be a gross oversight; it is a mistake to be unaware of the existence of vocational opportunities in a specific geographic location. Additionally, does the rehabilitation counselor have a thorough and grounded understanding of employer needs? For this to occur, rehabilitation counselors must be willing to establish professional business relationships with local employers (Bissonnette, 2002). One-on-one business relationships help rehabilitation counselors understand the needs of employers, including the essential functions of a number of jobs that exist within a particular business. Such relationships provide information relative to job culture and unspoken workplace expectations as well. Finally, will the client be able to pass necessary drug and background checks? A rehabilitation counselor may consider a client ready for placement only to learn, after the fact, that he or she cannot pass a drug screening.

Gathering information is the first step in the rehabilitation process. Information collected from multiple sources creates a vivid, dynamic picture of the individual seeking services. After collecting these data, an analysis of the information and a thoughtful, meaningful synthesis of this information is produced that yields pertinent, useful information in the form of suggestions and recommendations regarding an individual's vocational capacity for success. This process in concert with the rehabilitation counselor's knowledge about a client should result in job matching that is appropriate and satisfying to the client. A properly prepared vocational evaluation should provide data relative to potential job groupings that match client skills and abilities or point to further training or education. A rehabilitation counselor should be wary of reports that only provide recommendations in the form of potential jobs listed by job titles and occupational code numbers. Such information tends to ignore the uniqueness of an individual who is the consumer of vocational rehabilitation services. Reports that are not person-centered and positive in tone ignore a basic tenet of our field: *the belief that all people, regardless of disability, are worthy and unique beings* (Curtis, 1998). As a rehabilitation counselor, it is imperative to understand that evaluation reports do *not* yield "the right answer" or "the perfect job," yet a properly prepared vocational evaluation report provides information that may lead to further training, education, or direct placement within the labor market.

DEALING WITH ISSUES OF QUALITY. When the vocational evaluation report does not seem to be on target or have fully answered referral questions, what recourse does the rehabilitation counselor have? An examination of why counselors may experience disappointment with evaluation reports must begin, however, with our expectations. Were our expectations realistic regarding the information we had hoped to see in the form of suggestions and recommendations? Have we been thorough, behaviorally oriented, and specific in our referral questions?

Rehabilitation counselors may be hesitant to voice complaints regarding evaluations; however, if the purpose of doing such is to improve the rehabilitation system and yield quality services, then the effort is worth making. In this type of situation, the rehabilitation counselor should contact the vocational evaluator and provide a thorough description of what is lacking. By identifying areas that are consistently lacking, the originating organization has the potential to identify organizational issues, procedures, or methods that may be corrected. Alternatively, the requesting professionals and organizations have the right to make their concerns known and, if ignored, seek services elsewhere. This decision may be the final response when negotiations and attempts to communicate are not met with success.

Practical Considerations: Improvement in the Evaluation Process

ECOLOGICAL EVALUATIONS. One method to improve assessment outcomes and determine vocational potential is through the use of an ecological evaluation. An ecological evaluation is a type of assessment that is performed in the environment where a client lives, works, and interacts within the community (Havranek, Field, & Grimes, 2001). Data used in ecological evaluations include client files, perceptions of significant others, and observations in daily routines. This type of evaluation is person-centered and characterized by open communication throughout the process. At the end of the evaluation, the client receives a copy of the evaluation report. Using ecological evaluation is similar to a standard evaluation in terms of the sources of data sought and used for analysis and synthesis. The major difference in this type of evaluation is that it takes place over time and is not just a snapshot of the individual's behavior. Ecological evaluations occur where appropriate, based on the client's age and life complexity (Havranek, Field, & Grimes, 2001). Recommendations for places of observation include academic settings, occupational settings (carefully defining tasks performed and skills used), and settings in which an individual spends leisure time and engages in social or community events. In an ecological evaluation, content areas to be addressed are the person's (a) strengths, (b) weaknesses, (c) career interests and goals, (d) lifestyle in the community, (e) needed supports, and (f) probability of success. The advantage of using an ecological evaluation is that it gathers information from multiple sources across multiple settings, thereby giving the evaluator a much better opportunity to capture a dynamic picture of the client, observing the consistencies and inconsistencies of behavior. The use of an ecological evaluation format ensures that a holistic perspective of the client's situation is examined.

FOLLOW-UP: TYING CLIENT OUTCOMES WITH VOCATIONAL EVALUATION RECOMMENDATIONS. A common concern to most vocational evaluators is they are left out of the rehabilitation loop. If you were to ask most evaluators what happened to client Jane Doe who they last evaluated, they cannot tell you. This is not because the evaluator does not care or is not concerned about clients; rather, there simply is little or no communication after the evaluation report is completed. When evaluation is thought of as a one-time event, its usefulness quickly degenerates, and evaluation reports that appear rote, generic, and dull easily have the capacity to become commonplace. In instances such as this, there is generally little to no accountability associated with evaluation outcomes. For vocational evaluation to be an integral component of the rehabilitation process, open communication and feedback systems must be in place if the quality of evaluation recommendations and suggestions is to be realistic and achievable for the client.

AN ORIENTATION TOWARD SKILLS BUILDING VERSUS WORK ADJUSTMENT AND JOB PLACEMENT. A recommendation frequently seen in evaluation reports is for the client to engage in work adjustment activities. While work adjustment activities have their place in the rehabilitation process, not every person needs this service and its recommendation should not be *de rigueur*. Goals of work adjustment counseling include the following:

- Orient the person to the new work setting,
- Help the person to understand the demands of the new work environment,
- Interpret production standards and expectations for work behavior to the person,
- Counsel the person regarding adjustment problems in the work

setting,
• Recommend specific tasks and experiences that may provide personal growth,
• Help plan other services that would enhance the person's work adjustment (Havranek, Field, & Grimes, 2001, p. 60).

Work adjustment and job placement go hand-in-hand. Work adjustment, however, should not be a substitute for vocational evaluation, and vocational evaluation should not be a substitute for work adjustment. More specifically, recommendations for work adjustment do not need to supersede recommendations for the acquisition of skill building and development that are often a necessary prerequisite for successful job placement. If a client does not possess the skills needed to obtain employment, work adjustment services will not aid in the acquisition of those skills.

SUMMARY. When the vocational evaluation process is a viable, essential component of the rehabilitation process, it is most apparent. When this occurs, vocational evaluators produce meaningful, well-thought-out recommendations for clients that assist the rehabilitation counselor and client in planning, and ultimately in successful job placement. Communication between the rehabilitation counselor, vocational evaluator, and client is a key element that enhances the achievement of occupational goals. In such situations, a transparent understanding of the purpose and expectations of the evaluation report exist and can be articulated by all involved. Making the vocational evaluation a vital part of the rehabilitation journey is essential for client success. It is a win-win situation for all concerned.

Assistive Technology

Assistive technologies can prove to be necessary and helpful tools for individuals who may otherwise not be capable of performing the essential functions of a job. Oftentimes assistive technologies can be viewed as great equalizers because they have the power to minimize or remove previous and potential barriers to employment. This, in turn, affords individuals with disabilities a much broader range of opportunities. Assistive technologies can be used to enable an individual to maximize his or her chances to pursue the American Dream by competitively participating in the labor force. The Americans with

Disabilities Act of 1990 (ADA) made it possible for individuals with disabilities to include job accommodations and assistive technology when considering whether or not the individual can perform the essential functions of a job. Assistive technology needs, however, should not be confined to the realm of employment. It is also vital to consider the assistive technology needs of the consumer during activities of daily living. How can we expect individuals with disabilities to work effectively if they cannot fix their own breakfast, take a shower in the morning, or open their front door without the necessary technology aids? Therefore, we must first enable the client in his or her home environment prior to sending him or her out into the workforce.

While it is ultimately the employers' responsibility to provide reasonable accommodations, they often are at a loss as to what is needed or appropriate. Individuals with disabilities themselves may also not be aware of the options that are available to them. It is essential that the rehabilitation counselor educate both the individuals and the future employers about the appropriate assistive technology choices. Additionally, employers may worry that the assistive technology could involve extreme costs or extensive training periods. While it is true that some individuals will need expensive or complicated equipment, this tends to be the exception rather than the rule. Creativity coupled with a comprehensive knowledge base can lead to a variety of low and no-cost items. For example, an individual could be fitted for an expensive prosthesis costing hundreds or thousands of dollars when a simple Velcro strap with a loop and hook would be more beneficial and virtually cost-free.

In order to be truly effective, assistive technology should be considered during every phase of the rehabilitation process for all individuals being served. From the initial referral through vocational evaluation and continued on to placement and postemployment, assistive technology can be the defining factor in the ultimate goal of successful employment. The consumer should be at the crux of these assessments. While it may not be feasible to include a formal assessment during all stages of the rehabilitation process, informal evaluations should be given. When deemed beneficial, placement assessments should include a job/task analysis in addition to a thorough understanding of the individual's functional limitations and how they may impact job performance. It is vital that these assessments take place on the job, and a supervisor should be present. Including the supervisor during this process helps to alleviate concerns, answer questions, and build trust and support.

Assistive technology practitioners (ATPs) are professionals who have received a certification from the international organization Rehabilitation Engineering and Assistive Technology Society of North America (RESNA). These individuals can be utilized to provide personalized assessments and professional advice. It is also beneficial to establish a close working relationship with someone familiar with assistive technology such as an ATP because they have a wealth of knowledge on the subject as well as a list of suppliers and resources that are currently available. If a device needs fabrication or modifications, a rehabilitation engineering technologist (RET) should be contacted. These individuals are also certified by RESNA and can be found, along with ATPs, by visiting the directory on their Website (www.resna.org). This RET should accompany the client to the job-site to customize the assistive technology device to the work environment and specific job tasks.

When sending a client to an assistive technology professional, it is important to ask specific questions in your referral letter. Each referral letter should be tailored to the individual. A few examples of helpful referral questions are as follows:

- What assistive technology device(s) does the consumer need in order to perform activities of daily living?
- What assistive technology device(s) will enhance the consumer's general employability?
- What specific assistive technology device(s) may be necessary for various employment settings? (List some of the employment options that your client is considering.)
- What are some effective low-cost, low-tech devices?
- Is the assistive technology device a medical necessity and/or durable medical equipment?
- What are the costs, model numbers, and vendor information for each suggested device?
- Are there any devices that need to be fabricated or modified? If so, who do you recommend for this?
- What prior knowledge does the consumer have regarding specific devices?

- How motivated is the consumer for using assistive technology devices?
- What assistive technology services (i.e., training) will be necessary for each device?
- Who do you recommend to provide these services?
- How should the device be evaluated for effectiveness?

Once you receive the report back from the ATP, it is important to discuss the results with your client. Keep in mind that while it is the ATP's responsibility to focus on assistive technology needs, it is the rehabilitation counselor's task to integrate the technology needs into the entire picture of the client. The client's comfort level and willingness to use the assistive technology devices should be taken into consideration.

Cost often plays a large part in the under use of assistive technology. Many counselors neglect the long-term benefits of the technology on employability and instead concentrate on the short-term costs that may be involved. This is a tragic mistake to make. The following list identifies some funding options that should be carefully researched and explored:

- Medicaid and Medicare
- Private loans
- Company grants
- Family resources
- Local, state, or national grants
- Low- or no-interest loans through a statewide assistive technology program
- Used and recycled equipment
- Private trusts and foundations
- Workers' Compensation programs
- Income and business tax incentives
- Private/public health maintenance organizations
- Employer
- Social Security Administration
  - Plan for Achieving Self-Support (PASS)
  - Impairment-related work expenses (IRWE)
  - Blind work expenses
- Work incentive programs

Community resources should not be overlooked. Many service organizations are looking for venues to channel their funds and may also be interested in sponsoring fundraising events for specific consumers or equipment.

Rehabilitation counselors are responsible for including appropriate assistive technologies in the Individualized Plan for Employment (IPE). In the IPE, be sure to detail the steps that have been taken to evaluate the individual for suitable assistive technology needs. It is important to be as specific as possible. The plan should outline the following:

- The exact assistive technology device (including brand, make, model, color, size, etc.)
- From whom the device will be obtained/purchased
- Purchase price
- Specific funding sources
- Training that will be necessary prior to use
- Who will perform this training
- When the training will take place
- How the effectiveness of the assistive technology device will be evaluated
- Who will perform this evaluation
- What will be done if the device is found to no longer meet the desired goals

Because the technology is often such an essential ingredient to the future success of the client, the value of formally integrating such devices and services in the plan cannot be stressed enough.

Technologies are constantly changing, and it is often difficult to stay abreast of the vast array of assistive technology options that are available. Therefore, it is crucial to have a comprehensive assistive technology reference book on hand. One excellent choice is Cook and Hussey's (2002) *Assistive Technologies: Principles and Practice.* Ultimately, the most important thing to remember is to maximize the use of any resources that are available. Appendix D lists some additional resources that may be helpful in the integration of assistive technology into the rehabilitation process.

Using the Disability Guide Form

If the preponderance of assessments (medical and/or psychological, assistive technology, or vocational evaluation reports) indicates that an individual's medical impairment(s) do not impede the ability to perform work activity, the Disability Guide Form (see Appendix A) will help answer these important questions:

- Is the individual able to engage in his/her customary work (with or without assistive technology or accommodations)?
- Can the individual engage in some other work with a less strenuous exertional level?
- Does the individual have skills that may transfer to other types of work?
- Does the individual have the cognitive, social, and emotive capacity to sustain an educational or training program?

Appendix A contains a copy of the *Disability Guide Form.* Appendices B and C provide standard definitions for environmental conditions and for physical demands.

In order to ensure a full and clear evaluation of the major factors in disability determination, one of the more important uses of the guide will be to structure interviews with the person. The information from the individual's self-report can be compared with the medical reports so that discrepancies can be identified and areas requiring additional medical evaluation or opinion can be elucidated prior to the decision date.

Page 2 of the guide provides a concise summary of the individual's perceptions concerning his or her present functional ability. This information can be compared with those medical records which contain opinions concerning functional ability. Again differences are highlighted. Since these questions are designed to record functional ability in terms of strength and movement requirements inherent in all work, the highest exertional level at which the individual thinks he or she can function is quickly determined. When compared with the actual exertional requirements of their last job (p. 4), judgments as to whether the individual can perform their last job are readily made. In addition, conclusions as to whether the individual can function in work having the same or lower exertional levels can be reached.

The non-exertional requirements of functional ability are found on page 3 of the guide. This information can be obtained by direct questioning of the individual or by making inferences based on other data supplied by the individual and in the medical reports. This area is frequently given less consideration than it deserves in disability determination. The list of major symptoms on page 4 serves to ensure consideration of the more important subjective complaints. It is extremely important that the sources of information be identified and that the guide is not a compilation of information from all sources but that care is taken to differentiate the various sources and the implications this information has relative to the selected vocational objective and overall rehabilitation goal.

Conclusion

The concept of disability, at first glance, appears to be fairly straightforward. As demonstrated by the preceding narrative, however, the application of this concept to a particular individual become quite complex. While a definitive diagnosis of a particular medical condition or trauma is a necessary first step, vocational factors, work experience, application of assistive technology, and the implications of a vocational evaluation must be considered. The systematic evaluation of these factors will ensure the determination of disability that is ultimately reached will accurately and reliably portend the vocational and rehabilitation goals of the individual.

Appendix A

THE DISABILITY GUIDE

Date_____

Name _____   SSN_____

Address _____   Date of Birth_____

_____   Age_____

Highest grade completed_____   College major _____

Can you read or write?   Yes   No

List symptoms/disease or injury: Describe in terms of limitations imposed. (Specify current treatment including medications.)

_____

_____

_____

_____

_____

_____

Common Symptoms: (Check those you experience)

___ Anxiety   Relieved by medication   Yes   No
___ Shortness of breath   Relieved by medication   Yes   No
___ Headaches   Relieved by medication   Yes   No
___ Seizures   Relieved by medication   Yes   No
___ Depression   Relieved by medication   Yes   No
___ Frequent bowel movement   Relieved by medication   Yes   No
___ Pain   Relieved by medication   Yes   No
___ Frequent urination   Relieved by medication   Yes   No
___ Generalized weakness   Relieved by medication   Yes   No

RESIDUAL FUNCTIONAL CAPACITY
Exertional Factors

Give your best estimate. Any item not answered should be marked N/A. Complete in terms of what your client can do today. In terms of an 8-hour workday, "occasionally" equals 1% to 33%; "frequently," 34% to 66%; "continuously," 67% to 100%.

I. In an 8-hour workday, client can: (Circle full capacity for each activity)

Total at one time

A. Sit	0	1	2	3	4	5	6	7	8	(hours)
B. Stand	0	1	2	3	4	5	6	7	8	(hours)
C. Walk	0	1	2	3	4	5	6	7	8	(hours)

Total during entire 8-hour day *(alternating position)*

A. Sit	0	1	2	3	4	5	6	7	8	(hours)
B. Stand	0	1	2	3	4	5	6	7	8	(hours)
C. Walk	0	1	2	3	4	5	6	7	8	(hours)

II. Client can lift: Never   Occasionally   Frequently   Continuously
    A. Up to 10 lbs
    B. 11–15 lbs
    C. 16–20 lbs
    D. 21–25 lbs
    E. 26–50 lbs
    F. 51–100 lbs

III. Client can carry: Never   Occasionally   Frequently   Continuously
    A. Up to 10 lbs
    B. 11–15 lbs
    C. 16–20 lbs
    D. 21–25 lbs
    E. 26–50 lbs
    F. 51–100 lbs

IV. Client can use hands for repetitive action such as: (Circle yes or no)

	Simple Grasping	Pushing & Pulling	Fine Manipulation
A. Right	Yes No	Yes No	Yes No
B. Left	Yes No	Yes No	Yes No

V. Client can use feet for repetitive movement as in pushing and pulling of leg controls:

	RIGHT		LEFT	
	Yes	No	Yes	No

VI. Client is able to: Not at all   Occasionally   Frequently   Continuously
A. Bend
B. Squat
C. Crawl
D. Climb
E. Reach

VII. Highest possible exertional level indicated:

Sedentary   Light   Medium   Heavy

RESIDUAL FUNCTIONAL CAPACITY
Nonexertional Factors

NONE: *No impairment in this area.*
MILD: *Suspected impairment of slight importance which does not affect*
                             ability to function.
MODERATE: *An impairment which affects but does not preclude ability to function.*
MODERATELY SEVERE: *An impairment which seriously affects ability to function.*
SEVERE: *Extreme impairment of ability to function.*

I.   Estimated degree of impairment of ability to relate to other people:

     None   Mild   Moderate   Moderately Severe   Severe

II. Estmiated degree of restriction of daily activities, e.g., ability to attend meetings (church, lodge, store), work around the house, socialize with friends and neighbors:

     None   Mild   Moderate   Moderately Severe   Severe

III. Estimated degree of deterioration in personal habits:

     None   Mild   Moderate   Moderately Severe   Severe

IV. Estimated degree of constriction of interests:

     None   Mild   Moderate   Moderately Severe   Severe

V.   Estimated degree of limitation in ability to do the following on a sustained basis:

a) Comprehend and follow instructions:

     None   Mild   Moderate   Moderately Severe   Severe

b) Perform work requiring frequent contact with others:

      None   Mild   Moderate   Moderately Severe   Severe

c) Perform work where contact with others will be minimal:

      None   Mild   Moderate   Moderately Severe   Severe

d) Perform simple tasks:

      None   Mild   Moderate   Moderately Severe   Severe

e) Perform complex tasks:

      None   Mild   Moderate   Moderately Severe   Severe

f) Perform repetitive tasks:

      None   Mild   Moderate   Moderately Severe   Severe

g) Perform varied tasks:

      None   Mild   Moderate   Moderately Severe   Severe

h) Perform work requiring rotating shifts:

      None   Mild   Moderate   Moderately Severe   Severe

Environmental Factors *(Check those which will influence or modify the client's ability to function)*

____Inside	____Wet	____Mechanical hazards
____Outside	____Dusty	____Moving objects
____Hot	____Dirty	____Cramped quarters
____Cold	____Odor	____High places
____Sudden temperature changes	____Noisy	____Electrical hazards
____Humid	____Adequate lighting	____Explosives
____Dry	____Adequate ventilation	____Radiant energy
____Vibration	____Toxic condition	

WORK HISTORY

List all other jobs in the last 15 years before your client stopped working.

JOB TITLE *(Last job first)*	JOB DUTIES	DATES WORKED *(Month & Year)*	RATE OF PAY *(Per hour, day, week, month or year)*	FROM TO

_____

_____

_____

_____

_____

_____

OVERALL: Skill Level_____ Exertional Level_____

  • Did your client use machines, tools or equipment of any kind? *(Describe)*

  • Use technical knowledge or skills? *(Describe)*

  • Do any writing, complete reports or perform similar duties? *(Describe)*

  • Have supervisory responsibilities? *(Describe)*

In the last job estimate the number of hours in a working day spent:
    Walking   Standing   Sitting
    Bending: *(how often)*   Never   Occasionally   Frequently   Constantly
    Reaching: *(how often)*   Never   Occasionally   Frequently   Constantly

Lifting and Carrying: *(Describe kind of objects or material lifted, weight, frequency and distance carried.)*_____
_____
_____
_____

Skill Level_____ Exertional Level_____

Transferable
skills:_____
_____
_____

Appendix B

ENVIRONMENTAL CONDITIONS

Environmental conditions are the physical surroundings of a worker in a specific job.

1. *Inside, Outside, or Both:*

> I–Inside: Protection from weather conditions but not necessarily from temperature changes.
> O–Outside: No effective protection from weather.
> B–Both: Inside and outside.

A job is considered "inside" if the worker spends approximately 75% or more of the time inside, and "outside" if the worker spends approximately 75% or more of the time outside. A job is considered "both" if the activities occur inside or outside in approximately equal amounts.

2. *Extremes of Cold Plus Temperature Changes:*

> (1) *Extremes of Cold:* Temperature sufficiently low to cause marked bodily discomfort unless the worker is provided with exceptional protection.
> (2) *Temperature Changes:* Variations in temperature which are sufficiently marked and abrupt to cause noticeable bodily reactions.

3. *Extremes of Heat plus Temperature Changes*

> (1) *Extremes of Heat:* Temperature sufficiently high to cause marked bodily discomfort unless the worker is provided with exceptional protection.
> (2) *Temperature Changes:* Same as 2(2).

4. *Wet and Humid:*

> (1) *Wet:* Contact with water or other liquids.
> (2) *Humid:* Atmospheric condition with moisture content sufficiently high to cause marked bodily discomfort.

5. *Noise and Vibration:* Sufficient noise, either constant or intermittent, to cause marked distraction or possible injury to the sense of hearing, and or sufficient vibration (production of an oscillating movement or strain on the body or its extremities from repeated motion or shock) to cause bodily harm if endured day after day.

6. *Hazards:* Situations in which the individual is exposed to the definite risk of bodily injury.

7. *Fumes, Odors, Toxic Conditions, Dust, and Poor Ventilation:*

   (1) *Fumes:* Smoky or vaporous exhalations, usually odorous, thrown off as the result of combustion of chemical reaction.
   (2) *Odors:* Noxious smells, either toxic or nontoxic.
   (3) *Toxic Conditions:* Exposure to toxic dust, fumes, gases, vapors, mists, or liquids which cause general or localized disabling conditions as a result of inhalation or action on the skin.
   (4) *Dust:* Air filled with small particles of any kind, such as textile dust, flour, wood, leather, feathers, etc., and inorganic dust, including silica and asbestos, which make the workplace unpleasant or are the source of occupational diseases.
   (5) *Poor Ventilation:* Insufficient movement of air causing a feeling of suffocation; or exposure to drafts.

SOURCE: *Selected Characteristics Defined in the Dictionary of Occupational Titles,* U.S. Department of Labor, Employment and Training Administration, 1981.

Appendix C

PHYSICAL DEMANDS

The physical demands listed in this publication (*Dictionary of Occupational Titles*) serve as a means of expressing both the physical requirements of the job and the physical capacities (specific physical traits) a worker must have to meet those required by many jobs (perceiving by the sense of vision), and also the name of a specific capacity possessed by many people (have the power of sight). The worker must possess physical capacities at least in an amount equal to the physical demands made by the job.

THE FACTORS

1. *Strength:* This factor is expressed in terms of *Sedentary, Light, Medium, Heavy, and Very Heavy*. It is measured by involvement of the worker with one or more of the following activities:

a. Worker position(s):
    (1) Standing: Remaining on one's feet in an upright position at a workstation without moving about.
    (2) Walking: Moving about on foot.
    (3) Sitting: Remaining in the normal seated position.

b. Worker movement of objects (including extremities used);
    (1) Lifting: Raising or lowering an object from one level to another (includes upward pulling).
    (2) Carrying: Transporting an object, usually holding it in the hands or arms or on the shoulder.
    (3) Pushing: Exerting force upon an object so that the object moves away from the force (includes slapping, striking, kicking, and treadle actions).
    (4) Pulling: Exerting force upon an object so that the object moves toward the force (includes jerking).

The five degrees of Physical Demands Factor No. 1 (strength) are as follows:

S SEDENTARY WORK

Lifting 10 lbs. maximum and occasionally lifting and/or carrying such articles as dockets, ledgers, and small tools. Although a sedentary job is defined as one which involves sitting, a certain amount of walking and standing is often necessary in carrying out job duties. Jobs are sedentary if walking and standing are required only occasionally and other sedentary criteria are met.

L LIGHT WORK

Lifting 20 lbs. maximum with frequent lifting and/or carrying of objects weighing up to 10 lbs. Even though the weight lifted may be only a negligible amount, a job is in this category when it requires walking or standing to a significant degree, or when it involves sitting most of the time with a degree of pushing and pulling of arm and/or leg controls.

M MEDIUM WORK

Lifting 50 lbs. maximum with frequent lifting and/or carrying of objects weighing up to 25 lbs.

H HEAVY WORK

Lifting 100 lbs. maximum with frequent lifting and/or carrying of objects weighing up to 50 lbs.

V VERY HEAVY WORK

Lifting objects in excess of 100 lbs. with frequent lifting and/or carrying of objects weighing 50 lbs. or more.

2. CLIMBING AND/OR BALANCING

(1) Climbing: Ascending or descending ladders, stairs, scaffolding, ramps, poles, ropes, and the like, using the feet and legs and/or hands and arms.
(2) Balancing: Maintaining body equilibrium to prevent falling when walking, standing, crouching, or running on narrow, slippery, or erratically moving surfaces; or maintaining body equilibrium when performing gymnastic feats.

3. STOOPING, KNEELING, CROUCHING, AND/OR CRAWLING:

(1) Stooping: Bending the body downward and forward by bending the spine at the waist.

(2) Kneeling: Bending the legs at the knees to come to rest on the knee or knees.

(3) Crouching: Bending the body downward and forward by bending the legs and spine.

(4) Crawling: Moving about on the hands and knees or hands and feet.

4. REACHING, HANDLING, FINGERING, AND/OR FEELING:

(1) Reaching: Extending the hands and arms in any direction.

(2) Handling: Seizing, holding, grasping, turning, or otherwise working with the hand or hands (fingering not involved).

(3) Fingering: Picking, pinching, or otherwise working with the fingers primarily (rather than with the whole hand or arm as in handling).

(4) Feeling: Perceiving such attributes of objects and materials as size, shape, temperature, or texture, by means of receptors in the skin, particularly those of the fingertips.

5. TALKING AND/OR HEARING:

(1) Talking: Expressing or exchanging ideas by means of the spoken word.

(2) Hearing: Perceiving the nature of sounds by the ear.

6. SEEING:

Obtaining impressions through the eyes of the shape, size, distance, motion, color, or other characteristics of objects. The major visual functions are: (1) acuity, far and near, (2) depth perception, (3) field of vision, (4) accommodation, and (5) color vision. The functions are defined as follows:

(1) Acuity, far-clarity of vision at 20 feet or more. Acuity, near-clarity of vision at 20 inches or less.

(2) Depth perception–three-dimensional vision. The ability to judge distance and space relationships so as to see objects where and as they actually are.

(3) Field of vision–the area that can be seen up and down or to the right or left while the eyes are fixed on a given point.

(4) Accommodation—adjustment of the lens of the eye to bring an object into sharp focus. This item is especially important when doing near-point work at varying distances from the eye.

(5) Color Vision—the ability to identify and distinguish colors.

SOURCE: *Selected Characteristics Defined in the Dictionary of Occupational Titles,* U.S. Department of Labor, Employment and Training Administration, 1981.

Appendix D

SELECTED ASSISTIVE TECHNOLOGY RESOURCES

AbilityHub
http://www.abilityhub.com/
"AbilityHub.com's purpose is to help you find information on adaptive equipment and alternative methods available for accessing computers. Searching the Internet for accurate information on Assistive Technology is much like "looking for a needle in a haystack". This website attempts to reduced the size of the haystack and bring you the information in an organized fashion."

Abledata
http://www.abledata.com/
"ABLEDATA provides objective information on assistive technology and rehabilitation equipment available from domestic and international sources to consumers, organizations, professionals, and caregivers within the United States. We serve the nation's disability, rehabilitation, and senior communities."

Alliance for Technology Access
http://www.ataccess.org/
"The Alliance for Technology Access (ATA) is a network of community-based Resource Centers, Developers, Vendors and Associates dedicated to providing information and support services to children and adults with disabilities, and increasing their use of standard, assistive, and information technologies."

Assistivetech.net
http://www.assistivetech.net/
"Our mission is to provide access to information on AT devices and services as well as other community resources for people with disabilities and the general public."

Association of Assistive Technology Act Programs
http://www.ataporg.org/
"The mission of ATAP is to promote the collaboration of AT Programs with persons with disabilities, providers, industry, advocates and others at the state and national level and to increase the availability and utilization of

accessible information technology (IT) and assistive technology devices and services (AT) for all individuals with disabilities in the United States and territories. ATAP's role is to support AT Programs in implementing the AT Act and promote the rights of people with disabilities, family members, providers, etc. to access accessible IT and AT devices and services."

Cook, A. M., & Hussey, S. M. (2002). *Assistive technologies principles and practice.* St. Louis: Mosby.

Job Accommodation Network
http://www.jan.wvu.edu/
"JAN's mission is to facilitate the employment and retention of workers with disabilities by providing employers, employment providers, people with disabilities, their family members and other interested parties with information on job accommodations, self-employment and small business opportunities and related subjects. JAN's efforts are in support of the employment, including self-employment and small business ownership, of people with disabilities. JAN represents the most comprehensive resource for job accommodations available. JAN's work has greatly enhanced the job opportunities of people with disabilities by providing information on job accommodations since 1984. In 1991 JAN expanded to provide information on the Americans with Disabilities Act."

Langton, A. J. & Ramseur, H. (2001). Enhancing employment outcomes through job accommodation and assistive technology resources and services. *Journal of Vocational Rehabilitation, 16,* 27–37.

Rehabilitation Engineering and Assistive Technology Society of North America (RESNA) http://www.resna.org/
"We are an interdisciplinary association of people with a common interest in technology and disability. Our purpose is to improve the potential of people with disabilities to achieve their goals through the use of technology. We serve that purpose by promoting research, development, education, advocacy and provision of technology; and by supporting the people engaged in these activities."

REFERENCES

Bissonnette, D. (2002). *Beyond traditional job development.* Chatsworth, CA: Milt Wright & Associates.

20 C.F.R. pt. 404 (1950).

Curtis, R. S. (1998). Values and valuing in rehabilitation. *Journal of Rehabilitation, 64*(1), 42–47.

Cook, A. M., & Hussey, S. M. (2002). *Assistive technologies principles and practice.* St. Louis: Mosby.

Havranek, J., Field, T., & Grimes, J. W. (2001). *Vocational assessment: Evaluating employment potential* (3rd Ed.). Athens, GA: Elliott & Fitzpatrick, Inc.

JIST Works. (2002). The O*NET dictionary of occupational titles. Indianapolis, ID: Author.

Langton, A. J., & Ramseur, H. (2001). Enhancing employment outcomes through job accommodation and assistive technology resources and services. *Journal of Vocational Rehabilitation, 16,* 27–37.

U.S. Department of Labor. (1999). *Testing and assessment: An employer's guide to good practices.* Washington, DC: Employment and Training Administration.

U.S. Department of Labor. (1981). *Selected characteristics defined in the dictionary of occupational titles.* Washington, DC: Employment and Training Administration.

U.S. Department of Labor. (2004). *Occupational outlook handbook.* Washington, DC: Bureau of Labor Statistics.

U.S. Department of Labor. (1991). *The dictionary of occupational titles.* Washington, DC: Author.

Chapter 6

JOB DEVELOPMENT AND PLACEMENT: CONSIDERATIONS FOR THE REHABILITATION COUNSELOR

E. DAVIS MARTIN, JR., LARRY L. SINSABAUGH,
GEORGE R. JARRELL, AND RICHARD E. HARDY

The placement of individuals with disabilities into jobs through which such persons can maintain themselves and their loved ones is the concept that has allowed rehabilitation counseling to make a substantial contribution to individuals with disabilities and to society in general. Because rehabilitation counseling accepts the responsibility of job placement, this emphasis on the final outcome of the rehabilitation process is a variable that distinguishes rehabilitation counseling from all other forms of counseling and other applied disciplines in the social services.

Recent technological advances, new diagnostic techniques, and modes of medical treatment have prolonged the lives of people with chronic disease and disability. For a substantial number of these individuals, treatment has been life saving but medical science alone has not been able to facilitate return to a predisability level of functioning. As such, matching an individual with a disability to a job or career can be a difficult and complicated process. Liptak (2001) suggests that counselors view career choice as a series of five critical tasks:

- Career choice is a developmental process (that may be further complicated by the issue of disability).
- People continually acquire and process accurate as well as inac-

curate career information about themselves and the world.
- Career choice ultimately involves a matching of characteristics of the individual with the work environment.
- Most people do not possess a systemic, logical method for making such career-related decisions.
- All people experience, or hope to experience, intrapersonal and interpersonal satisfaction from the work they do. (p. 5)

Because a number of other factors, including age, education, prior work experience, and residual functional capacity must be integrated with vocational factors to determine a suitable career or occupational goal, occupational analysis and career planning are required. Moreover, Liptak (2001) suggests there is a connection between career counseling and personal growth. It is within this context that the rehabilitation counselor must be prepared to deal effectively with the physical and emotional issues that may emerge during the career planning aspects of the rehabilitation process.

Residual Functional Capacity

Medical reports serve as a basis for planning medical treatment as well as defining a suitable career or vocational goal. Well-written medical reports serve (a) to provide medical opinion as to the presence or absence of disease or injury, (b) to delineate periods and modes of treatment, and (c) to state a probable prognosis. These are important elements, although other aspects of the medical report, usually not as prominent, may be of greater utility in establishing an occupational or career plan. When the physician includes estimates of the effects of a diagnosed medical condition or injury upon the individual's ability to function in the occupational marketplace, these are of paramount importance. Frequently in the aftermath of illness or injury, an individual is unsure of restrictions, and this may be prudent from a medical standpoint. When this occurs, an aura of uncertainty permeates the process of career or vocational planning, job development, and placement. To eliminate uncertainty and provide direction, statements concerning an individual's physical ability (and cognitive and emotive functioning) are central to occupational selection and placement.

The resulting impediments from a medical impairment generally imply some diminished capacity to function resulting from chronic disease, accident, or developmental disability. Residual functional capacity (RFC) is the maximum degree to which the individual retains the capacity for sustained performance in terms of the physical/mental requirements of a job. Diminished ability may manifest itself in one or more of the following spheres and delineates areas of informed medical opinion needed to begin the process of career adjustment or selection and job accommodation: (a) *physical,* affecting ambulation, coordination, speech production, vision; (b) *mental,* affecting ability to think, remember, or comprehend or general learning ability; (c) *social,* affecting ability to communicate and establish relationships with other people; (d) *emotional,* affecting self-image, self-acceptance, mental health; and (e) occupational, affecting vocational, homemaking, or self-care abilities.

In reporting findings, physicians frequently use negative statements to describe a person's ability to function; "No heavy lifting, no prolonged standing, cannot bend repetitively, etc." is commonly used. What do these statements mean? "Heavy" may mean a hundred pounds to one physician while another may think in terms of forty to fifty pounds. Prolonged may mean anything from one to six hours. The rehabilitation counselor needs a more precise estimate of the individual's ability to function, preferably stated in positive terms. Physicians should be asked to complete a physical activities form (see Fig. 6-1). This requires the physician to be very precise in the estimation of physical function or residual functional capacity (RFC) and should serve to eliminate the counselor's need to infer physical capacity. Definitions utilized in the *Dictionary of Occupational Titles* (U.S. Department of Labor, 1991) or the *O***NET Dictionary of Occupational Titles* (U.S. Department of Labor, 2004) to describe strength requirements of jobs frequently serve as the basis for such a checklist. Factors other than residual physical ability, such as the effects of a psychiatric impairment on the individual's ability to perform physical activity in a work setting are equally as important. The functional overlay checklist serves to focus professional opinion upon the residuals of psychiatric or other non-exertional impairment (see Fig. 6-2).

Although Figures 6-1 and 6-2 represent generic information required by the rehabilitation counselor, the variety of formats and forms used to acquire information about a client's RFC are unlimited. Both of these checklists represent two common ways of summarizing such information. Physicians often complain about the lack of standardiza-

FIGURE 6.1. RESIDUAL FUNCTIONAL CAPACITY
Exertional Factors

Give your best estimate. Any item not answered should be marked N/A. Complete in terms of what your client can do today. In terms of an 8-hour workday, "occasionally" equals 1% to 33%; "frequently," 34% to 66%; "continuously," 67% to 100%.

I. In an 8-hour workday, client can: (Circle full capacity for each activity)

Total at one time

A. Sit	0	1	2	3	4	5	6	7	8	(hours)
B. Stand	0	1	2	3	4	5	6	7	8	(hours)
C. Walk	0	1	2	3	4	5	6	7	8	(hours)

Total during entire 8-hour day *(alternating position)*

A. Sit	0	1	2	3	4	5	6	7	8	(hours)
B. Stand	0	1	2	3	4	5	6	7	8	(hours)
C. Walk	0	1	2	3	4	5	6	7	8	(hours)

II. Client can lift:	Never	Occasionally	Frequently	Continuously
A. Up to 10 lbs				
B. 11–15 lbs				
C. 16–20 lbs				
D. 21–25 lbs				
E. 26–50 lbs				
F. 51–100 lbs				

III. Client can carry:	Never	Occasionally	Frequently	Continuously
A. Up to 10 lbs				
B. 11–15 lbs				
C. 16–20 lbs				
D. 21–25 lbs				
E. 26–50 lbs				
F. 51–100 lbs				

IV. Client can use hands for repetitive action such as: (Circle yes or no)

	Simple Grasping	Pushing & Pulling	Fine Manipulation
A. Right	Yes No	Yes No	Yes No
B. Left	Yes No	Yes No	Yes No

V. Client can use feet for repetitive movement as in pushing and pulling of leg controls:

RIGHT		LEFT	
Yes	No	Yes	No

VI. Client is able to: Not at all Occasionally Frequently Continuously
A. Bend
B. Squat
C. Crawl
D. Climb
E. Reach

VII. Highest possible exertional level indicated:

Sedentary Light Medium Heavy

FIGURE 6.2. RESIDUAL FUNCTIONAL CAPACITY
Nonexertional Factors

NONE: *No impairment in this area.*
MILD: *Suspected impairment of slight importance which does not affect ability to function.*
MODERATE: *An impairment which affects but does not preclude ability to function.*
MODERATELY SEVERE: *An impairment which seriously affects ability to function.*
SEVERE: *Extreme impairment of ability to function.*

I. Estimated degree of impairment of ability to relate to other people:

None Mild Moderate Moderately Severe Severe

II. Estmiated degree of restriction of daily activities, e.g., ability to attend meetings (church, lodge, store), work around the house, socialize with friends and neighbors:

None Mild Moderate Moderately Severe Severe

III. Estimated degree of deterioration in personal habits:

None Mild Moderate Moderately Severe Severe

IV. Estimated degree of constriction of interests:

None Mild Moderate Moderately Severe Severe

V. Estimated degree of limitation in ability to do the following on a sustained basis:

a) Comprehend and follow instructions:

None Mild Moderate Moderately Severe Severe

b) Perform work requiring frequent contact with others:

| | None | Mild | Moderate | Moderately Severe | Severe |

c) Perform work where contact with others will be minimal:

| | None | Mild | Moderate | Moderately Severe | Severe |

d) Perform simple tasks:

| | None | Mild | Moderate | Moderately Severe | Severe |

e) Perform complex tasks:

| | None | Mild | Moderate | Moderately Severe | Severe |

f) Perform repetitive tasks:

| | None | Mild | Moderate | Moderately Severe | Severe |

g) Perform varied tasks:

| | None | Mild | Moderate | Moderately Severe | Severe |

h) Perform work requiring rotating shifts:

| | None | Mild | Moderate | Moderately Severe | Severe |

Environmental Factors *(Check those which will influence or modify the client's ability to function)*

____Inside	____Wet	____Mechanical hazards
____Outside	____Dusty	____Moving objects
____Hot	____Dirty	____Cramped quarters
____Cold	____Odor	____High places
____Sudden temperature changes	____Noisy	____Electrical hazards
____Humid	____Adequate lighting	____Explosives
____Dry	____Adequate ventilation	____Radiant energy
____Vibration	____Toxic condition	

tion of reporting formats; sometimes it seems that there are as many different styles of forms as there are requesters. Many physicians will not complete the work capacities form without examining the person and/or without the benefit of a formalized work capacities evaluation (i.e., a standardized protocol measuring exertional capacities: amounts and durations of lifting and carrying, sitting, standing, stooping, pulling and pushing, reaching, and dexterity–both gross and fine motor movement–performed by an interdisciplinary team composed of physical therapist, occupational therapist, and vocational evaluator). This type of physical capacity evaluation, while very precise, can be time consuming and expensive. Its utility may be more applicable in the area of Workers' Compensation and forensic rehabilitation where precision is often demanded because of the legal issues involved. The Functional Capacities Checklist (FCC) or similar checklists may have greater utility for the rehabilitation counselor and physician to ascertain exertional and nonexertional capacities in less time and for less cost. The FCC is available in two formats: (a) as a paper-and-pencil instrument (Burke & Dillman, 1984) and (b) as a computer software program (Burke & Dillman, 1990). The value of this instrument or similar instruments for the rehabilitation counselor and the physician lies in the systematic methodology it employs to explore and understand the person's perception about the daily barriers encountered regarding exertional and nonexertional limitations (Burke & Dillman, 1990).

The physician's estimate of RFC should be recent enough to provide an adequate basis for evaluating the person's present state of functional ability relative to occupational planning, training, education, or work activities. Rehabilitation counselors in public sector programs may be less constrained by this factor than private sector counselors who are often required to have an RFC determination within a specified time frame. In some states, for example, a determination of job suitability under Workers' Compensation rules may not be made if the physician's decision about RFC is more than twenty-one days postinjury. Generally stated, the physician determines impairment, residual functional capacity and percentage of disability while the counselor determines eligibility, vocational impediments, work readiness, and access to the labor market (Klein, Swisher, Lynch, Krewson, 1982; McGowan & Porter, 1967; Weed & Field, (1991).

Readiness for Employment and Job Placement

Planning for placement begins when the counselor first reads the client's rehabilitation referral form. The rehabilitation counselor must constantly learn about the client in order to effectively help the person secure employment. This is a multifaceted determination based upon the client's residual functional capacity, vocational interests, and psychosocial factors. In determining readiness, the counselor is, in effect, diagnosing the assets and impediments faced by the client so appropriate interventions may be planned for and implemented. Figure 6-3 contains a useful checklist for the counselor to determine readiness that has been published by the Job Placement Division of the National Rehabilitation Association (1992).

FIGURE 6-3: CLIENT READINESS CHECKLIST

Criteria for Determining Job Readiness
A. Physical readiness
    1. Is the client at the maximum level of physical capacity?
    2. Can client travel to and from a job?
    3. Can client work a full work day? A full work week?
    4. Can client meet the physical demands of the kind of work sought?
    5. Does the client understand the nature of the disability and limitations imposed by the disability?
    6. Is client aware of activities and situations that would tend to aggravate the disability or impair general health?
    7. Does client know danger signs like fatigue or coughing as warning that rest or treatment may be necessary?

B. Psychological readiness:
    1. Do the client and the client's family accept the client's limitations?
    2. Do the client and the client's family recognize the client's capacity?
    3. Is client sincerely motivated toward employment?
    4. Is the client able to adjust to the strains and pressures of a work environment?
    5. Does the client react well to supervision?
    6. Does the client react well to other people?
    7. Is the client's behavior appropriate for the job demands?
    8. Are the client's personality traits in keeping with the job tasks?
    9. Are there personal or social problems that might affect the client's performance on the job?

C. Occupational readiness:
    1. Are the client's aptitudes, skills, knowledge, and experience commensurate with job requirements, current and future?
    2. Can the client meet the mental demands of the kind of work sought?
    3. Is the client really interested in job under consideration?
    4. Are the job's non-monetary, psychological rewards in keeping with client's needs, values, and long-range goals?
    5. Is client aware of opportunities and requirement of the job?
    6. Is client aware of wages? Hours? Special requirements of the job?
    7. Is client aware of possibilities and requirements for advancement in this field?
    8. Has client's preparation been flexible enough for reassignment to other jobs or tasks?
    9. Are the client's work habits and attitudes suitable for successful job performance?

D. Placement readiness:
1. To what extent can client participate in job-finding process?
2. Does client know sources of job leads?
3. Can the client develop a personal information packet?
4. Can the client satisfactorily complete an application?
5. Can the client present himself/herself adequately in a job interview?
6. Is the client prepared for the possibility of taking employment tests?
7. Would the client continue the job search if a number of turndowns were initially experienced?
8. Could the client conduct himself/herself appropriately if work were to begin tomorrow?
9. Has the client's need for job related clothing been assessed?
10. If client has less than high school education, has there been an assessment of his/her ability to obtain a GED?

SOURCE: Job Placement Division of the National Rehabilitation Association (1992, pp. 7–8), adapted and reprinted with permission.

Vocational Diagnostic Interview

In assessing job/work readiness, the counselor completes a vocational diagnostic interview (VDI). The VDI is a specific, structured clinical interview that is used for the express purpose of acquiring vocationally relevant background data to determine whether the person has the ability (a) to perform work or to undertake a training or educational program; (b) to get along with others; (c) to acquire knowledge about the job or occupation, training, or education; (d) to be dependable and fit a company/employers' work image if offered work or training or education; and (e) to understand personal, medical, or environmental limitations that may present impediments to employment (Cormier & Cormier, 1985; Strum, Otto, & Bakermann, 1972). Strum et al. (1972) suggest that counselors organize information obtained from the VDI around the following areas: (a) job goal, (b) functional capacities (i.e., physical, learning), (c) job-seeking and retention issues, (d) environmental concerns (e.g., health, impairment prognosis, medical release, medications, limitations); (e) transportation; and (f) special concerns (e.g., marital and family, financial, legal, housing, chemical dependency). These data are then organized into an assessment format such as that displayed in Figure 6-4, the Vocational Appraisal Form.

FIGURE 6-4: VOCATIONAL APPRAISAL FORM

I. <u>Job Goal</u>

    1. <u>What is job goal?</u> _____   Alternative job goal_____
        a. Experience _____
        b. Related Experience _____   IV. <u>Environmental</u>
        c. Training _____   1. Health:_____
        d. Education _____   a. Prognosis_____
        e. Skills _____   b. Medical release_____
        f. Licenses _____   c. Medications_____
        g. Interest(s) _____   d. Limitation(s)_____
        h. Expectations _____
             salary _____
             job duties _____

    2. <u>Physical Capacities</u>   2. Transportation _____
        a. Sit _____
        b. Stand _____   3. Family/Marital_____ _____
        c. Lift _____
        d. Bend _____   4. Financial_____
        e. Climbing _____   a. Garnishments_____
        f. Reaching _____   b. Budgeting_____
        g. Handling
        h. Sight _____   5. Legal:
        i. Hearing _____   a. Workers' Compensation
                                        _____
    3. <u>Learning Capacity</u>   b. Felony Conviction(s) _____
        a. Reading level _____   c. Felony Charges Pending
        b. Math ability _____
        c. Memory _____   _____
                                6. Housing:_____

    4. <u>Job Availability</u>   7. Leisure Time: _____
        a. Labor Market _____
        b. Openings: _____   8. Personal_____

II. <u>Job Seeking</u>   9. Chemical Dependency_____
    1. Work history _____
    2. Length of time since last job _____   V. Statement of Problems & Impressions
    3. Reason for leaving last job _____
    4. Frequency of job search _____   _____
    5. Knowledge of sources _____
    6. Explain Skills _____   _____
    7. Problem questions _____
    8. Appearance/grooming _____   _____
    9. Enthusiasm _____
    10. Money for job search _____   _____
    11. Job readiness _____   _____

III. Job Retention   Comments:
    1. Absenteeism   _____   _____
    2. Tardiness   _____
    3. Co-Workers   _____   _____
    4. Supervisors   _____
    5. Quality & Quantity of Work _____   _____

SOURCE: Strum, T. E., Otto, V. R., & Blakeman, M. (1972). *Vocational diagnostic interviewing.* Minneapolis, MN: Multi-Resource Center, Inc., p. 6, adapted and reprinted with permission.

Overall, the VDI is designed to assess work assets and impediments by determining (a) if the person is appropriate for vocational rehabilitation (VR) services or direct return to work with or without accommodations; (b) what the person wants or expects to accomplish using VR services; (c) the person's vocational problems, (d) personal, educational, and vocational assets; and (e) services that are needed. During the VDI, issues concerning job goals, job-seeking skills, and issues affecting job retention and environment are explored. This information along with other relevant medical and psychosocial information is used as a basis for a vocational diagnosis (Strum et al., 1972). All further job development and placement interventions are then based upon the client's readiness.

Role playing is an excellent method to use in preparing a person for employment interviews. In role playing, it is helpful for the counselor as well as the client to play the role of the employer. Current practice is to expose clients to didactic and experiential preparation, which includes role playing in what is known as *Job-Seeking Skills* (JSS). This practice emerged out of research conducted by the Minneapolis Resource Center (MRC). The MRC JSS approach emphasizes that clients must do four things within the first few minutes of a job interview to successfully demonstrate that he or she is the "right" candidate for the job: (a) explain skills and abilities, (b) answer problem questions about disability with short positive statements; (c) dress appropriately for the job; and (d) show enthusiasm. The specific performance factors that must be mastered by clients are detailed in Figure 6-5.

FIGURE 6-5: JOB SEEKING SKILLS

Ability to explain skills

> Did I use several different statements to support my job choice such as: past work experience, related work experience, training aptitude or intelligence, hobbies?
> Did I describe work skills using names of machines or other terms appropriate to my job goal?
> Did I answer the question, "Why should we hire you?" by explaining my skills?
> Did I explain my skills within the first few minutes of the interview?
> Did I respond to open ended questions such as "Tell me a little about yourself," by mentioning my work skills and abilities?

Ability to answer problem questions

> Did I explain my answers to all questions on the application blank especially in the areas of physical, history, little education, age, no experience in job for which I am applying, et cetera?
> Were my answers to questions in these areas short and did they end in a positive statement about my being able to do the job?
> If the problem is visible to the interviewer (age, physical, et cetera) did I mention it within the first few minutes of the interview?

Appropriate appearance and mannerisms

> I was neat and clean, wearing clothes similar to those worn by people who do the kind of work for which I am applying.
> I maintained good eye contact with the interviewer, and tried not to show my nervousness.

Enthusiasm for work

> I stated sometime during the interview that I wanted to work or indicated a desire to work by asking, e.g., about overtime.
> I walked in and out of the interview situation briskly.
> I had a firm handshake.
> I asked specific questions about the job.
> I used a "call back" closing.

SOURCE: Multi-Resource Center (1972). *Job Seeking Skills Manual,* adapted and reprinted with permission.

Some of the first research regarding reasons clients were not getting jobs resulted from the work of the MRC. In a landmark study (1966), the MRC found that many VR clients had difficulty in adjusting to the world of work in three areas: (a) lack of an appropriate job goal, (b) problems with job retention, and (c) poor job-seeking skills.

Astoundingly, the MRC found that:

- 80 percent of the clients did not look for work frequently enough.
- 85 percent of the clients could not explain their skills and abilities to employers.
- 40 percent of the clients demonstrated inappropriate mannerisms.
- 90 percent of the clients could not effectively answer problem questions that arise during a job interview. (p. 3)

Many of the job techniques used by employment specialists today address these same problems noted by the MRC.

After role playing a mock interview(s) that includes a variety of questions, the counselor can provide feedback relative to how the person may improve his or her performance during an actual job interview. There are a large variety of instructional and job development techniques and job-seeking skills formats and videos available to counselors to employ in role-playing activities. Videos such as the *Very Quick Job Search* and others that have been subsequently produced teach the basic approach necessary to access jobs in both the traditional and nontraditional job markets (Farr, 1991a; 1991b).

Clients must realize that getting a job is not an easy task and, to be successful, a person must actively participate in job securing activities. Bose, Geist, Lam, Slaby, and Arens (1998) concluded that compliance with job search strategies was a major predictive factor in obtaining employment. When the client is able to, in fact, secure a job without counselor assistance, this may serve to indicate effectiveness of rehabilitation services. The ability of clients to do this will vary depending upon degree of motivation and the severity of disability.

For many clients, vocational training may provide only a partial solution to many of the impediments experienced by workers with a disability. In each case, the counselor should take an individualized approach to helping. For individuals who have educational, developmental, or social impediments, various remedial programs may be necessary before actual work training programs can begin. The counselor must exercise considerable judgment concerning what a client needs in order to be totally ready for employment.

On-the-job training can be an effective arrangement for some clients to gain entry or reentry into a particular occupation. It may be necessary for the counselor to assist the employer in arranging an appropriate payment schedule for the client, since the person during training is not a skilled employee and would not receive an amount equal to the earnings of a skilled employee. Some clients take longer than others to gain competitiveness in an on-the-job training situation. In certain cases, exemptions to the minimum wage requirements of the Fair Labor Standards Act of 1938 (as amended, 2004) can be requested when lower productivity may be expected as a result of significant impediment.

Regardless of the technique that is employed, the focus of job placement has centered on assisting the person to prepare for, find, and keep a job (Vandergoot & Worrall, 1979). For years, rehabilitation counselors have traditionally followed two primary models of job placement: *selective placement* and *client-centered placement* approaches. Both of these models focus on jobs identified as existing in significant numbers in the labor market. Counselors who follow the selective placement approach emphasize services such as (a) appraisal of readiness, (b) resume development, and (c) job-seeking skills while assuming major responsibility for job development and placement. Counselors following the client-centered model acquire information for the client and place greater emphasis upon the client to take a leadership role in locating and securing employment. Although each model has its particular strengths and weaknesses, both are generally referred to as the *traditional method of job development.*

The *entrepreneurial job development* model popularized by Denise Bissonnette (1994) has emerged as another viable approach to job placement. This model emphasizes creativity and marketing skills of both the counselor and the client. In many ways, this model builds upon traditional approaches, but differs as the counselor attempts to develop jobs that do not exist within a particular segment of the labor market. The entrepreneurial model focuses upon the hidden job market and upon determining employer needs. In many ways, this is an employer-focused model. The differences between the two methods are examined and compared in Figure 6-6.

The entrepreneurial approach to job placement represents a very innovative method that is consistent with the precepts identified in the 1998 amendments to the Rehabilitation Act regarding the Individualized Plan for Employment.

FIGURE 6-6: A COMPARISON OF TRADITIONAL AND
ENTREPRENEURIAL JOB DEVELOPMENT

Traditional Job Development	Entrepreneurial Job Development
Sees a limited job market	Sees a world of possibility
Views the corporate world as impenetrable	Views the corporate world as a frame for approachable human systems
Sees organizations as static institutions	Sees organizations as ever-changing processes
Expects organizations to make sense	Expects the unexpected from the people who make up the organization
Focuses on the decision to hire, wants to talk to the decision maker	Focuses on the need to hire, the screening and recruitment process, and the decision to hire, will talk to anybody
Recognizes employers as experts in hiring	Recognizes employers as experts in the business they are running but possible amateurs at hiring (especially people with disabilities)
Defines a job by the duties and minimum qualifications	Defines a job by the results produced or needs met
Works to give applicants the best edge against competing job seekers	Works to remove applicants in the hidden job market
Responds to job orders for existing positions	Proposes to create new employment
Sees scarcity of identified employment	See abundance of as yet unidentified employment opportunities
Hears, "We're not hiring."	Hears, "We're not hiring yet."
Reacts to the whims of employers	Proacts to the needs of the business community

SOURCE: Bissonnette, D. (1994). *Beyond traditional job development: The art of creating opportunity*. Chatsworth, CA: Milt Wright & Associated, Inc., reprinted with permission.

Private Sector Job Placement

The International Association of Rehabilitation Professionals in the Private Sector (IARPPS) Website contains the Primary Care Vocational Service Delivery Standards–Standards and Ethics (2006) for successful job placement and placement interventions that can be summarized into three necessary conditions for successful placement: (a) the client's readiness to participate in selective placement on the basis of skills, attitudes, and appropriateness of prospective jobs; (b) clearly defined expectations for the client and the provider; and (c) the communication and confirmation of job offers. According to Holmes and Karst (1989), the rehabilitation case record should reflect that the rehabilitation counselor has developed a:

- Clear and concise definition of the problem(s).
- Description of the investigation of solution(s).
- Clear definition of specific and concrete change(s) to be achieved.
- Specific attempt at the formulation of a plan to produce the desired change(s).
- Summary of major contacts, time, and events.
- Clear sense of the documentation of findings and conclusions developed from: (a) assessments, (b) evaluations, (c) activities, and (d) interventions.

Processes such as those described by IARP (2006) and Holmes and Karst (1989) require that the counselor keep reasonable progress notes. Liptak (2001) suggests that all significant activities, comments, plans, and client interactions be recorded in a SOAP format. SOAP is an acronym that allows for differing levels of commentary related to (S) subjective comments, (O) objective comments, (A) assessment/analytical comments, and (P) comments related to future planning. More recently, Spencer (2006) asserts it is an ethical requirement of all counselors to keep records pertaining to career plans, goals, and progress interactions for all items researched, pending, interrupted/discontinued, or continued including the reasoning and justifications for all interventions accepted or declined by the client. Spencer (2006) further maintains that all goals established must be monitored for success or failure to achieve such goals. Prudent counselors would agree that if the service (i.e., assessment, evaluation, analysis, plan, intervention, and follow-up) is not documented, it probably did not occur. For purposes of ethical practice, thorough documentation is a *mandatory* professional activity.

Bridges (1946) many years ago offered four guiding criteria that are involved in the successful employment of persons with disabilities (regardless if placement is facilitated by a private or public sector rehabilitation counselor). These continue to remain as important considerations for counselors today, so much so, that these provisions (*Bridges Criteria*) were incorporated into the Americans with Disabilities Act:

- The worker should have the ability to accomplish the task efficiently—that is, to be able to meet the physical demands of the job.
- The worker should not be a hazard to himself [*sic*].
- The work must not jeopardize the safety of others.

- The job should not aggravate the disability or handicap [*sic*] of the worker.

Job placement is a major function of rehabilitation counselors in both the public and private sectors of rehabilitation; however, greater emphasis is placed upon this aspect in the private sector due to the nature of private sector rehabilitation (Bose, Geist, Lam, Slaby, & Arens, 1998). Sinsabaugh (1994), in a review of private sector literature regarding this issue, noted that employers (responsible for paying for rehabilitation services for injured workers) began voicing concerns about public sector VR policies that emphasized long term training as a primary rehabilitative strategy. From this major concern, a new set of priorities for VR services in the private sector emerged. Known as the *Welch Model*, return-to-work (RTW) decisions were organized in six hierarchical steps (Deneen & Hessellund, 1986; Field & Sink, 1981; Field & Weed, 1988; Schwartz & Carbine, 1987; Weed & Field, 1990). According to this model, private rehabilitation providers structured rehabilitation efforts in the following hierarchy:

1. Same job, the same employer,
2. Same employer, a modified job,
3. New employer, the same job,
4. New employer, a different job,
5. Short term training, and
6. Self-employment.

The primary criteria for placement interventions with clients receiving Workers' Compensation have been this hierarchical model. A continuing criticism of the private sector of rehabilitation concerns the setting of standards for delivery of job placement services and for engagement in inappropriate practices like *job stuffing*. This is a practice of placing Workers' Compensation claimants into any job for which the person is physically qualified without first considering the claimant's past work experience, education, or skills (Sinsabaugh, 1994; Sinsabaugh & Martin, 1999; Ayella & Crook, 1989; JLARC, 1990; Smolkin et al., 1987; The Maryland Rehabilitation Association and the Chesapeake Association of Rehabilitation Professionals in the Private Sector, 1988).

On the other hand, private sector rehabilitation specialists have enhanced the practice of job placement by developing standardized protocols that are typically followed by all rehabilitation counselors. Once a suitable job has been located, for instance, certain practices should be followed to ensure that all stakeholders will be appropriately notified regarding job placement. The O'Connor (1988) Return-to-Work model, as noted in Figure 6-7, is a widely accepted protocol for determining job suitability and for notifying the client and other stakeholders about reporting to work. Another feature of the O'Connor model is its emphasis on successful postemployment follow-up of newly employed workers.

Generally, the rehabilitation counselor should attempt to place clients in jobs that they can manage and do not require modification. In some cases, however, minor modifications can be made with little or no re-engineering effort. The counselor will have to be careful in suggesting re-engineering of a job, since this may be a costly undertaking. However, the major objective should be that of assisting individuals with disabilities to integrate effectively into the total work force regardless of modifications, accommodations, or change in the work situation. As with other areas involving job placement, rehabilitation counselors must continually update their base of knowledge. Blackwell, Conrad, and Week (1992) developed a guide, *Job Analysis and the ADA: A Step by Step Guide,* to assist counselors in meeting the employment standards required by ADA. This guide provides useful information regarding accommodations and is recommended to the reader.

Deneen and Hesselund long ago suggested that rehabilitation counselors observe certain key concepts when developing placement plans: (a) objectives must be reasonable, (b) accomplishing plan objectives must be cost effective, and (c) client agreement to established objectives is a primary consideration that must be recognized. Moreover, Deneen and Hesselund (1981) have noted that a completed vocational rehabilitation plan will stand alone when supported with clear documentation and that minimum plan justification will include the following elements:

- Compatibility of job demands with physical capacities of the client
- Labor market and wage information

FIGURE 6-7: O'CONNOR RETURN TO WORK MODEL

1. Identify the medical restrictions and limitations.

2. Conduct an assessment interview with the person with a disability to identify a) the medical, work and environmental needs and b) the return to work (RTW) work attitude.

3. Conduct a job analysis for the following purposes: a) determine the need for job accommodation; b) identify alternative, light duty or transitional employment compatible with the physical restrictions set by the treating or consulting physician; and or c) determine if a task analysis or training analysis is required.

4. Obtain medical approval for the RTW alternative. The specialist will: a) explain the job described in the job analysis to the treating physician, and b) obtain the physicians's approval for the job description.[1]

5. Arrange and communicate job offer:

    a) The *written job offer* will include the following:

       (1) type of work,
       (2) job starting date,
       (3) where and to whom to report for work,
       (4) that medical approval has occurred,
       (5) scheduled hours expected to be worked,
       (6) whom to call if problems develop,
       (7) expected salary and benefits if applicable.

    b) *Notification*–The best practice is to deliver a job offer "in-person". The next best method is to send the notification by certified mail so that a written acknowledgment can be obtained. The RTW notice should be provided to the client during a face-to-face consultation. Copies documenting notification should be sent to: (1) the employer, (2) the claims representative, (3) the physician, (4) any other interested party authorized by the principal and client.

6. Conduct a timely RTW follow-up in order to:

    a) determine the adequacy of the regular or accommodated work,
    b) deal with adjustment problems so as to minimize any loss of time.
    c) re-evaluate the job to determine if it continues to match the workers' medical condition,
    d) keep in mind the Bridges (1946) Criteria.

SOURCE: O'Connor, S. (1988). Management of individuals with disabilities in the workplace. *Journal of Job Placement* 4(2), 18-21. National Rehabilitation Association, Job Placement Division, reprinted with permission.

1. Some employers will attempt to circumvent the medical approval by changing the job so the job actually performed by the claimant is not the same job which has medical approval. Therefore, jobs which are allowed by the employer must be re-approved by the treating physician. To avoid any misunderstanding the consultant should always attempt to have the employer sign or acknowledge that he or she understands the claimant's medical restriction and approved work authorized by the treating physician.

- Confirmation of interests and aptitudes
- If schooling is chosen, documentation of why transferable skills are not applicable
- Confirmation of the credibility of content areas if on-the-job (OJT) training is involved
- Justification of how placement is to be accomplished (p. 62)

Job placement has been characterized by some as a competency best left to employment development specialists. The utilization of an employment specialist as an adjunct or as a service directed by the rehabilitation counselor is appropriate; however, it is inappropriate for the counselor to refer clients to this type of specialist without maintaining supervision, direct contact, or involvement during this most crucial aspect of the rehabilitation process. The counselor is the focal point for the client throughout the rehabilitation process. The rehabilitation counselor must recognize and heed the following eight common misconceptions about job placement:

1. Because placement occurs toward the end of the rehabilitation process, the counselor's responsibility to the client diminishes.
2. Placement is an activity that requires no counselor training and is a matter of matching an available client with an available job.
3. Client location of a job or "self-placement" cannot be effective rehabilitation work.
4. When a client is ready for vocational placement, the information in the case folder is no longer of value to the counselor since the client has been, in a sense, readied for employment.
5. Follow-along after placement always can be handled easily by telephone or mail communications with the employer or client.
6. Labor market trends, job information, and analysis are the responsibilities of placement specialists and employment services counselors, not of general rehabilitation counselors.
7. An employer will notify the counselor and the rehabilitation agency when dissatisfied with a client placement.
8. An employer will automatically call upon the rehabilitation agency to furnish additional employees when needed.

Follow-Along after Placement

A rehabilitation counselor is often tempted to consider the job completed when the client is placed in employment that appears suitable; however, this phase of the rehabilitation process, which begins immediately after the person has secured employment, is one of the most complex and critical. Follow-along involves the counselor's ability to work between the employer and the client in order to assist the client in solving problems related to impediments that may emerge after being hired. The counselor must be diplomatic and resourceful in maintaining the employer's confidence in the client's ability to do the job. At the same time, the counselor must let the client know that he or she has the counselor's full faith. The counselor, as well, must evaluate how the client is performing on the job and be available to help if issues arise which the client cannot solve.

The client who chooses to not disclose disability and requires no accommodation(s) or prefers to request an accommodation(s) that may be needed to perform the essential functions of a job poses a differing situation for the counselor. The same resources and guidance that are needed by all clients to be successful in obtaining employment are available; however, the role of the counselor and/or employment specialist in the provision of services shifts to that of a consultant for the client who prefers to seek employment or accommodations on their on accord.

In addition to the rehabilitation counselor's service to the client during follow-along, this period can offer real public relations opportunities for the VR agency especially when an employer notes the interest with which the counselor follows the client. The frequency of follow-along varies according to the counselor's judgment of the client's job adjustment, agency guidelines, and/or need for postemployment services.

Conclusion

The rehabilitation counselor's responsibility in job placement must not be underrated. The decisions made at this stage in the rehabilitation process affect not only the client's immediate feelings of satisfaction and achievement but also, of course, long-term physical and mental health. The counselor has a responsibility to prepare or to assure the preparation of the client for employment by providing that person the type of information needed to secure a job and about retaining employment once it is achieved. Counselors need to focus placement and career planning interventions toward the *primary labor market,* the area of the labor market where the client can experience career and wage growth, as opposed to jobs in the secondary labor market, where advancement and growth are limited (Hagner, 2000; Vandergoot & Worrall, 1979). In doing so, the counselor will assist the client in achieving career growth.

Placement should always be client centered with strong emphasis given to the client's opinion about work and how it will affect this person and his or her family. Counselors must be ready to answer the questions that employers will ask about hiring persons with disabilities and about the VR program. In the alternative, counselors must prepare clients to adequately respond to these types of questions as well.

The counselor must be knowledgeable about occupational information and job analysis regarding the synthesis of medical, psychological, educational, economic, vocational, and social data in order to afford the client the greatest probability of success. Once placement has been achieved, the counselor must follow-along the client in order to make certain that the person is doing well on the job. Effective placement requires good planning, and counselors must constantly evaluate and update their knowledge of the world of work to ensure their ability to achieve success in job placement for individuals with disabilities.

CASE ABSTRACTS

Occupational Analysis, Job Development, and Placement

The following case abstracts have been developed to provide the reader with an opportunity to analyze and evaluate various vocational factors commonly found in persons whose disability poses a barrier or impediment to employment. Being abstracts and not fully developed presentations, an element of ambiguity is, thus, introduced. The point of these abstracts is to allow the reader, either individually or in a small group exercise, to examine and explore the concepts of occupational analysis and placement previously presented in the text. For each case abstract, you are to determine an alternative vocational goal for consideration by the person. Such documents as the *O*NET*

Dictionary of Occupational Titles, Dictionary of Occupational Titles, Occupational Outlook Handbook, and *Enhanced Guide to Occupational Exploration* and other resources, as appropriate, will need to be consulted during this exercise. Assumptions may be made as long as those assumptions conform, in general, to the data provided in the case abstract. For each case, assume that maximum medical improvement has resulted in the exertional and nonexertional capacities stated in the abstract.

The below noted questions should serve to guide the reader in this process of exploration and examination:

- What further information/data would be helpful in determining an alternative vocational goal?
- Consider the person's residual functional capacity to engage in work. Based on this assessment, what level(s) of work activity (e.g., sedentary, light, medium, heavy, very heavy) can the person do? Why? or Why not?
- Consider the person's nonexertional residual functional capacities, if any, that may present a barrier to employment (e.g., pain). What effect will this have on the selection of an alternative vocational goal?
- Consider the factors of race and gender (make race one of your assumptions). Will these attributes influence placement? If so, how? And, what would the elements of a plan for placement include to counter these effects?
- Did the person's previous work provide any transferable skills? If so, what are the transferable skills?
- What resources would be needed to achieve the alternative vocational goal? How long would it take? How much would it cost?

Gina T.

Ms. T., twenty-six years old, is currently recuperating from a back injury sustained in a work-related accident last June. At that time she was working as a manager for a fast food restaurant. Her treating physician has not released Ms. T. for full-time work as of this date (six months post injury). As a result of this injury, she has constant but tolerable pain in her right leg. Prolonged walking (two to three hours at a time) causes her back to hurt. Once this occurs, Ms. T. must sit for a period of thirty or so minutes in order to gain relief from the pain.

She is not able to walk for prolonged periods of time and cannot lift more than twenty pounds. Ms. T. is not able to perform the wide range of tasks associated with her previous employment. Her managerial duties included (a) inventory control, (b) purchasing, (c) monitoring preparation and quality of food, (d) preparation of financial forms and (e) training and supervising all employees. Ms. T. was also required to fill in for employees who were absent and on numerous occasions performed the duties of cashier/clerk, cleaner, and sandwich maker. This was a fast-paced job that required the manager to stand and/or walk for long periods of time, lifting weights in excess of fifty pounds throughout the work day.

Ms. T. received an academic diploma from high school with a high B average. After high school, she enrolled in the local community college with the intent of majoring in data processing and computer programming. She completed forty-two semester hours of credit with a grade point average (GPA) of 3.2. During her last two semesters she was a dean's list student. Her college board scores and grades in mathematics, in both high school and college, demonstrated ability and area of particular strength.

Ms. T. appears highly motivated to complete her college education or return to, in her words, "a suitable job."

Tom R.

Mr. R., thirty-six years old, is still receiving treatment for a rotator cuff tear to his left shoulder. This injury was the result of an accident while playing baseball. As a result of that injury, Mr. R. cannot raise his left arm above shoulder level. Any attempt to do so or to lift heavy objects with his left arm causes sharp pain that can only be relieved by a steroid injection. Mr. R. can manipulate small objects with his arms below shoulder level and he can lift objects up to twenty pounds, waist high without discomfort. He can no longer reach above his head with his left arm; therefore, Mr. R. cannot perform the full range of activities required in his usual occupation of master fitter and mechanic.

While an employee of Brand X Foods, he completed the following courses:

• Brand X Training Course: Master Craftsman

- Training Systems Course: Maintenance Management for First-Line Supervisors
- Training Systems Course: Air Conditioning and Refrigeration Maintenance
- General Education Development: Successfully completed requirements.

The results of the Strong-Campbell Interest Inventory recently taken by Mr. R. indicated a very high interest in mechanical activities. Mr. R. enjoys creating things with his hands and would prefer to work with objects such as tools or large machines. This independent career assessment suggests that Mr. R. should pursue a career in the mechanical/fixing area. His stated interests are compatible with and support the results obtained by the Strong-Campbell. Mr. R. prefers to work on those tasks that provide closure. He likes to know when a task is completed. The Self-Directed Search supported a preference for technical jobs.

Mr. R. worked for two years as a master mechanic and fitter. Prior to that, he has four years' experience as a heating equipment mechanic. The majority of his vocational experience has required activities utilizing hand tools. Regardless of other considerations, Mr. R. prefers activities using these skills. He does not want a desk job or a job where desk work is prominent.

Joe J.

Mr. J., fifty-eight years old, injured his back while working as a general laborer. This job involved heavy physical activity requiring constant walking, standing, pulling, and lifting heavy objects. Mr. J.'s prior work experience has been in similar types of jobs.

Dr. C. stated in her latest report: "It is my opinion that he could be employed in a sedentary capacity, and it is also my feeling that if he goes back to heavy laboring work, he could anticipate a recurrence of his problems. If he had suitable training, I think it would be preferable to employ him in a sedentary capacity."

From an educational perspective, Mr. J. received a high school diploma in general business and has completed thirty semester hours of courses in business-related subjects over the past five years at the local community college, where his grade point average (GPA) is 2.1.

Logic would dictate that this is an extremely strong area of interest. His stated interests and motivation appear to be directed toward a career in business, and administration of psychological or education tests appears to be redundant and would be of little value.

Elliott E.

Mr. E., a twenty-nine-year-old journeyman iron worker, has just reached maximum medical improvement. He sustained serious bilateral upper extremity injuries approximately one year earlier in a fall from the building on which he was working. His medical rehabilitation required multiple surgeries, extensive physical therapy, and aggressive hand therapy. Mr. E.'s treating physician has refused to approve his return to a job as an iron worker. Mr. E. is in agreement with the exertional restrictions that the doctor established for his physical activities; that is, working an eight-hour day, where lifting and carrying would be restricted to ten pounds. Other physical activities such as squatting, crawling, and climbing are permitted only occasionally, while bending is permitted on a frequent basis. Mr. E. can use his hands to perform such activities as simple grasping and fine manipulation. Pushing or pulling activities must be avoided because of bilateral upper arm weakness. Mr. E. briefly sought psychiatric treatment for intrusive dreams as a result of the fall; however, he has no continuing nonexertional limitations. Mr. E. described having pain routinely at a level 1 on a scale of 0 to 10. Mr. E. is worried about the future. He frequently remarks, "How will I care for my wife and child?" "Iron work is the only trade I know." He reports disliking school. He says that he does not learn well from books, although he easily grasps an idea when someone takes the time to show him. Results from a vocational interest test suggest that he is drawn toward occupations in which one can visualize the results of the work. He enjoys building and repair activities. His lowest results were associated with jobs involving work with others. Mr. E. stated he "hates inside or desk work." Temperament testing revealed Mr. E. as flexible, quiet, active, consistent, and reticent. In the past he has supervised up to five ironworkers and six apprentices, but he does not eagerly seek leadership positions. Mr. E. lost his driving privileges approximately nine years ago because of a reckless driving conviction. He is not eligible to regain his driver's license until he pays a court imposed fine and is re-examined by the State Bureau of Motor Vehicles. He has no felony or misdemeanor convictions. Mr. E. wants to become a fork lift (lift truck), crane, or heavy equipment operator.

Dr. N.

At age fifty-six, Dr. N. (a physical medicine specialist), was diagnosed as having chronic fatigue syndrome. Memory, alertness, and the ability to focus were her major nonexertional limitations. She experienced daily headaches and fatigue to the point where she remained in bed for the majority of each day. She was granted permanent disability from a private long-term disability policy she held. She was denied Social Security Disability Insurance benefits and made the decision not to pursue these benefits as it was too stressful.

Recently (two years after receipt of long-term disability benefits), her stamina and alertness increased to about four hours per day for three days per week. Her headaches now occur every other day and are no longer severe. She can use the computer for up to two hours per day. Forgetting no longer seems to be much of a problem. With this increased endurance, Dr. N. called her insurance company requesting a consultation with a qualified rehabilitation counselor for the purpose of determining what work she may be qualified to perform within her current limitations.

REFERENCES

Bissonnette, D. (1994). *Beyond traditional job development: The art of creating opportunity.* Chatsworth, CA: Milt Wright & Associates.

Blackwell, T. L., & Conrad, A. D. (1990). *Job analysis for private sector rehabilitation.* Athens, GA: Elliott & Fitzpatrick.

Bose, J. L., Geist, G. O., Lam, C. S., Slaby, M., & Arens, M. (1998). Factors affecting job placement success in proprietary rehabilitation. *Journal of Applied Rehabilitation Counseling, 29*(3), 19–24.

Bridges, C. C. (1946). *Job placement of the physically handicapped.* New York: McGraw Hill.

Burke, L. K., & Dillman, E. G. (1990). *Functional Capacity Checklist* [computer software program]. Athens, GA: Elliott & Fitzpatrick.

Burke, L. K., & Dillman, E. G. (1984). *Functional Capacity Checklist* [vocational instrument]. Athens, GA: Elliott & Fitzpatrick.

Cormier, W. H., & Cormier, L. S. (1985). *Interviewing strategies for helpers: Fundamental skills and cognitive behavioral interventions* (2nd Ed.). Monterey, CA: Brooks/Cole.

Deneen, L. J., & Hesselund, T. A. (1986). *Counseling the abled disabled: Rehabilitation counseling in disability compensation systems.* San Francisco: Rehab Publications.

Deneen, L. J., & Hesselund, T. A. (1981). *Vocational rehabilitation of the injured worker.* San Francisco: Rehab Publications.

Farr, J. M. (1991a). *The very quick job search* [video]. Indianapolis, IN: JIST Works.

Farr, J. M. (1991b). *The very quick job search: Get a good job in less time.* Indianapolis, IN: JIST-Works.

Field, T. F., & Field, J. (1992). *The classification of jobs* (revised edition). Athens, GA: Elliott & Fitzpatrick.

Habeck, R. V. (1991). Managing disability in industry. *NARPPS Journal & News, 6*(4), 141–146.

Hagner, D. (2000). Primary and secondary labor markets: Implications for vocational rehabilitation. *Rehabilitation Counseling Bulletin, 44*(1), 22–29.

Holmes, G. E. & Karst, R. A. (1989). Case record management: A professional skill. *Journal of Applied Rehabilitation Counseling, 20*(1), 36–40.

International Association of Rehabilitation Professionals. (2006). Primary Care Vocational Service Delivery Standards, IARP Standards and Ethics, Section D, Job Development and Placement. Retrieved on March 31, 2006 from http://www.rehabpro.org/vocationalservice_frameset.html

Job Placement Division, National Rehabilitation Association. (1992, April-June). Job readiness evaluation and criteria. *Job Placement Digest, 27*(2), 7–8 [Reprint of the Placement Handbook of the State of Iowa Division of Vocational Rehabilitation Services].

Klein, M., Swisher, J., Lynch, R., & Krewson, C. (1982). The rehabilitation counselor and the medical consultant. *Rehabilitation Counseling Bulletin, 25*(4), 239–242.

Liptak, J. J. (2001). *Treatment planning in career counseling.* Stamford, CT: Brooks/Cole Thomson Learning.

McGowan, J. G., & Porter, T. L. (1967). *An introduction to the rehabilitation counseling process.* Washington, DC: U.S. Government Printing Office.

Meyers, D. W. (1992). *Human resources management: Principles and practice* (2nd Ed.). Chicago: Commerce Clearing House.

Multi-Resource Center (1972). *Job seeking skills manual.* Minneapolis, MN: Author.

National Institute on Disability and Rehabilitation Research. (1989). Rehabilitation counselors: Qualifications, credentials, and confidence. *Rehab Brief, 11*(12), 1–4.

O'Connor, S. (1988). Management of individuals with disabilities in the workplace. *Journal of Job Placement, 4*(2), 18–21.

Salomone, P. R. (1996). Career counseling and job placement: Theory and practice. In E. M. Szymanski & R. R. Parker (Eds.), *Work and disability: Issues and strategies in career development and job placement* (pp. 365–420). Austin, TX: PRO-ED.

Sinsabaugh, L. L. (1994). *A study of issues critical to the private rehabilitation industry.* Unpublished doctoral dissertation, Virginia Commonwealth University.

Sinsabaugh, L. L., & Martin E. D., Jr. (1999). A survey of private sector practitioners in the state of Virginia. *The Rehabilitation Professional, 7*(1), 29–35.

Spencer, B. (2006). *Applied ethics for behavioral health practitioners.* Nashville: TN: Cross Country Education.

Strum, T. E., Otto, V. R., & Bakeman, M. (1972). *Vocational diagnostic interviewing.* Minneapolis, MN: Minneapolis Rehabilitation Center.

Szymanski, E. M., Hershenson, D. B., Ettinger, J. M., & Enright, M. S. (1966). Career development interventions for people with disabilities. In E. M. Szymanski & R. R. Parker (Eds.), *Work and disability: Issues and strategies in career development and job placement* (pp. 255–276). Austin, TX: PRO-ED.

The Fair Labor Standards Act of 1938 (as amended, 2004). U.S. Department of Labor Employment Standards Administration Wage and Hour Division, [WH Publication 1318,

Revised March 2004; (29 U.S.C. 201, et seq.) in PDF format]. Retrieved on March 31, 2006, from http://www.dol.gov/esa/regs/statutes/whd/FairLaborStandAct.pdf

U.S. Department of Labor. (1990). *OWCP rehabilitation manual.* Washington, DC: U.S. Department of Labor, Employment Standards Administration, Office of Workers Compensation Programs.

U.S. Department of Labor. (1991). *Dictionary of occupational titles* (4th Ed.). Washington, DC: Author.

U.S. Department of Labor. (1991). *Revised handbook for job analyzing jobs.* Washington, DC: Author.

U.S. Department of Labor. (2004). *Occupational outlook handbook* (Bulletin 2570). Washington, DC: Author.

U.S. Equal Opportunity Commission. (1993). *Laws enforced by the U.S. Equal Employment Opportunity Commission* [Publication # 355-218/90016]. Washington, DC: U.S. Government Printing Office.

Vandergoot, D., & Worrall, J. D. (1979). *Placement in rehabilitation: A career perspective.* Baltimore, MD: University Park Press.

Weed, R., & Field, T. (1991). *Rehabilitation consultant's handbook* (revised edition). Athens, GA: Elliott & Fitzpatrick.

Witt, M. A. (1992). *Job strategies for people with disabilities.* Princeton, NJ: Peterson Guides.

Chapter 7

ETHICS AND THE
REHABILITATION COUNSELOR

E. DAVIS MARTIN, JR., REBECCA S. CURTIS, AND KEITH C. WRIGHT

The ethical treatment of persons with disabilities is the responsibility of all professionals who participate in the rehabilitation process. Because of the continuity of the counselor-client relationship and the counselor's coordination of services responsibility, this professional, perhaps more so than others, is placed in a position to set high standards of conduct. The rehabilitation counselor is the focal point for the client during the rehabilitation process; this is the person who coordinates this process, managing the delivery of services, and providing the client with continuity and consistency. Ethical behavior for the rehabilitation counselor, or for that matter any human service professional, represents an ideal in terms of personal traits and characteristics that must be constantly pursued (Corey, Corey & Callanan, 2003). Corey, Corey and Callanan (1984) have noted ". . . that counselors who are willing to continually look within themselves and struggle toward becoming more effective human beings are the ones who are most likely to make a positive difference in the lives of their clients" (p. 26). Moreover, Corey (1996) has further expanded on the meaning of a being a counselor and the characteristics that model such behavior. The identification and subsequent development of a listing of personal qualities or characteristics, according to Corey, was not to define a "fixed model of perfection" but rather to identify ways counselors may assess themselves relative to the growth and development of their clients. From an ethical perspective, the identification and aspiration to such values and beliefs would frame the counselor-client relationship from a posture of counselor effectiveness. Corey (1996) proffers the following markers of counselor effectiveness for our consideration:

- Effective counselors have an identity.
- They respect and appreciate themselves.
- They are able to recognize and accept their own power.
- They are open to change.
- They are expanding their awareness of self and others.
- They are willing and able to tolerate ambiguity.
- They are developing their own counseling style.
- They can experience and know the world of the client, yet their empathy is nonpossessive.
- They feel alive, and their choices are life-oriented.
- They are authentic, sincere, and honest.
- They make mistakes and are willing to admit them.
- They generally live in the present.
- They appreciate the influence of culture.
- They are able to reinvent themselves.
- They are making choices that shape their lives.
- They have a sincere interest in the welfare of others.
- They become deeply involved in their work and derive meaning from it.
- They are able to maintain healthy boundaries. (pp. 16–19)

Personal effectiveness, as revealed through these characteristics, certainly represents an ideal for the counselor to strive toward. The rehabilitation client deserves no less.

The focus of this chapter will be to examine the values upon which moral and ethical precepts have developed and the application of these precepts to the rehabilitation counselor from both an agency-counselor perspective and a counselor-client perspective. Issues arising in both of these contexts will be examined and explored.

Values and Valuing in Vocational Rehabilitation

Rehabilitation service providers must identify what is valued in terms of client goals and outcomes. On a practical level, service providers must assess if values guide the provision of services or if, in actuality, standard practices shape the values that professionals hold toward clients and services provided. In the latter instance, one may wonder if values evidenced by service providers reflect clients' needs or service providers' needs. It is therefore significant to propose values that influence rehabilitation counseling and understand their potential for impacting services.

Values are indicators of what is held in esteem (Gordon, 1975; Rokeach, 1973). Values act as standards or beliefs that guide actions and judgments across situations and time. Typically, values are organized by priority into what is known as a value system, thereby resulting in a continuum along which judgments are made regarding behaviors and actions (Kluckhohn, 1951; Rokeach, 1973; Schwartz, 1990). Values and resulting value systems operate at the individual or personal level, the institutional or professional level, and a societal or national level (Rescher, 1969; Schwartz, 1990). Personal values, for instance, are values that do not necessarily involve interaction with others. Personal values are expressed by an individual's behavior that generally brings about value satisfaction (e.g., someone who works diligently on a job because he or she values a strong work ethic; Gordon, 1975). Institutional or professional values, alternatively, may be described as a specified prioritization or constellation of values that serve to express and encourage the identification and advancement of the group's values (Schwartz, 1990). In this sense, professional values serve as a group's standards and have the propensity to set the direction toward which an organization works (NICHCY News Digest, 1993). This happens whether values are clarified by the group and stated up-front or are ambiguous because they have not been formally identified. When values are not articulated, assumptions are made about what is considered to be of value. Unspoken values and assumptions made about what is of value to the group, however, will continue to influence and shape the behavior and actions of the group.

The Relationship of Values to Rehabilitation Counseling

Values have been defined as enduring beliefs that become standards for guiding actions (Rokeach, 1973). Values are constants that guide our actions and judgments across situations and time. Bergin (1985) described values in the context of counseling as being ". . . orienting beliefs about what is good for clients and how that good should be achieved" (p. 99) and indicated values are "necessarily embedded in the treatment process [that] . . . should be made explicit and . . . openly used to guide and evaluate change" (p. 99).

The purpose of exploring values is to increase the understanding about the impact that values have upon individuals and systems. Values that influence rehabilitation counseling, however, fall within a global framework of values and valuing. It is, therefore, beneficial to explore the relationship of values, in theory and practice, to the field of vocational rehabilitation.

When initially exploring the role of values in rehabilitation counseling, a definition of values that is conceptually person-centered in its orientation, is a logical choice. Vocational rehabilitation (VR) may be described as a service provider system, and while it is a system, it was established to work for and with persons with disabilities. The overall design of VR is such that, even when values are discussed about things (e.g., a work sample system) or behaviors (work performance), such a discussion takes place in relationship to a person or groups of people. Additionally, such discussions may take place in relationship to services that are being provided for people (persons with disabilities) by other people (e.g., rehabilitation counselors, vocational evaluators).

It is also logical to define values in the sense of such authors as Kluckhohn, Rokeach, and Williams, wherein values serve as standards by which to make evaluative decisions. In this way, values serve as the basis by which judgments are made and about the rehabilitative process. Values serve as the basis for defining standards that the quality of services provided to persons with disabilities are appraised. Rokeach (1973) stated evaluation of values and value-related behaviors can be accomplished using behavioral, cognitive, or affective terminology. This concept is vital, in that, values have the potential to serve as the basis for making judgments regarding the quality of life that persons with disabilities will sustain.

In discussing the properties of values, Rokeach (1973) described two types of values: a means or an end-result of actions that are appraised as to their desirableness. Both terminal and instrumental values play a role when setting goals and objectives that are personally and socially preferable to other alternatives. A practical illustration of this concept can be seen when a counselor and client set short- and long-term goals and objectives. Values that motivate long-term goals are, more frequently, terminal in nature. That is, the value that drives an overall goal is usually the desired end-state (e.g., when someone who dropped out of high school sets the long-term goal of obtaining a GED). Instrumental values can be seen in the short-term objectives and goals that constitute the steps it takes to successfully reach long-term goals. Again, these values concern themselves with *modes of conduct* dealing with moral, competence, or self-actualizing behaviors (Rokeach, 1973).

The manifestation of values in the field of VR can be seen in prime directives that helped to establish and continue to propel the system. Values have served as an impetus in the establishment of federal laws and regulations that concern themselves with the quality of life and civil rights of persons with disabilities (e.g., Americans with Disabilities Act, Individuals with Disabilities Education Act and subsequent amendments, 1973 Rehabilitation Act and subsequent amendments). The constellation of values that steers an organization also govern how an organization functions daily and establishes the standards and goals that motivate employees (Wilson, 1988). In rehabilitation, values are inherent in mission or goal statements, professional codes of conduct, and standards establishing competency requirements for certification, licensure, educational degrees, and the provision of services.

On the state level as well, values are often evidenced in the Purpose (or mission) and Philosophy Statements of the state-federal VR systems. The following, taken from the Alabama Department of Rehabilitation Services Blueprint for the 21st Century (Annual Report, 2004) is one such example that is quite instructive:

> Mission–to enable Alabama's children and adults with disabilities to achieve their maximum potential. (p. 2)

Based on that mission statement, a listing of value statements follow that detail actions and behaviors that correspond to the specific value:

We VALUE the worth, dignity, and rights of people with disabilities and we will:

- Provide an easily accessible, integrated continuum of services;
- Ensure quality services that are family-centered, culturally sensitive, and community-based;

- Promote and respect consumer choice regarding provision of services;
- Advocate for the rights of persons with disabilities and promote self-advocacy;
- Include people with disabilities, their families and advocates in agency planning and policy development. (Alabama Department of Rehabilitation Services, Annual Report, 2004, p. 2).

A total of six guiding values are stated in this document; each value statement followed by a number of corresponding statements identifying how that value will be expressed by individuals working in the Alabama Department of Rehabilitation Services.

Finally, when discussing the acquisition of values in relationship to rehabilitation, it is imperative to remember that the acquisition of values is not static (Corey, Corey, & Callanan, 2003; Smith, 1977). As individuals and institutions grow and change, values also change. As both Maslow and Rogers stated, the ultimate expression of human needs is found in values that promote self-actualization. Intrinsic to the system of rehabilitation should be values that promote the process of self-actualization for individuals with disabilities.

Values are embedded in the definition, philosophy, and purpose of the VR system in the United States. When there is a discrepancy between the values that drive service provision and the values that clients perceive as advancing the self-actualization process, these values need to be clearly identified and stated. Values associated with this process need to be articulated in such a way that individuals with disabilities know the system promotes their development and enhances their quality of life. Values that drive this system are presented in Table 7-1. Core values are highlighted with accompanying value statements listed below each core value.

- **Altruism:** The value of altruism represents the "Moral Argument" for rehabilitation (Hotz, 1992). As a society, we believe in the value of the individual (Emener, 1991). Accordingly, each and every person is regarded as holding inherent worth and dignity. Our society also holds the belief that people should and will better themselves (or move toward self-actualization).
- **Choice:** The value of choice is the belief that one should be able to determine, to the fullest extent possible, the manner in which one lives. Within the value of choice are concepts such as com-

TABLE 7-1. VALUES AND VALUE STRUCTURE IN REHABILITATION

Altruism
    Individual dignity
    Individual worth
    Self-actualization process

Choice
    Community participation
    Integration
    Least restrictive environment
    Mainstreaming normalization

Empowerment
    Independence
    Self-control
    Self-determination

Equality and Individualism
    Autonomy
    Freedom
    Responsibility
    Self-reliance

munity participation, integration, least restrictive environment, mainstreaming, and normalization (Racino, 1992).

- **Empowerment:** This value indicates one's ability to act upon choice (Parent, 1993). Empowerment is a value that indicates one has an awareness of choice and the opportunity and independence to act upon one's choices. Found within the value of empowerment are the concepts of self-control and self-determination.

- **Equality and individualism:** Equality is a value that is also based upon the belief of individual worth and dignity. Individuals in our society often seek equal opportunities in order to maintain autonomy as much as possible within the general structure of our society. Autonomy and freedom require an individual to maintain self-reliance and personal responsibility in order to function individually and as a member of society.

The values of altruism, choice, empowerment, equality, and individualism have the potential and should serve as standards guiding professional codes of conduct and the provision of services in vocational rehabilitation.

A Study of Ethics

Ethics is concerned with value judgments regarding human behavior. Ethics as a philosophical discipline is concerned with conduct that uses such moral predicates as *ought, should, right, wrong,* and *good* as they apply to our behavior. Ethics concerns principles or norms that ought to govern conduct rather than those that do. Cottone and Tarvydas (1998) noted that "ethics, as a philosophy, cannot be separated from morality" (p. 6). Moreover, "morality deals with human conduct where judgments are made as to whether a human act conforms to the accepted rules of righteousness or virtue" (p. 6).

Garrett (1966), many years ago, defined ethics as "the science of judging specifically human ends and the relationship to means to those ends . . . and . . . the art of controlling means so that they will serve specifically human ends" (p. 4). He added that "ethics really is or should be involved in all human activities" (p. 4).

Recognizing that all professions have codes of ethics and noting also, that many civic organizations and businesses have creeds and ethical standards, it becomes apparent that no single or simple guide or rule could suffice for everyone, especially if we support the concepts of flexibility and innovativeness as positive values. Alfred North Whitehead observed "the simple minded use of the notions 'right or wrong' is one of the chief obstacles to the process of understanding." Acceptance of this statement thus leads to a rejection of the *Golden Rule* as the answer to our ethical issues: "Do unto others that which you wouldst have others do unto you." Judaism teaches more than 613 commandments or mitzvahs of the *Torah,* or laws of righteousness. Rules and guides for effective and proper living have been handed down to us for centuries through various commandments, maxims, proverbs, and fables. Books directed toward effective living and ethics abound, yet so do ethical problems exist in government, business, education, and everyday social situations. Parents, schools, churches, movies, television, and limitless other sources are blamed for these ethical violations.

Is sportspersonship a myth? Is the intentional foul a proper ethic? Are the following quotations indicative of today's ethics?

- All is well that ends well. (John Heywood)
- The end justified the means. (Publilius Syrus)
- Do you remember this poem?
    For when the one great scorer comes
    To check against your name,
    It's not whether you won or lost
    But how you played the game.

Do you believe this? Do most coaches or managers? Do most athletes? Do you trust car salespersons, politicians, mechanics, or lawyers? Is there a specific segment of our population you don't trust? Have you given thought to the image of rehabilitation counselors?

Recognizing that the study of ethics is related to rightness and wrongness (appropriateness), let us consider wrongness but emphasize rightness. In rehabilitation, we consider disability and impediment but emphasize ability. Our very philosophy is opposed to discrimination due to disability. We are concerned with the dignity of the individual. Ethics and rehabilitation have grown up together. Rousseau provides us with an apt analogy: "Those who would treat politics and morality apart will never understand the one or the other."

Vash (1981/2004), commenting on a conservative U.S. senator's pronouncement that "You can't legislate morality," states:

> . . . morality is just what we do legislate—or try to. The Constitution put forth a moral order, and statutory law attempts to maintain it. Ideally, the goals of the law are what's right, fair and moral to the best of the lawmaker's ability to foresee and implement. (p. 141)

Ethical principles are derived from the general understandings or fundamental assumptions of the larger society regarding what is considered to be right and wrong (Cottone & Tarvydas, 1998). Cottone and Tarvydas (1998) have noted that ". . . principle ethics involves objectivity applying a system of ethical rules and principles to determine what is the right or moral decision when an ethical dilemma arises" (p. 135). Beauchamp and Childress (1983) identified these principle ethics as: beneficence, nonmaleficence, autonomy, justice, and fidelity. Corey et al. (2003) have included another principle ethic, that being veracity. Veracity, very simply, means being truthful; being truthful, for instance, about the implications of a particular diagnosis, testing, confidentiality, or scope of practice of the counselor all related to the concept of informed consent. Veracity and fidelity are similar in that both principle ethics relate directly to honesty and, for that matter, all of these principle ethics center on honesty in relationships.

Rubin, Wilson, Fischer, and Vaughn (1992) further amplify the five principle ethics of beneficence, nonmaleficence, autonomy, justice, and fidelity to rehabilitation counseling as follows:

BENEFICENCE. The principle of beneficence applies to acting in a manner that promotes the growth and well-being of the client. For example, rehabilitation practitioner actions that would be compatible with the principle of beneficence might be:

1. Providing a client with vocational training compatible with the recommendations contained in the client's vocational evaluation report.
2. Advocating for the client in the job placement process.
3. Funding a service such as surgery to prolong a client's productive life.
4. Providing support services to the family that is necessary to facilitate the client's rehabilitation gain.
5. Providing a client with home modifications in order to make their residence accessible.
6. Assisting a client to obtain needed medical services. (p. 10)

NONMALEFICENCE. The principle of nonmaleficence applies to acting in a manner that does no harm to clients or prevents harm to clients. For example, rehabilitation practitioner actions that would be compatible with the principle of nonmaleficence might be:

1. Confronting a client concerning his or her self-destructive lifestyle.
2. Intervening to meet the specific health care and safety needs of a client.
3. Withholding distressing information from clients who are not prepared to handle it.
4. Assisting a client to leave an abusive home situation. (p. 13)

AUTONOMY. The principle of autonomy applies to acting in a manner that respects the freedom of clients to control their own lives (to make their own choices). For example, rehabilitation practitioner actions that would be compatible with the principle of autonomy might be:

1. Supporting a specific type of training requested by the client.
2. Supporting a client's selection of a particular vocational objective or independent living goal.
3. Providing a client with the requested information about job opportunities in the local community.
4. Providing clients with complete information to enable them to make informed choices.
5. Providing a client with requested case file information.
6. Supporting a client's choice to move from a group home to an apartment.
7. Encouraging a client to take responsibility for obtaining needed services. (p. 15)

JUSTICE. The principle of justice applies to treating clients fairly. For example, for many rehabilitation counselors the principle of justice generally applied to the fair allocation of available caseload monies to clients, as well as the fair allocation of their limited time to provide direct client services and to complete other job tasks. The fact that client needs and the time demands of the job role generally exceed available resources places rehabilitation counselors in the position of having to distribute limited money and professional work time among clients in a fair or just manner. Rehabilitation practitioner actions that would be compatible with the principle of justice might be:

1. Refusing to provide an extremely expensive service requested by an individual client when limited funds are available.
2. Keeping individual case service costs down in order to provide services to a large number of clients in need.
3. Providing an individual with a severe disability with expensive adaptive equipment to enable him or her to have equal access to the community.
4. Being equally accessible to all clients on your caseload.
5. Refusing to continue to provide funds or spend limited available

time assisting an unmotivated client who is not working toward his or her independent living or vocational goals.

6. Limiting the amount of time spent with any one client in order to provide services to a large number of clients in need.
7. Spending a large portion of one's available service delivery time with an individual who has complex independent living service needs to enable him or her to have equal access to the community. (p. 18)

FIDELITY. The principle of fidelity applies to keeping promises or commitments, both stated and implied. For example, for rehabilitation counselors the principle of fidelity generally applies to counselor-client, counselor-colleague, and counselor-agency relationships. Service delivery actions that would be compatible with the principle of fidelity might be:

1. Adhering with agency case movement guidelines.
2. Providing all services agreed to in the client's Individualized Written Rehabilitation Plan [now Individualized Plan for Employment].
3. Providing clients with case file information they request.
4. Carrying out a previous rehabilitation counselor's commitment to the client.
5. Completing required case file documentation.
6. Refusing to provide information on a client to other agencies without having the written permission of the client.
7. Abiding by a supervisor's recommendations.
8. Adhering to organizational policy. (p. 20)

Situational Ethics

Joseph Fletcher (1966), in his classic treatment of ethics, *Situation Ethics: The New Morality,* permits us to look at ethics from three vantage points. By doing so, we are able to get a better perspective as to the enormity and complexity of the problem.

He describes *legalism ethics* as not too different from state rehabilitation agency standards and procedures as exemplified in the state plan and policy manual with rules and regulations. With this approach, Fletcher stated:

> . . . one enters into every decision-making situation encumbered with a
> whole apparatus of prefabricated rules and regulations. Not just the spir-
> it but the letter of the law reigns. Its principles, codified by rules, are not
> merely guidelines or maxims to illuminate the situation; they are direc-
> tives to be followed. Solutions are present, and you can "look them up
> in a book." (p. 18)

Legalism ethics makes it difficult to honor individual differences in
both counselors and clients. It is suggested that the word *uniqueness*
may be unique in legalism thinking. Counselor flexibility, innovativeness, and imaginative planning can be seriously hampered. To be sure,
we do need laws, rules, regulations, manuals, state plans, codes, and
guidelines; yet, these should not inhibit or eliminate necessary services to people. Perhaps many current legal requirements were initiated
because of counselor malpractice or misinterpretation of program
philosophies and principles. Fletcher states that

> rules are like punt or fourth down or take a pitch when the count is
> three balls. These rules are part of the wise player's know-how and dis-
> tinguish him [*sic*] from the novice. They are not unbreakable. The best
> players are those who know when to ignore them. (p. 28)

Fletcher also discusses *antinomianism ethics,* a polar opposite of legalism ethics (literally, "against the law"). Here we can relate to counselors, for instance, who have manipulated agency regulations illegal-
ly for client benefits. These counselors are certainly client-centered. In
their own minds, they may have considered themselves as right and
professional. It was the agency, with its regulations and pressures, that
was wrong. These counselors were breaking the law. We have seen,
not too long ago, situations whereby groups with vested interests,
believing the law to be too slow or wrong, took the law into their own
hands. They were ethical but against the law. Many revolutionaries
practice antinomianism ethics.

Fletcher then discusses *situation ethics.* Here ". . . situational factors
are so primary that we may say "circumstances alter rules and principles" (p. 29). He qualifies this by stating "it is necessary to insist that
situation ethics is willing to make full and respectful use of principles,
to be treated as maxims but not as laws or precepts. We might call it
principled relativism" (p. 31).

The Agency and Ethics

The state-federal VR agency must be concerned with ethical practice in a variety of ways. True, it must detect and correct unethical practice either through dismissal of the offending counselor(s) or through rehabilitation measures. Detection and correction are not enough, however. The state VR agency and its leadership must set the tone and caliber of professional practice by example.

Accountability criteria for state VR agencies have been a topic of discussion for some time and may be of significance when discussing ethics. Rehabilitation counselors, educators, and others had long ago challenged what has been referred to as the "quota system" or "numbers game" (Rule and Wright, 1974). Perhaps, as suggested by the National Citizen's Advisory Committee on Vocational Rehabilitation which pre-dated Rule and Wright's observation may very well be correct that the "numbers game . . . resulted in a perversion of both program objectives and counselor satisfaction" (p. 30). Certainly, the consumerism movement starting with the passage of the Architectural Barriers Act in 1968 to the landmark 1973 Rehabilitation Act (and its subsequent amendments) to the Americans with Disabilities Act (1990) has had the effect of lessening the emphasis on "numbers." And, as a result of these watershed legislative acts, persons with significant disabilities are being afforded a greater opportunity to seek remunerative employment or to gain independent living skills through the provision of rehabilitation services.

The Government Accountability Office (GAO) (2005), however, has recently revisited this issue of accountability noting there is inconsistency and considerable variation of the eighty state VR agencies in the success ratios or performance indicators that denote the effectiveness and efficiency of the state-federal VR program; that is, the number of persons who were successfully rehabilitated and those who, for other reasons, exited the VR system before gaining employment. This GAO report noted that of the 650,000 persons exiting the VR system in fiscal year 2003, approximately one-third of this number were successfully employed for at least ninety days following receipt of substantial VR services. The remaining two-thirds of cases were closed without gaining employment for a variety of reasons:

• Failed to cooperate or refused services–46%.

- Unable to contact or locate–24%.
- No disabling condition–6%.
- Disability too significant–3%
- Other–22% (includes individuals who exited because of institutionalization, transfer to other state VR agencies, death, transportation problems, unavailability of extended services, extended employment, or "all other" reasons [in 17% of all cases]). (p. 13)

While the GAO has highlighted this finding as an accountability issue, it nevertheless remains as an ethical issue for the agency. One successful closure does not necessarily equal another successful closure in the VR system if one considers the nature and severity of the disability. Certainly, there is a significant difference between the costs–the time, services, and assistive technology–needed by a person who has, for instance, a paralysis disability and a person who has a less involved physical disability vis-à-vis successful rehabilitation. A lack of funds allocated to state VR agencies has caused a number of state VR agencies to declare an order of selection for those who will receive VR services. It may well be just as discriminatory to serve only persons with the most significant disabilities rather than serving a representative number of persons with all levels of disability severity. From an ethical perspective, the principle ethic of nonmaleficence would seem to be compromised as well as the principle ethic of justice. It would seem that our accountability systems have yet to recognize these factors.

Analyses of agency reports might reflect several ethical concerns expressing values and the integrity of a program. The inference that rehabilitation is a one-time expense that returns an investment of a few dollars to twenty-fold in tax dollars for every dollar expended by the agency might seriously affect a counselor's values and practice. Placement, if judged only by this standard, ignores a qualitative standard, for example, of positioning persons to compete in the primary labor market. When this occurs persons with disabilities and their families and/or significant others are afforded a greater opportunity to access the American Dream. A job in the primary labor market is truly an investment that continuously yields dividends for the individual and for society. A job in the secondary labor market, while valuable, does not yield the same return and, in general, does not provide the same opportunity to access the American Dream. Within this GAO report, it was concluded that a performance measure with a single criterion (e.g., employment for ninety days) to measure success makes it difficult to evaluate the VR system. Because the eighty state VR agencies vary considerably in the achievement of this goal, for instance, a low of 20 percent to a high of 74 percent relative to employment rates, it makes it difficult to judge the quality of the VR program. Additionally, the GAO noted that the Department of Education's untimely feedback to the state VR agencies relative to key populations, such as students transitioning from school to work or those who are currently receiving services, compromises the ability to develop or disseminate best practices.

Employment of qualified rehabilitation counselors has long been an issue for rehabilitation educators and has been emphasized within rehabilitation legislation beginning with the 1973 Rehabilitation Act continuing to the present. The Rehabilitation Services Administration, along with its constituent programs, gave birth to and helped develop professional training programs for rehabilitation counselors in 1954. Millions upon millions of dollars have been invested over the years in support of this training, yet incredibly, the standards and regulations for employment of rehabilitation counselors have only recently been given increased emphasis primarily through the Comprehensive System of Personnel Development (CSPD). An illustration of how recent this change was may be noted in a study by Froehlic, Garcia, and Linkowski (1998) regarding minimal hiring standards for rehabilitation counselors. This study revealed that nationally, at that time, no state required its rehabilitation counselors to hold the certification certified rehabilitation counselor (CRC), although thirty states encouraged such certification; only thirteen states required a master's degree in rehabilitation counseling or a related area, twenty-four states encouraged such degrees, ten states required only a bachelor's degree for its rehabilitation counselors, and four states did not even require this level of educational attainment. A study conducted by Lynch and McSweeney seventeen years earlier produced similar results. They noted that counselor education training programs and the certification program for rehabilitation counselors were often taken lightly by the employing organization. Froehlich et al. (1998) noted that "the goal of raising the minimum hiring standards for rehabilitation counselors is to provide better services and to improve the vocational outcomes for persons with disabilities" (p. 201). The often-cited studies (Cook &

Bolton, 1992; Szymanski & Danek, 1992; Szymanski & Parker, 1989) regarding client outcomes and level of education of the rehabilitation counselor are particularly relevant and point to the ethical need, not only for the establishment of minimal standards of education but also for the adherence of those standards when hiring persons as rehabilitation counselors. The current CSPD initiative has, for the most part, been extremely successful in remedying this situation, producing increased numbers of qualified rehabilitation counselors through quality educational programs. This programmatic emphasis has, as well, facilitated stronger relationships between the various educational programs and the state VR agencies, a relationship that may be characterized as mutually beneficial. In the end, VR clients gain the most from the CSPD initiative.

With this increase in education and new skills, CSPD graduates, however, are looking to practice these skills and be paid accordingly. The irony of the successfulness of the CSPD initiative may be that once the payback obligation is met, a number of these graduates could leave the state agency for practice in an environment where these skills can be applied and appropriately remunerated.

The Counselor and Ethics

Ethics is related to many things: to perceived benefits of a particular situation, to the philosophies that rehabilitation counseling is based upon, and to the principles of morality and to codes of ethics that define and guide ethical behavior. Ethics is measured by behavior. One aspect of counselor practice related to ethics is attitude. Many years ago, a very perceptive and still quite timely document (Rusalem and Baxt, 1969) referred to "attitudinal barriers" whereby the attitudes of a small minority of insecure, frightened, misdirected, and immature practitioners damage the image of the agency and the profession. They fail to realize that their attitudes (and actions) speak not only for themselves but also for their co-workers, their employer, and their profession. One study cited revealed that "neither costs nor rehabilitation techniques, neither transportation nor severity of the disability, was found to be as critical as the attitudes of key professional workers" (p. 41). The attitudes and behaviors of counselors almost always reflect on the employer (and profession) wherever the counselor may be. Perhaps the most direct and compelling statement of ethics is embodied in the Commission on Rehabilitation Counselor Certification's (2002) preamble to the Code of Professional Ethics for Certified Rehabilitation Counselors. In part, it reads:

> Rehabilitation counselors are committed to facilitating the personal, social and economic independence of individuals with disabilities. In fulfilling this commitment, rehabilitation counselors work with people, programs, institutions, and service delivery systems. Rehabilitation counselors provide services within the Scope of Practice for Rehabilitation Counseling (see Scope of Practice document) and recognize that both action and inaction can be facilitating or debilitating. It is essential that rehabilitation counselors demonstrate adherence to ethical standards and ensure that the standards are enforced vigorously. The Code of Professional Ethics for Rehabilitation Counselors, henceforth referred to as the Code, is designed to facilitate these goals.
>
> The fundamental spirit of caring and respect with which the Code is written is based upon five principles of ethical behavior. These include autonomy, beneficence, nonmaleficence, justice, and fidelity as defined below:
>
> Autonomy: To honor the right to make individual decisions
> Beneficence: To do good to others
> Nonmaleficence: To do no harm to others
> Justice: To be fair and give equally to others
> Fidelity: To be loyal, honest, and keep promises
>
> The primary obligation of rehabilitation counselors is to their clients, defined in the code as individuals with disabilities who are receiving services from rehabilitation counselors. Regardless of whether direct client contact occurs or whether indirect services are provided, rehabilitation counselors are obligated to adhere to the code. At times, rehabilitation counseling services may be provided to individuals other than those with disabilities, such as a student population. In all instances, the primary obligation remains with the client and adherence to the code is required.
>
> The basic objective of the code is to promote public welfare by specifying ethical behavior expected of rehabilitation counselors. The Enforceable Standards within the code are exacting standards intended to provide guidance in specific circumstances and will serve as the basis for processing ethical complaints initiated against certificants.
>
> Rehabilitation counselors who violate the Code are subject to disciplinary action. Since the use of the Certified Rehabilitation Counselor (CRC) designation is a privilege granted by the Commission on Rehab-

ilitation Counselor Certification (CRCC), CRCC reserves unto itself the power to suspend or to revoke the privilege or to approve other penalties for a violation. Disciplinary penalties are imposed as warranted in accordance with published procedures and penalties designed to assure the proper enforcement of the Code within the framework of due process and equal protection under the law. (http://www.crcertification.com)

Corey (1996) has noted that professional codes of ethics serve a number of purposes: (a) to educate the public about the profession and its responsibility (for the practitioner and the general public), (b) to act as an accountability mechanism (to protect against unethical practice), and (c) to improve practice (through reflection and self-monitoring). Because codes of ethics describe such a broad range of issues and expected behavior, only minimal standards of excellence are articulated for the practitioner to follow. Corey (1996) has stated that "there is a real difference between merely following the ethical codes and making a commitment to practicing with the highest ideals" (p. 55). As such, ethics may be viewed from two vantage points:

- *Mandatory ethics* entails a level of ethical functioning at which counselors simply act in compliance with minimal standards.
- *Aspirational ethics* pertain to striving for the optimum standards of conduct.

Tarvydas (1997) similarly has written that codes of ethics are an attempt by the professional organization to determine appropriateness. Moreover, Tarvydas has observed that codes of ethics are not absolute formulas to be followed, but rather are normative standards.

Virtue Ethics

Virtue ethics or the ethics of care relate to the personal characteristics of the rehabilitation counselor. Meara, Schmidt, and Day (1996) provide a clear differentiation between principle ethics and virtue ethics by noting that principle ethics center on moral issues, providing a means of resolving dilemmas that give insight as well as implications for future ethical behavior. Virtue ethics, on the other hand, center on the counselor doing the very best for his or her clients, focusing on an ideal outcome for each client exemplified by four core virtues. These are prudence, integrity, respectfulness, and benevolence. In the context of rehabilitation counseling, *prudence* as a virtue embodied by the rehabilitation counselor infers wisdom in terms of making good judgments that are in the best interest of clients; *integrity* means straightforwardness and honesty regarding demeanor in all situations with clients; *respectfulness* means the counselor holds his or her clients in esteem regarding their determination to succeed; and *benevolence* is exemplified by the rehabilitation counselor's compassion and will to do good for his or her clients.

Meara et al. (1996) provide the following characteristics as noted in Coret et al. (2003) of virtuous professionals which are quite instructive:

- They are motivated *to do what is right for the right reasons.* They do what is right not simply because they feel obligated or fear the consequences.
- They possess *vision and discernment,* which involve sensitivity, judgment, and understanding and lead to decisive action.
- They possess *compassion* that involves a regard for the welfare of others and sensitivity to the suffering [*sic*] of others.
- They possess *self-awareness.* They have a capacity for self-observation; they know how their assumptions, convictions, and bias are likely to affect their interactions with others.
- They are *connected with and understand the mores of their community* and the importance of community in moral decision-making, policy setting, and character development. (p. 14)

In addition to these core personal characteristics, virtuous rehabilitation counselors must be passionate and persistent regarding the desired outcomes for all of his or her clients. Passion, in this sense, refers to a commitment to the values of independence (having choice and control over your life), productivity (a recognition that in order to access the American Dream, each client must acquire employment in the primary labor market, or in instances where that is not possible, as close an approximation as possible), and inclusion (living, working, and recreating in the community of choice). Persistence means the counselor is dedicated to continuing, not giving up on the client, allowing the person the right to fail and to learn from those experiences.

Ethical Issues Encountered in Rehabilitation Counseling Practice

The preceding discussion noted the difference between principle ethics and virtue ethics; however, the differences are artificial as both are complementary, necessary, and required prerequisites to ethical practice. Virtue ethics, or an ethic of care, relates to the deliverer of services and to the perspective of that professional. The rehabilitation counselor is more than a counselor; this is a person who is a harbinger of hope–a messenger of hope–for the rehabilitation client and those who share in that person's life. It is, therefore, incumbent upon the rehabilitation counselor to maintain a transparent sense of prudence, integrity, respectfulness, and benevolence. Specific issues that relate to both principle and virtue ethics that must be addressed by the counselor on a daily basis are:

CONTINUING MAINTENANCE OF PROFESSIONAL SKILLS OR COMPETENCY. This refers to the need to develop a pattern of life-long learning. Change is a constant within our environment. In order to provide services that are timely and that meet the needs of clients, rehabilitation counselors must avail themselves of a variety of continuing education opportunities ranging from formal educational programs to professional organization meetings to home study to a regular schedule of journal reading and discussion with colleagues. A practitioner's scope of practice must constantly be examined by the rehabilitation counselor regarding maintenance of existent skills and the acquisition of new skills that will benefit clients.

THE APPROPRIATE USE OF TESTS AND TEST RESULTS. Not withstanding the issue of who has the appropriate authority or competency to perform testing, the rehabilitation counselor must assure that the testing protocol allows for appropriate accommodation(s) to reveal the true attributes of a client. Issues related to race, gender, religion, national origin, and disability are particularly relevant. Testing should be done to screen people, not to screen people out. Assessments should be used to determine what people can do, not what they cannot do.

THE ACCEPTANCE OF GIFTS (EITHER FROM CLIENTS OR FROM VENDORS). The giving of a gift, particularly for the client, may have great meaning. Obviously, only gifts of nominal monetary value may be accepted by the rehabilitation counselor. However, to decline a gift may be interpreted as a very harsh statement or as rejection. Larger gifts, of course, may not be accepted by the counselor but may, under certain circumstances, be accepted by the organization to fund or further notable client-related activities. Conflict of interest statues define acceptable monetary limits and organizational guidelines should, likewise, offer guidance. Situational ethics, as noted by Fletcher, should be the controlling guideline in these situations. Gifts from vendors, as well, should fall within professional and/or organizational guidelines. Publicly funded agencies must be representative, for the most part, in the award of contracts for services. In the selection of a vendor, client outcome should be the guiding principle, not extraneous factors unrelated to the service.

DUAL RELATIONSHIPS. The essence of the rehabilitation process is the client-counselor relationship, and it is always based on a professional plane. A personal relationship compromises the effectiveness of the counselor-client relationship and must be avoided. The rehabilitation counselor's role may, at times, be that of a mentor, employment coach or specialist, or other roles that occur within the community (recreation, independent living, social, or residential where life skills are being taught or acquired). Boundaries in these instances may become blurred. The rehabilitation counselor must maintain primary responsibility to assure healthy and appropriate relationship boundaries. Herlihy and Corey (1992) recommended five safeguards to assist counselors in the maintenance of healthy relationships as noted in Cottone and Tarvydas (1998):

- *Informed consent:* The counselor should fully inform the client of all possible risks involved, the limitations of the relationships, and the safeguards in place.
- *Ongoing discussions:* The counselor should have periodic discussions with all the parties involved in the relationships to identify and work through any conflicts or concerns that develop.
- *Consultation:* If the counselor does proceed with the dual relationship, an ongoing consultation with a colleague should be in place so that all aspects of the situation will be evaluated to guard against overlooking a problem.
- *Supervision:* If the situation involves a high risk for harm, more continuous supervision may be warranted.
- *Documentation:* Counselors should document all aspects of the

dual relationships and issues that arise with the process, including the techniques used to manage the situation. (pp. 338–339)

Relationships involving intimacy or a business partnership with other professionals when services for a mutual client are involved also fall under the category of a dual relationship (Cottone & Tarvydas, 1998). Relationships such as these may be potentially harmful to the client if one of the professionals exerts pressure (knowingly or unknowingly) on the other.

CONFIDENTIALITY. Clients must be assured that all aspects of the counselor-client relationship are confidential and that the counselor may not reveal the essence or any part of that relationship without the expressed consent of the client. The quality of the client-counselor relationship is based on trust. The basis for trust is established by the counselor's assurance of confidentiality. Issues that have the potential to pose ethical dilemmas for the rehabilitation counselor were identified by Patterson and Settles (1992) in a survey they conducted with certified rehabilitation counselors and reported in Cottone and Tarvydas (1998):

(a) Maintaining confidentiality in institutional settings,
(b) Knowing that a client is driving with poorly controlled seizures,
(c) Recommending a client who is suspected of abusing substances to an employer,
(d) Sharing information with family members about a client with chronic mental Illness,
(e) Conflicts between Workers' Compensation and state laws related to confidentiality,
(f) The requirement to report client information to an agency that results in disciplinary action against the client,
(g) Learning that a client who has AIDS is not practicing safe sex, and
(h) Discussing clients with others without signed written consent. (p. 334)

Confidentiality and privileged communication are not the same; they are, however, similar concepts although, in many ways, very different. Privileged communication is granted by statute and extended to licensed professionals, not through professional certification.

Privilege, as such, varies from state to state dependent on factors related to required qualifications to practice as a rehabilitation counselor or licensed professional counselor.

INFORMED CONSENT. A central concept in rehabilitation counseling is the involvement of the client in the process of rehabilitation or habilitation. With the passage of the 1973 Rehabilitation Act and through its subsequent amendments, most notably the 1998 amendments, client involvement has been continuously encouraged and mandated. The exercise of informed choice has matured into a consumer-centered and-directed process. Rehabilitation counselors must respect this major change, particularly for persons with significant disabilities, and assume a posture of assisting clients to successfully effectuate this responsibility. The intent of informed choice ". . . is to be sure that clients have a sufficient understanding of the circumstances so they can exercise their autonomy and make informed choices" (Cottone & Tarvydas, 1998, p. 336).

PERSONAL AND ORGANIZATIONAL VALUES AND CLIENT CHOICE. A rehabilitation counselor's personal beliefs and values may seep into the counselor-client relationship intentionally or more likely unintentionally. Counselors must be aware of their beliefs and values and the impact these beliefs and values may play in the rehabilitation process. For example, when participating in career planning and counseling, clients are expected to value work and to exhibit the desire and willingness to be productive. What happens to clients seeking career guidance when vocational advice that seems to lead toward the secondary labor market or occupational choice is sidestepped by issues of time and cost? There may be little or no attempt to understand the phenomenological view of the client when organizational pressures for successful closures are needed. In such instances, client choice may not be honored as the client must agree with the organization's or counselor's understanding of the world and base goals and outcomes on standards and values that may not be truly their own.

These issues and others encountered in day-to-day practice require the counselor to develop *responsibleness,* as noted by Tennyson and Strom (1986) that goes beyond the mere application of professional standards. They have stated that ". . . counseling is a moral enterprise requiring responsibleness; that is, action should be based on careful, reflective thought about which response is professionally right in a particular situation" (p. 298). Tennyson and Strom further advise that counselor effectiveness may be enhanced when ". . . their beliefs, attitudes and actions are grounded in reasons that are openly examined through critical reflection" (p. 302).

The resolution of ethical dilemmas poses a significant responsibility upon the rehabilitation counselor to consciously understand the principle ethics of beneficence, nonmaleficence, autonomy, justice, fidelity, and veracity. Several models of resolving ethical dilemmas are available to the rehabilitation counselor (Corey, 1996; Cottone, 2001; Cottone & Tarvydas, 1998; Forester-Miller & Davis, n.d.; Hill, Glaser, & Harden, 1995; Rubin, Wilson, Fischer, & Vaughn, 1992; Tarvydas, 1997; Walden, 1997), and the reader is advised to consult one or more of these citations for more detailed information. Corey et al. (2003) in a review of ethical decision-making models suggests the following steps be followed in the resolution of ethical dilemmas. This approach has the advantage of embracing the feminist model of ethical decision-making, the social constructivism model, and Walden's inclusion of clients in the ethical decision-making process:

- *Identify the problem or dilemma.* Ethical dilemmas do not have "right or wrong" answers, so you will be challenged to deal with ambiguity. Consultation with your client begins at this initial stage and continues throughout the process of working through an ethical problem, as does the process of documenting your decisions and actions.
- *Identify the potential issues involved.* Consider the basic moral principles of autonomy, beneficence, nonmaleficence, justice, fidelity, and veracity and apply them to the situation. Good reasons can be presented that support various sides of a given issue, and different ethical principles may sometimes imply contradictory courses of action.
- *Review the relevant ethics codes.* Ask yourself whether the standards or principles of your professional organization offer a possible solution to the problem.
- *Know the applicable laws and regulations.* It is essential for you to keep up to date on relevant state and federal laws that apply to ethical dilemmas. In addition, be sure that you understand the current rules and regulations of the agency or organization where you work.
- *Obtain consultation.* Consultation can help you think about infor-

mation or circumstances that you may have overlooked. In making ethical decisions, you must justify a course of action based on sound reasoning. Consultation with colleagues, whether it is formal or informal, provides an opportunity to test your justification. Remember to document the nature of your discussions with those whom you consult.

- *Consider possible and probable courses of action.* As you think about the many possibilities for action, discuss these options with your client as well as with other professionals.
- *Enumerate the consequences of various decisions.* Consider using the six fundamental moral principles (autonomy, beneficence, nonmaleficence, justice, fidelity, and veracity) as a framework for evaluating the consequences of a given course of action.
- *Decide on what appears to be the best course of action.* Once you have made what you consider to be the best decision, do what you can to evaluate your course of action. Reflecting on your assessment of the situation and the actions you took are essential if you are to learn from your experience. (pp. 20–21)

Corey (1996) has admonished counselors regarding the importance of continuously reviewing their professional and ethical responsibilities. Toward that end, Corey provides a listing of guidelines that counselors should periodically consider and reflect upon that is highly instructive:

- Counselors need to be aware of what their own needs are, what they are getting from their work, and how their needs and behaviors influence their clients. It is essential that the therapist's own needs not be met at the client's expense.
- Counselors should have the training and experience necessary for the assessments they make and the interventions they attempt.
- Counselors need to become aware of the boundaries of their competence, and they should seek qualified supervision or refer clients to other professionals when they recognize that they have reached their limit with a given client. They should make themselves familiar with the resources in the community so that they can make appropriate referrals.
- Although practitioners know the ethical standards of their professional organizations, they are also aware that they must exercise

their own judgment in applying these principles to particular cases. They realize that many problems have no clearcut answers, and they accept the responsibility of searching for appropriate solutions.

- It is important for counselors to have some theoretical framework of behavior change to guide them in their practice.
- Counselors need to recognize the importance of finding ways to update their knowledge and skills through various forms of continuing education.
- Counselors should avoid any relationships with clients that are clearly a threat to therapy.
- It is the counselor's responsibility to inform clients of any circumstances that are likely to affect the confidentiality of their relationship and of any other matters that are likely to negatively influence the relationship.
- It is important that counselors be aware of their own values and attitudes, recognize the role that their belief system plays in their relationships with their clients, and avoid imposing these beliefs, either subtly or directly.
- It is important for counselors to inform their clients about matters such as the goals of counseling, techniques, and procedures that will be employed, possible risks associated with entering the relationship, and any other factors that are likely to affect the client's decision to begin therapy. Counselors must realize that they teach their clients through a modeling process. Thus, they should attempt to practice in their own lives what they encourage in their clients.
- Counseling takes place in the context of the interaction of cultural backgrounds. You bring your culture to the counseling relationship, and your client's cultural values also operate in the process.
- Counselors need to learn a process for thinking about and dealing with ethical dilemmas, realizing that most ethical issues are complex and defy simple solutions. The willingness to seek consultation is a sign of professional maturity. (pp. 79–80)

Conclusion

The ethical treatment of rehabilitation clients, as noted throughout this chapter, is dependent upon a multitude of factors, the most central of which is the good will and intent of the counselor. The employer of this professional, whether in the public or private sector of rehabilitation is, likewise, an integral participant in the broader issues of ethics as they affect individual clients.

The increased awareness of ethical concerns by the client, as noted by Stadler (1986) has created an atmosphere where clients have been encouraged ". . . to demand that services be delivered ethically" (p. 291). This trend assuredly must be recognized as good for those who receive services and for those who deliver and administer such services. Certainly, the consumerism embodied within the spirit and letter of 1973 Rehabilitation Act (and subsequent amendments), the Individuals with Disabilities Act (and subsequent amendments), and the 1990 Americans with Disabilities Act require that services be delivered from a consumer-centered posture.

Professional codes of ethics, while not always totally inclusive, have, nevertheless, provided a structure for counselor behavior and responsibility (Mable and Rollin, 1986). The Commission on Rehabilitation Counselor Certification's *Code of Professional Ethics for Rehabilitation Counselors* represents one such effort. This statement of ethical concern for the individual rehabilitation client and his or her family when coupled with the notion of *responsibleness* represents a most laudable ideal. Responsibleness in decision-making will be of great importance as the ethical issues of the future become more apparent in our day-to-day existence. Preventive rehabilitation with its emphasis and concern on safety, for example, has in the recent past led a number of legislators to champion mandatory seat-belt laws, the desired effect being a decrease in the number of head and spinal cord injuries. The effect of such legislation may, however, further complicate the ethical issue and concern as to how much safety is necessary without unnecessarily invading individual freedom of choice. Ethical issues involving persons born with significant disabilities and the withholding of medical treatment as well as other similar issues will pose dilemmas requiring responsibleness in the decision-making process. Legislative solutions for many of these ethical issues may infringe on individual responsibility and may not always result in the best decision. These and other institutional issues regarding the conduct of the state-federal program of vocational rehabilitation will command our attention now and in the future. We must employ our ethic of care for these issues and for those dilemmas we face in day-to-day professional practice. As we strive for excellence in the ethical treatment of persons with disabilities, we, as rehabilitation counselors, must continually examine the attitudes, beliefs, and values of our profession and, most importantly, our personal beliefs and values as they relate to persons with disabilities.

REFERENCES

Alabama Department of Rehabilitation Services. *Blueprint for the 21st century.* Annual Report, 2004, 1–2.

Americans with Disabilities Act of 1990. Public Law 101–336.

Beauchamp, T. L., & Childress, J. F. (1983). *Principles of biomedical ethics.* Oxford: Oxford University Press.

Bergin, A. E. (1985). Proposed values for guiding and evaluating counseling and psychotherapy. *Counseling and Values, 29*(2), 99–116.

Cook, D. W., & Bolton, B. (1992). Rehabilitation counselor education and case performance: An independent replication. *Rehabilitation Counseling Bulletin, 36*(1), 37–43.

Corey, G., Corey, M. S., & Callanan, P. (1993). *Issues and ethics in the helping professions* (4th Ed.). Pacific Grove, CA: Brooks/Cole.

Corey, G. (1996). *Theory and practice of counseling and psychotherapy* (5th Ed.). Pacific Grove, CA: Brooks/Cole.

Cottone, R. R. (2001). A social constructivism model of ethical decision making in counseling. *Journal of Counseling and Development, 79*(1), 39–45.

Cottone, R. R., & Tarvydas, V. M. (1998). *Ethics and professional issues in counseling.* Upper Saddle River, NJ: Prentice-Hall.

Curtis, R. S. (1998). Values and valuing in rehabilitation. *Journal of Rehabilitation, 64*(1), 42–47.

Emener, W. G. (1991). An empowerment philosophy for rehabilitation in the 20th century. *Journal of Rehabilitation, 57*(4), 7–12

Froehlich, R. J., Garcia, J., & Linkowski, D. (1998). Minimum hiring requirements for rehabilitation counselors in the states: A comparison across federal regions. *Rehabilitation Education, 12*(3), 193–203.

Forester-Miller, H., & Davis, T. E. (n.d.). *A practitioner's guide to ethical decision making.* Alexandria, VA: American Counseling Association.

Foundation for Rehabilitation Education and Research (1997). *Rehabilitation counseling: The profession and standards of practice.* Rolling Meadows, IL: Author.

Gordon, L. V. (1975). *The measurement of interpersonal values.* Chicago: Science Research Associates.

Hill, M., Glaser, K., & Harden, J. (1995). A feminist model for ethical decision making. In E. J. Rave & C. C. Larsen (Eds.), *Ethical decision making in therapy: Feminist perspectives* (pp. 18–37). New York: Guilford Press.

Hotz, J. C. (1992). *Study guide for the certified rehabilitation counselor (CRC) examination.* St. Cloud, MN: Distinctive Ink.

Individuals with Disabilities Education Act of 1990 (IDEA), Public Law 101–476.

Individuals with Disabilities Education Act of 1997, Public Law 101–476.

Individuals with Disabilities Education Act Amendments of 1997, Public Law 105–17.

Kluckhohn, C. (1951). Values and value-orientations in the theory of action. In T. Parsons & E. A. Shils (Eds.), *Toward a general theory of action* (pp. 388–433). Cambridge, MA: Harvard University Press.

Lynch, R., & McSweeney, K. (1981, Winter). The professional status of rehabilitation counseling in state/federal vocational rehabilitation agencies. *Journal of Applied Rehabilitation Counseling, 12*(4).

Mabel, A. R., & Rollin, S. A. (1986). The role of a code of ethical standards in counseling. *Journal of Counseling and Development, 64*(5), 294–297.

Maki, D. R., & Riggar, T. F. (1997). *Rehabilitation counseling: Profession and process.* New York: Springer.

Maslow, A. H. (1959). *New knowledge in human values.* New York: Harper.

NICHCY News Digest (National Information Center for Children and Youth with Disabilities) (1993, March). *Transition summary: Transition services in the IEP, 3*(1). Washington, DC: Author.

Oberman, C. E. (1972). *A code of ethics for rehabilitation counselors.* National Rehabilitation Counseling Association.

Parent, W. (1993). Quality of life and consumer choice. In P. Wehman (Ed.), *The ADA mandate for social change* (pp. 19–41). Baltimore, MD: Paul H. Brookes.

Patterson, J. B., & Settles, R. (1992). The ethics education of certified rehabilitation counselors. *Rehabilitation Education, 6,* 179–184.

Racino, J. A. (1992). Living in the community: Independence, support, and transition. In F. R. Rusch, L. Destefano, J. Chadsey-Rusch, L. A. Phelps, & E. Szymanski (Eds.), *Transition from school to adult life* (pp. 131–145). Pacific Grove, CA: Brooks/Cole Publishing.

Rasch, J. D. (1985). *Rehabilitation of workers' compensation and other insurance claimants.* Springfield, IL: Charles C Thomas.

Rehabilitation Act of 1973. Public Law 93–112.

Rehabilitation Act of 1978. Public Law 95–602.

Rehabilitation Act Amendments of 1992. Public Law 102–569.

Rehabilitation Act Amendments of 1993. Public Law 103–73.

Rescher, N. (1969). *Introduction to value theory.* Englewood Cliffs, NJ: Prentice-Hall.

Rogers, C. R. (1964). Toward a modern approach to values: The valuing process in the mature person. *Journal of Abnormal and Social Psychology, 68*(2), 160–167.

Rokeach, M. (1973). *The nature of human values.* New York: Free Press.

Rubin, S. E., & Roessler, R. T. (1995). *Foundations of the vocational rehabilitation process* (4th Ed.). Austin, TX: PRO-ED.

Rubin, S. E., Wilson, C. A., Fischer, J., & Vaughn, B. (1992). *Ethical practice in rehabilitation: A series of instructional modules for rehabilitation education programs.* Student's workbook. Carbondale, IL: Rehabilitation Institute, Southern Illinois University.

Rubin, S. E., Wilson, C. A., Fischer, J., & Vaughn, B. (1992). *Ethical practices in rehabilitation: A series of instructional modules for rehabilitation education programs.* Instructor's manual. Carbondale, IL: Rehabilitation Institute, Southern Illinois University.

Rule, W. R., & Wright, K. C. (1974). A new slant to established values: Accountability and counselor reward. *Journal of Applied Rehabilitation Counseling, 5*(4), Winter.

Rusalen, H., & Baxt, R. (1969). *Delivering rehabilitation services.* Washington, DC: U.S. Department of Health, Education, & Welfare.

Schroeder, F. K. (1998). *The rehabilitation act amendments of 1998, Information Memorandum, RSA-IN-98-20.* Washington, DC: Rehabilitation Services Administration, United States Department of Education.

Schwartz, B. (1990). The creation and destruction of value. *American Psychologist, 45*(1), 7–15.

Smith, M. (1977). *A practical guide to value clarification.* La Jolla, CA: University Associates.

Stadler, H. (1986). Preface to special issue. *Journal of Counseling and Development, 64*(5), 291.

Tarvydas, V. M. (1997). Standards of practice: Ethical and legal. In D. R. Maki & T. F. Riggar (Eds.), *Rehabilitation counseling: Profession and practice* (pp. 72–94). New York: Springer.

Walden, S. L. (1997). The counselor/client partnership in ethical practice. In B. Herlihy & G. Corey (Eds.), *Boundary issues in counseling: Multiple roles and responsibilities* (pp. 40–47), Alexandria, VA: American Counseling Association.

Williams, R. M. (1968). *International encyclopedia of social sciences.* New York: Macmillan.

PART 3

PSYCHOSOCIAL CASE STUDIES

CASE STUDY INSTRUCTIONS

E. DAVIS MARTIN, JR. AND GERALD L. GANDY

The following case studies have been developed to provide the reader with an opportunity to analyze and evaluate thirteen differing situations representative of physical, mental, cognitive, and sensory disabilities. Although the cases in this text are composites of various persons, they do, nevertheless, represent reality concerning the challenging circumstances that people with disabilities and their families or significant others are faced with on a daily basis.

A major feature of each case is the manner in which it is presented. The social evaluation for each case provides an overview and backdrop for the medical, psychological, vocational, educational, and economic assessments. Discussion questions that follow each case are designed to facilitate thinking and the ultimate resolution of a particular case whether in a group situation, or an individual basis, or some combination of both. For instance, the medical information needed for each case may be gathered in groups, while the resolution of a case may be achieved on an individual basis. Each case will require a considerable investment of time in researching the various medical conditions, seeking information regarding community resources including other social service organizations and agencies as well as discussion with practicing professionals to adequately resolve a case. Cases represent varying degrees of difficulty and complexity requiring knowledge in the application of medical and psychological interventions, counseling, occupational analysis, career planning, location and utilization of community resources, and job development and placement strategies within a context of multiculturism, disability rights, and advocacy. The ethnic or cultural construct for each case study can be designated by the instructor or selected by the student and/or group. The ethnic or cultural construct, then, may be anticipated, and the effects, if any, may be confronted in the rehabilitation process.

A focus for each case is for the student or participant to (a) determine eligibility to receive vocational rehabilitation services and then, if appropriate, (b) the formulation of the IPE, (c) coordination and delivery of vocational rehabilitation services, (d) job placement, and (e) follow-along and case closure. Consequently, the student or participant must be knowledgeable of the state-federal program of vocational rehabilitation as well as the role, function, and responsibilities of the rehabilitation counselor. The persona assumed in the resolution of each case is that of the rehabilitation counselor. The structure for resolution is signified in the utilization of actual case management forms used by the vocational rehabilitation agency within each student's or participant's home state or, for that matter, any other state.

Case Presentation and Evaluation Guidelines

The role and function of the rehabilitation counselor are discussed in the various chapters contained in Part 2 of this text. Based on that information, previously completed rehabilitation counseling coursework, and clinical experience(s), the following structure is provided for the resolution of each case. Assumptions may be made as long as assumptions are consistent with the facts provided in the case narrative. Because varying assumptions may appropriately be made, varying case resolutions may result realistically emphasizing the individualized nature of vocational rehabilitation.

In the formulation of an employment goal, the vocational objective must be in the primary labor market, or if that is not obtainable and the job objective is in the secondary labor market, a rationale and plan for approximating the primary labor market are required. Within the IPE, for all services provided or coordinated, costs for each must be included. The case narrative should reflect a logical progression from referral to case closure.

The final written product should be of sufficient quality to demonstrate excellence. Clients accepted for and *provided* vocational rehabilitation services deserve no more or no less. Following each case are a series of questions that have been formulated relating to the medical, psychological, social/family/community, vocational, and economic aspects of the case to facilitate the analysis. Appendixes A and B, respectively, provide sample resolutions for the cases of Barbara (deafness) and James (cardiovascular disease) that are illustrative of the below provided structure that may be utilized in case analysis.

Case Resolution Structure

Medical Overview

- Cause/What Is It? (Etiology)
- Course and Prognosis of the Medical or Psychiatric Impairment(s)
- Functional Limitations/Impediments to Employment and Activities of Daily Living
- Medications (patient teaching, compliance, side effects)
- Assistive Technology (identification, availability, and accessibility)

Assessments

- Initial Interview
- Clarification of Assessment(s) Contained in the Case Narrative (Part 3 of the textbook)
- Additional Diagnostics Required (order specialized medical or psychological/psychiatric diagnostics (e.g., letter[s] to specialist, response to rehabilitation counselor)
- Assumptions (consistent with the facts present in the case)

Establishment of Eligibility

- Documentation of Disability
- Identification of Functional Limitations/Impediments to Employment
- Clearly Articulated Rationale and Need for VRS

Individualized Plan for Employment

- Vocational Goal (DOT and O*NET Code Number)
- Intermediate Objectives (a series of steps designed to assist the client to achieve the vocational objective)
- Services (specific services to be provided and/or coordinated,

search for comparable benefits)
- Duration of Services
- Evaluation of Services
- Terms and Conditions

Delivery of Services

- Case Notes that Clearly Define the Client-Counselor Relationship
- Clear Timeline for the Delivery of Services

Job Placement

- Rationale for Job (inclusive of transferability of skills)
- Career Orientation (primary labor market)
- Consumer Preparation
- Employer Preparation
- Employer Incentives

Follow-along/Postemployment Services

- Anticipated Need for Postemployment Services
- Closure Memorandum (to referral source, client, others, and for the agency file)

Suggested References for Case Analysis

The following reference sources have been particularly helpful in the analysis and subsequent resolution of the case situations contained in this part of the textbook. This listing of references is not exhaustive, merely illustrative of the many sources of information available:

American Psychiatric Association. (2000). *Diagnostic and statistical manual of mental disorders, IV, TR.* Washington, DC: Author.

Andrew, J. (2000+). *The disability handbook.* Fayetteville, AK: University of Arkansas.

Beers, M. H., & Berkow, R. (1999). *The Merck manual.* Rahway, NJ: Merck, Sharp and Dohme Research Laboratories (or the *Merck manual of medical information, home edition*).

Bissonnette, D. (1994). *Beyond traditional job development: The art of creating opportunity.* Chatsworth, CA: Milt Wright and Associates.

Buelow, G., & Herbert, S. (1995). *Counselor's resource on psychiatric medications: Issues of treatment and referral.* Pacific Grove, CA: Brooks/Cole Publishing Company (or a comparable reference).

Commission on Rehabilitation Counselor Certification. (1997). *Rehabilitation counseling: The profession and standards of practice.* Rolling Meadows, IL: The Foundation for Rehabilitation Education and Research.

Cook, A. M., & Hussey, S. M. (2002). *Assistive technologies principles and practice.* St. Louis: Mosby.

Crimando, W., & Riggar, T. F. (2003). *Utilizing community resources: An overview of human resources.* Prospect Heights, IL: Waveland Press, Inc.

Farr, J. M., & Ludden, L. L. (2004). *The O*NET dictionary of occupational titles* (3rd Ed.). Indianapolis: JIST Publishing.

Farr, J. M., Ludden, L. L., & Shatkin, L. (2001). *Guide for occupational exploration* (3rd Ed.). Indianapolis: JIST Publishing.

Farr, J. M., Ludden, L. L., & Shatkin, L. (2005). Enhanced occupational outlook handbook (5th Ed.). Indianapolis: JIST Publishing.

Fischler, G., & Booth, N. (1999). Vocational impact of psychiatric disorders: *A guide for rehabilitation professionals.* Gaitherburg, MD: Aspen Publishers (or a comparable reference).

Hood, A. B., & Johnson, R. W. (1991). *Assessment in counseling: A guide to the use of psychological assessment procedures.* Alexandria, VA: American Counseling Association (or a comparable reference).

Power, P. W. (1991). *A guide to vocational assessment.* Austin, TX: Pro-Ed (or a comparable reference).

Rybacki, J. J., & Long, J. W. (2003). *The essential guide to prescription drugs.* New York: Harper Perennial (or a comparable reference).

Stolov, W. V., & Clowers, M. R. (1981). *Handbook of severe disability.* Washington, DC: U.S. Government Printing Office (or a comparable reference).

Thomas, C. L. (1997). *Taber's cyclopedic medical dictionary.* Philadelphia: F.A. Davis (or a comparable reference).

United States Department of Labor (1991). *Dictionary of occupational titles* (4th Ed.). Washington, DC: United States Government Printing Office.

Witt, M. A. (1992). *Job strategies for people with disabilities.* Princeton, NJ: Peterson's Guides.

Appendix A

HEARING IMPAIRMENT AND DEAFNESS: THE COMPLETED CASE OF BARBARA

Deafness and Hearing Disability: Practical Implications of the Case of Barbara

ALLISON E. SHIPP

When I first read over the case of Barbara, I felt that this would be a simple fairly straightforward task that would require minimal effort. However, after getting started I quickly realized what an intricate and involved process case management truly is. I began by visualizing Barbara and trying to put myself in the position of her rehabilitation counselor. I then consulted two vocational rehabilitation counselors and asked their opinion on how best to approach a case such as Barbara's. Both gave me very similar responses, so I used those as benchmarks and guidelines as I worked through this case. During the process, I contacted many departments and services only to discover that case management can be a slow and arduous process because often it is necessary to rely on the timelines of others. While this can be a frustrating aspect of case management, patience and persistence will prevail most of the time.

Medical Overview

Etiology

Barbara had cerebrospinal meningitis as a complication of measles when she was five years old. She was left with permanent damage to the inner ear resulting in bilateral sensorineural deafness.

Course and Prognosis

Sensorineural hearing loss cannot be corrected medically or surgically. Barbara's hearing loss is expected to remain stable, getting neither better nor worse with time. Although Barbara has some capacity for hearing sound, she does not benefit from hearing aid equipment.

Functional Limitations/Impediments to Employment and Activities of Daily Living

Barbara experiences functional limitations in processing speech and other auditory cues. She also has very mild, virtually negligible, speech impairment. Barbara occasionally has problems maintaining her balance, but this feeling of vertigo is not severe and can be easily controlled. Barbara wishes to become a teacher, however, the colleges that her family can afford do not have adequate educational accommodations for students who are deaf or hard of hearing. Therefore, even though Barbara is a very bright and accomplished individual, her disability constitutes an impediment to employment through limited educational options. The activities of daily living that are affected by Barbara's hearing loss include (a) the inability to use the telephone without assistance or assistive technology and (b) the inability to hear an alarm clock, a smoke or fire alarm, or the doorbell, for example.

Medications

Barbara is not taking any prescribed medications at this time, nor is it anticipated that she will need any due to her disability in the future.

Assistive technology

Barbara does not benefit from hearing aid equipment. She uses a TTY/TDD machine to communicate on the telephone. Barbara will also require a flashing light to provide her with a visual cue when the smoke/fire alarm goes off. She will need a vibrating alarm clock and something that provides visual cues and/or vibrations when the telephone rings and when the doorbell chimes.

Assessments

Initial Interview

My initial interview with Barbara took place on February 1. Barbara and I established a great rapport immediately, and this continued throughout the delivery of services. Barbara and I both looked forward to our meetings, and she would frequently stop by or call to update me on her progress.

Clarification of and Additional Assessments

Barbara received a medical evaluation in November of the preceding year. I did not need another medical assessment, but I did obtain the recent records from her physician. The clinical psychologist administered the WAIS-IV to Barbara and she received IQ scores in the superior range (scores ranged from 124 to 126) on both the verbal and performance scales. Before meeting Barbara I thought that a language and communication assessment may be necessary, but I changed my mind after interactions with her. Barbara's excellent communication skills along with her superior score on the verbal section of the IQ test did not warrant any further testing or assessments in this area.

Barbara was administered the Strong-Campbell Interest Inventory in high school. After discussing the results with her, I found them consistent with her expressed vocational interests. She stated that her first career choice was to become a high school English/creative writing teacher. Her ability and interest scores from previous assessments echoed and supported this goal. Therefore, I did not see the need for any additional vocational testing.

Assumptions

I made the assumption that Barbara met the disability "listing" and economic need to receive SSI benefits. I also made the assumption that she scored a 29 on her ACT.

Eligibility

Barbara was found eligible for VR services because:
1. Barbara is an individual with a documented sensory disability (bilateral sensorineural hearing loss). This was documented through her medical report and audiogram.
2. Barbara's hearing loss constitutes a substantial impediment to employment that will make it very difficult for her to prepare for employment consistent with her capacities and abilities.
3. Barbara requires VR services to prepare for employment.

Individualized Plan for Employment

Vocational Goal

Barbara's vocational objective was to obtain a four-year college degree and the other necessary certifications/qualifications to prepare her to become a high school English/creative writing teacher (DOT Code 091.227-010/O*NET Code 25.2031.00). I approved this goal because it was consistent with her educational success in high school and her vocational interests and aptitudes. Barbara talked to me about her father's desire for her to go into something technical, but she admitted that teaching was her true passion. I encouraged her to follow her heart to become a teacher. She was excited about making this dream a reality.

Intermediate Objectives

Barbara's intermediate objective was to attend college at Auburn University beginning this coming fall. She was to keep up her grades in order to maintain in good standing and also to continue to receive her scholarship monies. Barbara was an excellent student and thrived in the college environment. Upon graduation from college, Barbara was to seek gainful employment with the assistance (if needed) from our office.

Services

ASL interpreter services were provided for Barbara during class. The cost of these services was $25/hour. VRS paid for half and Auburn University's Program for Students with Disabilities (PSD) covered the other half. The director of the PSD, Dr. Nancy Jamison, offered real-time captioning services to Barbara, provided by RapidText and paid for by the Program for Students with Disabilities. Barbara was eager to try these services out. The cost was $60/hour, and VR was to reimburse PSD the $12.50/hour that was originally agreed upon for the interpreter services. Dr. Jamison had received "earmarked" funding for these captioning services, but she was very grateful for VR's contribution. Barbara discovered that she liked the captioning service for classes that were "heavy lecture" but preferred the interpreter services for those classes involving more class participation. The reason for this was that the professor wears a microphone during captioning, and any conversation that the microphone does not pick up (i.e., student questions and comments) is not captioned. After making the appropriate adjustment, Barbara felt very satisfied with her "mixture" of accommodations.

Barbara received some scholarship and grant money, but she needed additional assistance in covering the remainder of her tuition. Because she was late in applying for the Pell Grant, she did not receive any funds for her first semester. Barbara did, however, receive the Pell Grant for the rest of her college career. VRS paid for 85% of the remaining tuition not covered by grants or scholarships and Barbara's family covered the remaining 15%. This number varied from semester to semester, depending on the actual cost of tuition (based on the number of hours that Barbara was registered for) and the amount that was covered by other sources. VR also provided Barbara with room and board expenses. The remaining costs were paid by grants and her parents. VR also paid for the amount not covered by her scholarships for her textbooks.

The flashing and vibrating fire/smoke alarm was provided by student housing services since Barbara lived in the dorms. Student housing also created a special set-up for Barbara that caused the lights to flash when someone was at her door or if the telephone rang. This required installing a doorbell and additional rewiring to connect these to the lights in her room. VR provided assistance to Barbara in requesting this, but did not provide any financial support. Barbara received a TTY machine from the Alabama Statewide Technology Access and Response Project (STAR). VR also provided Barbara with the appropriate means of contacting STAR, but did not cover any expenses of the TTY machine. Barbara already had a vibrating alarm clock, so she used this one during all four years of college.

Posteducation services to better prepare Barbara for employment included interviewing skills and resume-building skills. These were available to Barbara at no cost. However, Barbara chose to use the career services center on campus and found their office to be very helpful and accommodating. They assisted her with creating a resume, setting up interviews, and keeping her informed about the career and teacher interview days.

Duration of Services

The financial services for Barbara's schooling lasted for four years from the time that she entered college. Job placement services were to be available until a job was obtained and successfully maintained for ninety days. Post-education services (resume-building skills training, interviewing skills training) were also available during this time. Because Barbara procured a full-time position on her own during her last semester at Auburn, she did not need any additional assistance in this area.

Evaluation of Services

Barbara met with me, her hometown VR counselor, at least once per semester. At the end of each semester, Barbara was required to turn in her grades for the previous term and discuss any potential problems with me. Any minor issues, or those not involving funding, were handled by Auburn University's VR counselor, Mr. Joe Hanson. No major issues were encountered during Barbara's four years at Auburn University. She always expressed her gratitude and appreciation for the financial and emotional support provided by VR.

Terms and Conditions

Barbara understood that her funding would only cover four years at Auburn University. If she had to extend her stay, then it would be at her own expense. This was determined because it was found to be within Barbara's educational capabilities to maintain a full load to enable her to complete her degree in the allotted four years. It was also noted that should her disability ever prevent her from completing her degree in four years, an extension could have been added as an additional accommodation. Typically, VR does not cover coursework that is completed during the summer. However, there was one summer when Barbara needed to take a class that was only offered during that time. I got special permission to grant her funding for that class for the summer. Barbara completed within the allotted four years.

Delivery of Services

Case Notes

2/1–Begin case notes for session #1 (Initial Interview): Before the interview began, I gave Barbara the option of transferring her case to Tracey Cooley of Andalusia, who specializes in services for the deaf. I gave Barbara an information sheet about the services for the deaf along with Tracey Cooley's contact information. Barbara said that the Opp office was more convenient for her (Andalusia is approximately thirty minutes away), and she felt confident that she would receive appropriate services at our office.

For Barbara's initial interview, I had an ASL interpreter present. Barbara said that she appreciated the presence of the interpreter, but she felt comfortable speech-reading since we were in a close setting. I told her that the interpreter would be available if she changed her mind later on in the interview. I also encouraged Barbara to feel comfortable asking me to repeat myself or to clarify anything that she may have misunderstood. She encouraged me to do the same. Barbara's communication skills were excellent. I had no problems understanding her speech, and she only has minimal difficulties reading my lips. When she did not understand, she did not hesitate to ask for clarification.

I talked to Barbara about SSI benefits and Medicaid. I gave her some information on both services. Barbara stated that she was already in the process of obtaining SSI and Medicaid since she recently turned eighteen. She felt confident that she would be eligible for both services and assured me that she would let me know as soon as she found out anything more from either agency.

I discussed with Barbara the three-prong criteria process to determine eligibility for vocational rehabilitation services. She was already knowledgeable about the process of eligibility determination and the subsequent services that may follow. I also gave her information about SACAP (State of Alabama Client Assistance Program). As an advocate herself, she was well aware of the CAP.

I briefly discussed Barbara's medical records with her, assuring their accuracy. Barbara went for a second examination and testing in March. She anticipated that updated records would be needed either for VR services or at her college or university. I did not have the most recent test results, so I got Barbara to sign a release for those records. Barbara spoke freely about her meningitis as a child and her subsequent hearing loss. She did not seem bitter or angry about the loss and in fact spoke of her hearing loss as an interesting challenge that has only made her a stronger person. She said that she is an active advocate for the deaf community as well as for persons with disabilities in general.

I asked Barbara about the two colleges in her home area. She said that both Enterprise State Junior College and Lurlene B. Wallace Junior College in Andalusia had discouraged her from attending since they did not have the adequate services to accommodate Barbara. I reminded her that if she chose to go to either one of these universities, they would be legally responsible to make appropriate accommodations for her based on Section 504 of the Rehabilitation Act of 1973 and the ADA. I told her not to be discouraged or feel limited in her decision-making. Barbara also mentioned McArthur Douglas State, a technical college in Opp. She mentioned that her father thought it might be a good idea for her to be trained in a more specialized trade or craft at this local college. Without asking, I could tell that Barbara was not excited about that prospect, but that she would be willing to do that if it were her only option. She said on more than one occasion that she did not want to put a financial strain on her family. However, she also spoke passionately about her desire to teach. Her main areas of interest were in teaching high school English and/or creative writing.

I discussed with Barbara the urgency of choosing a college since fall classes would be starting in a few short months. I also informed Barbara that if she were found eligible, VR could not pay for out-of-state tuition. I encouraged Barbara to look at public colleges and universities in the state. She expressed interest in attending Auburn University but said that she wanted to visit the campus first to make sure she liked it. I encouraged her to make a visit as soon as possible to help her with her decision. I gave Barbara an accommodation availability checklist to complete when she spoke with disabilities services personnel at Auburn.

Before leaving, I gave Barbara a list of Websites that contained valuable information regarding transition from high school to college for deaf and hard of hearing students. Barbara and I set up our second meeting for March 8.

2/1–End case notes for session #1 (Initial Interview)

3/7–Begin case notes for Barbara's visit to Auburn University: Barbara visited Auburn University to help her decide if this college would meet her educational goals. She spoke with people at the College of Education and the Program for Students with Disabilities. She received a lot of information and filled out quite a bit of paperwork. Barbara also picked up an application for Auburn University and received some information about financial aid, Pell Grants, and loans.

3/7–End case notes for Barbara visited Auburn University

3/8–Begin case notes for session #2: Barbara arrived at the session bubbling with excitement. She had visited Auburn University the day before and could not wait to tell me all about it. She met with a representative of the College of Education who gave her the requirements for their program. Barbara also met with the director of the Program for Students with Disabilities, Dr. Nancy Jamison. Barbara said that both the College of Education and Dr. Jamison were excited about the possibility of her attending Auburn. They encouraged her to get her application in as soon as possible with the hopes of starting classes in the fall.

Barbara told me about a captioning service that Dr. Jamison was going to begin starting fall semester. She is going to use RapidText to produce real-time captioning for deaf students who are in heavy lecture classes. Dr. Jamison offered this service to Barbara as an alternative to interpreter services. Barbara was eager to try this out since she had never been exposed to it during her secondary education.

3/8–End case notes for session #2

12/16–Begin case notes for session #4: Barbara met with me to discuss her first semester at Auburn University. She happily informed me that she received all As except for one B. She loved being away at college but also dearly missed her family back home and was excited to return for the break. Barbara said that the Program for Students with Disabilities was very helpful if she ever needed anything and that housing was also equally accommodating. She was very pleased with her first semester. I told her how proud I was of her accomplishments and told her to keep up the good work.

12/16–End case notes for session #4

Case notes at the end of each semester were very similar to the one above. Barbara never encountered any major problems during her time at Auburn. She always seemed excited to be back home with her family but equally as eager to return the following semester. Barbara was an absolute pleasure to work with. Her abilities and strengths were complemented by her excellent attitude and bubbly personality. She obtained employment upon graduation at Opelika High School (OHS), where she interned the previous spring. Barbara made frequent calls when she was first placed. She adjusted well to her new job and found it very rewarding.

Barbara was conscientious and responsible throughout her college career. She joined a sorority and became an active member of the SGA. Barbara also wrote numerous articles for the school newspaper and won a regional poetry contest during her junior year. Barbara became president of the Advocates for Disabilities Awareness (ADA) her senior year and was vice-president of her sorority her sophomore year. Barbara was an active participant in a variety of college activities, enjoying various clubs and sporting events. However, Barbara never neglected her studies. She made excellent grades, graduating with a 3.65.

Job Placement

Rationale for Job

Barbara interned for OHS during spring semester, year 4. OHS was a little hesitant at first when Barbara's disability was made known. They voiced their concerns regarding her ability to communicate with the students and the costs of interpreter services and questioned the safety of her inability to hear the fire alarm. I assured them that Barbara had excellent communication skills. Since the class size was no more than 25, Barbara felt that she would be able to speech read and would not need an ASL interpreter. Barbara did ask for an interpreter for any meetings or activities that occurred in a larger setting, such as in an auditorium. After meeting with Barbara, OHS quelled all of their anxieties and concerns regarding her disability. They saw her as a capable young woman with a passion for teaching. Instead of being troublesome about providing some simple accommodations and modifications, they were eager to make their school more accessible for Barbara. Barbara absolutely loved interning at OHS. She was thrilled when they offered her the opportunity to return for a full-time position.

Follow-along/Postemployment Services

Postemployment Services

Barbara and I discussed postemployment services, and did not see any need for them. She felt that she could make the proper adjustments within the ninety days prior to closure. I agreed with Barbara on this and did not include any postemployment services in her IPE.

Closure Memo

I wrote a closure memo to Barbara, congratulating her on her success and told her what a pleasure she had been to work with. I also sent letters to Dr. Jamison and Mr. Joe Hanson at Auburn University. They were both key participants in accommodating her during her college career. They were very eager to help Barbara in any way and seemed genuinely motivated by her success as both a college student and as a person with a disability.

My final letter was sent to OHS. I thanked them for allowing Barbara the opportunity to shine and flourish at their school. I assured them that I had no doubts that she would become one of their best teachers. I also told them to contact me if they had any questions or comments about Barbara or her accommodations.

November 8
Dear Barbara,

I am writing this letter to inform you that you have been successfully employed for 90 days. At this time I am going to close your case. I want to congratulate you on all that you have achieved. From the moment you walked into my office for the first time I knew that you were destined for greatness. I am so glad that I had the opportunity to see you "in action" with your students. It is very apparent how passionate you are about your students and your job. You are truly a success, and I am very proud of you!

Please don't hesitate to call me if you ever need anything or if you have any questions. Good luck with your future endeavors!

Sincerely,
Allison Shipp

Dear Dr. Jamison,

I am writing this letter to inform you that Barbara has been successfully employed at Opelika High School as a 10th grade English teacher for 90 days. At this time I am going to close out her case. I want to thank you for all that you did to help Barbara achieve her goal. It has been a pleasure working with you, and I will recommend Auburn University to all of my future consumers as a disability-friendly environment. I had the opportunity to see Barbara "in action" with her students. It is very apparent how passionate she is about her job. You have been an essential piece of her success, and I want to again thank you for your willingness and eagerness to make Barbara's education opportunities consistent with her capabilities and potential.

Please don't hesitate to call me if you ever need anything or if you have any questions. I am looking forward to working with you again in the near future.

Sincerely,
Allison Shipp

Dear Joe Hanson,

I am writing this letter to inform you that Barbara has been successfully employed at Opelika High School as a 11th grade English teacher for 90 days. At this time I am going to close out her case. I want to thank you for all that you did to help Barbara achieve her goal. It has been a pleasure working with you, and I will recommend Auburn University to all of my future consumers as a disability-friendly environment. I had the opportunity to see Barbara "in action" with her students. It is very apparent how passionate she is about her job. You have been an essential piece of her success, and I want to again thank you for your willingness and eagerness to make Barbara's education opportunities consistent with her capabilities and potential.

Please don't hesitate to call me if you ever need anything or if you have any questions. I am looking forward to working with you again in the near future.

Sincerely,

Allison Shipp

Postscript

The case in its entirety was over 100 pages in length. I put all of the documentation, my narrative, and all of the completed forms in a three-ring binder. I put a picture of Barbara on the front. The purpose of the picture was to remind myself and the readers that I was working with a real individual. Putting a "face with a case" made things a little more realistic, and I found myself truly identifying with Barbara. I filled out all of the various forms and applications as if I were Barbara or the party responsible for the information. I downloaded some of the forms from the internet and obtained others by directly visiting the source (i.e., Auburn University's Program for Students with Disabilities, Vocational Rehabilitation Services, College of Education). Much of the information that I "gave" to Barbara was found online or in journals. In addition, I printed out some information for Barbara such as a college guide for students who are deaf and hard of hearing. Due to space constraints the forms and additional information are not included this replication. However, I have listed below various sections and pages found in the completed case notebook:

- Photocopy of the chapter/case of Barbara–seven pages total
- Alabama Department of Rehabilitation Services forms–twenty-one pages total
  - Alabama's Interagency Electronic Linkage System agreement–one page
  - Personal information–two pages
  - Employment worksheet–two pages
  - Application intake worksheet–two pages

- ○ Medical history and questionnaire–two pages
- ○ Authorization, disclosure, and release of information–four pages
- ○ Individualized Plan for Employment–three pages
- ○ Plan review worksheet–one page
- ○ Job readiness worksheet–two pages
- ○ Employment worksheet–two pages
- ○ Alabama Department of Rehabilitation Services information–seventeen pages total
- ○ Services for the deaf information–two pages
- ○ Client Assistance Program handout–one page
- ○ Transitional goals–one page
- ○ Social Security Income/Medicaid–thirteen pages
- Auburn University College of Education documents–five pages total
  - ○ Secondary English language arts curriculum guide–one page
  - ○ Completed curriculum worksheet–one page
  - ○ Teacher education student checklist–three pages
- Auburn University's Program for Students with Disabilities–twenty pages total
  - ○ Treating physician's disability documentation form–two pages
  - ○ Personal and background information form–two pages
  - ○ Authorization to obtain information form–two pages
  - ○ Accommodation/memo worksheet–one page
  - ○ Accommodations memo for professor–one page
  - ○ Confidentiality/information sharing agreement–two pages
  - ○ Parental permission to receive information release–one page
  - ○ Permission to release information–one page
  - ○ Criteria for disability documentation–three pages
  - ○ "Serving students with hearing impairments" handout–one page
  - ○ Accommodation descriptions–four pages
- Miscellaneous worksheets/information–thirty-three pages total
  - ○ Medical information on hearing impairments–two pages
  - ○ Hearing Disabilities book chapter–twenty-two pages
  - ○ Resource list for hearing impaired students entering college–one page
  - ○ Realtime Captioning: Access Equal Success article–four pages
  - ○ Postsecondary program interview accommodation checklist–one page
  - ○ "My career inventory" worksheet–one page
  - ○ "My work values" worksheet–two pages
- Workplace/job documents–ten pages total
  - ○ DOT/O*NET job listings, requirements, and descriptions–one page

- ○ Alabama's highly qualified teacher criteria–two pages
- ○ Alabama teacher certification requirements–three pages
- ○ Guide to determine "highly qualified" requirements–four pages

Appendix B

CARDIOVASCULAR DISEASE:
THE COMPLETED CASE OF JAMES

Cardiovascular Disease:
Practical Implications of the Case of James

J. CHAD DUNCAN

At first glance, I thought this would be a class project that I could spend a long weekend or so and complete. This project, however, was a different story. The good news was I started early in the semester, rather than waiting, as it took considerably more time to complete than I had anticipated. The complexity of the case required that I research many resources. Because students were encouraged to seek advice from professionals in the resolution of the case, I found myself engaged in many useful and fruitful discussions with a variety of community resources–physicians, rehabilitation counselors, cardiac rehabilitation personnel, hospital administrators, community credit counselors, and other social service workers. I was able to gain useful and insightful information on finding resources, and how each professional approached this case situation with similar cases such as James.

I must give credit to David Patterson, C.R.C., Angela Scarborough, C.R.C., Amanda Ingram, C.R.C., and Keith Brown, C.R.C. for helping me in the completion of James's case. Mr. Patterson, a rehabilitation counselor located at Auburn University assisted me in understanding the Alabama Department of Rehabilitation Services' procedures and processes, while Angela, Amanda, and Keith (fellow students and now practicing rehabilitation counselors in Alabama and Kentucky) provided me with some guidance in how they presented this case to fellow students in the "Principles and Practices of Case Management in Rehabilitation Counseling" class at Auburn University. In the day-to-day existence of vocational rehabilitation, I know that James's case may have been more complex than the assumptions I made in the resolution of the case. James was very optimistic and responsive to his situation, which may not have occurred as quickly as it did in my case resolution. Yet, it is our responsibility to motivate and assist clients in adopting a perspective of optimism and hope.

Case Resolution

Medical Overview–Etiology

Primary Issue: James is a forty-four-year-old man who experienced a myocardial infarction with no prior history of heart disease. Three months after the myocardial infarction, James underwent triple bypass surgery.

Secondary Issues: Six months after the heart attack, James became progressively depressed. James was diagnosed with the following heart conditions:

1. S/P anteroseptal myocardial infarction
2. S/P coronary artery bypass ×3
3. Class IIC cardiac disease
4. Dyspnea on slight exertion

The American Heart Association (AHA) lists six risk factors that contribute to coronary heart disease. These factors are tobacco smoke, high blood pressure, high blood cholesterol, physical inactivity, obesity, and diabetes. Of these risk factors, we know that James has two (smoking and high blood pressure).

Course and Prognosis

The Centers for Disease Control and Prevention has reported that there is one death every thirty-four seconds due to cardiovascular disease each year. Cardiovascular disease is the leading cause of death among any group of people in the United States.

Myocardial infarction: A myocardial infarction is more commonly known as a heart attack. This occurs when there is an interruption of blood flow (coronary artery) to the myocardium (heart muscle), resulting in damage to the heart muscle. This damage invariably leads to congestive heart failure. Thus, one can conclude that heart failure is progressive in nature and can worsen over time if proper steps are not taken. James's myocardial infarction occurred at the anterior part of the intraventricular septum.

Coronary artery bypass: An invasive medical procedure that uses blood vessels to go around or "bypass" clogged coronary arteries of the heart. This allows proper blood flow through the new vessels to the heart muscle. Normally these blood vessels are harvested from the patient's leg.

Class IIC heart disease: James was classified as having Class IIC heart disease according to the New York Heart Association's *Nomenclature and Criteria for Diagnosis of Disease of the Heart and Great Vessels.* There are four different classes that fall under functional capacity ranging from Class I (without limitation) to Class IV (inability to carry on any physical activity). James has been classified with Class II, which the New York Heart Association (1994) describes as "Patients with cardiac disease resulting in slight limitation of physical activity. They are comfortable at rest. Ordinary physical activity results in fatigue, palpitation, dyspnea, or anginal pain." The second set of criteria in the New York classification system is *objective assessment.* There are four assessments ranging from A to D. James currently has been classified with "C." C means that James has a moderately severe case of cardiovascular disease. A complete listing of criteria can be accessed from The Criteria Committee of the New York Heart Association: *Nomenclature and Criteria for Diagnosis of Diseases of the Heart and Great Vessels* (9th Edition). Boston, MA: Little, Brown & Co; 1994: pp. 253–256.

Dyspnea: The *Merck Manual* describes *dyspnea* as an unpleasant sensation and difficulty in breathing. There are seven clinical types of dyspnea: pulmonary, physiologic, cardiac, chemical, circulatory, psychogenical, and central. James's dyspnea occurs from slight exertion. This is consistent with the symptoms of physiologic type.

Secondary issue: Depression–Etiology of depression: Information on depression may be obtained from several internet sites and the *DSM-IV-TR.* Some Internet sites that can be accessed are: http://www.continuinged ucation.com/pharmtech/depression/depression.pdf and http://www.psy chologyinfo.com/depression/major.htm

Major depression: The *DSM-IV-TR* (2000) criteria for major depressive Episode are that "Five (or more) of the following symptoms have been present during the same two-week period and represent a change from previous functioning; at least one of the symptoms is either (1) depressed mood or (2) loss of interest or pleasure." The symptoms can include fatigue occurring everyday; indecisiveness, feeling empty or sad everyday, insomnia everyday, or hypersomnia everyday, and/or recurring thoughts of death. To obtain further information on depression refer to the *DSM-IV-TR* in the Mood Disorders section.

Functional limitations/impediments to employment ADLs, general limitations/considerations: Cardiovascular: According to *The Disability Handbook* by Jason Andrew (2000+):

1. Mobility
2. Standing for prolonged periods
3. Lifting , pushing, pulling, reaching, pressing
4. Stamina
5. Endurance

6. Temperature extremes
7. Dizziness (under what conditions?)
8. Tolerance to environmental changes (gases, fumes, air quality, altitude changes)

Specific limitations to James's case: Limitations were taken from the cardiologist's report:

1. Walking: one-half to one mile
2. Stairs: four flights
3. Lifting: 10–20 lbs
4. Standing: 50 percent of the time
5. Stooping, bending, twisting: Restricted
6. Temperature extremes: Avoid

Common limitations/considerations: Depression: According to *The Disability Handbook:*

1. Interpersonal skills
2. Dependability
3. Decision-making
4. Dealing with frequent change
5. Stamina
6. Strength
7. Judgment
8. Motivation or initiative
9. Follow-through or ability to follow instructions
10. Drowsiness from interrupted sleep
11. Concentration
12. Memory
13. Stability and consistency of behavior

Specific limitations to James's case: No specific limitations were documented by a professional prior to the intake interview. James mentioned in the intake interview that his relationship with his wife and daughters has been strained, and because of financial pressures he feels progressively depressed.

Medications: The only reported medication that James has been taking is Aldomet®. James has noted that he has not always taken this medication as directed. Best sources to refer to regarding medications are the *Physician's Desk Reference* and *PDR Nurse's Drug Handbook.* Other information may be obtained on the Internet (i.e., www.rxlist.com) but do not rely entirely on these types of resources.

Aldomet: methyldopa: Aldomet is used to treat high blood pressure. It has been reported there are various side effects, e.g., dizziness, decreased sexual ability, headaches that one may encounter when taking this drug.

Assistive technology: No assistive technology is being used at the present time. It was noted in the cardiologist's report that James was nearsighted and has no glasses. At the interview, James stated that he currently did not wear or have glasses.

Assessments

Initial Interview

My initial interview with James took place at the Alabama Department of Rehabilitation Services (ADRS) office in Opelika, Alabama, on April 1. James was referred to me by a caseworker at the local hospital. James was prompt in arriving for his appointment. James presented himself as a well-mannered, middle-aged man during the interview. His physical stature was medium build, and his appearance may be characterized as being neatly groomed. During the initial intake, James did not make consistent eye contact, especially when asked about his financial situation. James, however, appeared to be very honest and upfront about his situation. James has been married for twenty years to his wife, Sarah. His last completed grade was seventh at the age of sixteen. He and Sarah have three girls ages fourteen, sixteen, and eighteen. He stated that his oldest child is graduating from high school this year and plans to go to college. James is very proud of his daughters and their accomplishments. His relationship with his family was considered excellent prior to his heart attack, but now his relationships with Sarah and the girls is somewhat strained due to a lack of resources and the resultant impediments of his heart attack and inability to return to his former work. Currently his wife and two eldest daughters are working. Financially, James reports that the mortgage is two months past due (their home of fifteen years) and that he cannot pay the hospital charges. James stated that his girls volunteered their savings to help. I could tell that this bothered James by his nonverbal cues (looking away, shrugging, arms crossed, and lowered voice). Current transportation issues include the reliability of the family car (ten years old and in constant need of repair). James said that his wife has made contact with the local department of social services. At the conclusion of the initial interview, James was asked if he smoked. James replied, "Yes, but I am trying to stop." His clothing did smell of smoke.

When asked about his health and what physicians he has seen, James stated that he was seeing only one physician at this time. James mentioned that he did not feel comfortable asking his physicians any questions. On further questioning, James confided that he felt that his medication was causing sexual problems and that he did not want to ask questions about this because his physician was treating him *pro bono.* I obtained permission from James to contact this physician to inquire about other medications that James could take without this side effect. James stated that he would go by the physician's office to fill out proper Health Insurance Portability and Accountability Act (HIPAA) paperwork to allow me to ask about his medication.

Clarification of and Need for Additional Assessments

James's history in supporting a family, buying a house, and owning a car with little formal education demonstrates that he is a fighter. James is willing to succeed and is much more capable than what his IQ testing shows. Because of James gender and past cardiac history, interventions in nutrition and health habits will be necessary. Because of his depression and stress, he may need psychological counseling. James will also need financial assistance to help offset his current unemployment and to alleviate stress occurring from this debt.

James received a medical evaluation from a cardiologist two months after his wife contacted social services. Other medical evaluations are needed to determine the extent of dyspnea, the effects of the hydrocele, and the effect of a hole in his left eardrum as well as to determine James's general health.

Plan: Empower James to establish goals for himself and personalize them for better meaning.

Assumptions

I made several assumptions about James and his situation:

- The hospital where James was treated had not transferred James's outstanding bill to a collection agency.
- James's family income fell within the income guidelines to receive Alabama Hospital Care Program Assistance.
- James wants to change his negative lifestyle habits (i.e., to stop smoking, begin exercising, and eating more appropriately).
- James and family were found to be eligible for food stamps and cash assistance through Temporary Assistance for Needy Families (TANF) concurrent with his eligibility to receive vocational rehabilitation services.

Eligibility

James was found eligible for vocational rehabilitation services. James was determined eligible on the basis of having both a physical (coronary artery disease) and a mental (depression) impairment that constituted substantial limitation/impediments to employment. James presented with significant attendant factors as well: James's disabilities presented a substantial barrier to employment without assistance and services from the Alabama Department of Vocational Rehabilitation. James met the criterion of expanded services because he requires more than three months of physical restoration services (cardiac rehabilitation). Finally, James is eligible due to his low educational achievement, limited financial resources, and limited employment opportunities due to the geographic area where he lives (rural) and narrow work history, all significant impediments to his obtaining employment.

Individualized Plan for Employment

Vocational Goal

James's vocational goal is to obtain employment in a vocational area and atmosphere similar to his past job as a material handler in a machine shop. James commented that he likes and works best in a team-oriented atmosphere. James will be a good candidate for job placement because of his motivation to return to work. James was very enthusiastic about his return to work because he wants to provide for his family and pay his bills. Vocational exploration for James has identified the occupation of Assembly Inspector, DOT Code: 763.684-010 and O*NET Code: 51-9061.05 Production Inspectors, Testers, Graders, Sorters, Samplers, and Weighers.

Intermediate Objectives

James's intermediate objectives are to address his depression, quit smoking, and attend a cardiac rehabilitation program. James appears as a well-motivated candidate for cardiac rehabilitation program due to his age, desire to obtain employment, and desire to provide for his family. For James to achieve his vocational objective, he must attend a cardiac rehabilitation program to prepare him to take better care of himself physically and to understand his limitations due to coronary artery disease. Another objective for James is to obtain job-seeking skills. He may achieve this by taking job search classes through referral to the agency's employment specialist.

Services

Services that need to be coordinated for James are (a) cardiac rehabilitation program, (b) family counseling sessions, (c) credit counseling sessions,
(d) physician consultations (i.e., optometrist, internist, cardiologist examinations), and (e) job placement inclusive of job search classes. These services
will be provided by the ADRS. The costs of these services range considerably and will need to be researched to find the most cost efficient. A typical
cardiac rehabilitation program for sixteen weeks will cost in excess of $4,000.
James needs this program to assist him in obtaining his proposed lifestyle
changes. Optometry services plus obtaining a pair of glasses will cost around
$400. James needs to be seen by an optometrist to obtain glasses, due to his
myopia. Psychological services may range from $500 or greater depending
on the number of sessions James may require (secured from community
mental health and on a sliding scale). James needs counseling services to
address the depression he is currently experiencing. Cardiology and internist
services may exceed $1,000 depending on testing and services provided. Job
placement program costs are provided as a service absorbed by the VR
agency. Job placement services and job search classes will benefit James considerably in obtaining the job of his choice.

Evaluation of Services

James maintained contact with this VR counselor throughout the VR
process, reporting on his progress in counseling and cardiac rehabilitation.
When James secured employment, contact was made every two to four
weeks for ninety days. Upon James's successful case closure, he stated his
appreciation for the concern and assistance that VR provided him. He was
especially thankful and appreciative of the unconditional acceptance and
support from this counselor.

Terms and Conditions

James agreed that upon successful completion of his cardiac rehabilitation
program and job search classes that he would pursue employment. James
was also notified about the client assistance program (CAP). James's medication coverage will be discontinued after his case closure. Necessary pre-
cautions have been taken to make sure James gets his medication. To help
James with payment of his medications, a prorated drug assistance plan from
the drug manufacturer was arranged.

Delivery of Services

Case Notes

Work history: James has had a consistent work history since leaving school at the age of sixteen. James's jobs have always been in the area of heavy manual labor. James's work is consistent with his ability. *Vocationally,* James would like to go back to work in the same field. *Financially,* James feels there is a lot of pressure to make his house payment and meet other necessities of living. James is worried that he will lose his house and that his girls will not be able to go to college because they have no money. James is also concerned about paying his medical bills and feeling like he is a burden to his current physician. At the end of the initial interview, James was asked if he was informed about the Alabama Hospital Care Program. James acknowledged that he knew about it because the case manager at the hospital had mentioned it to him. James further explained that he did not ask if he was eligible because he was embarrassed to say anything in front of his family. James was asked about his wife's contacts with the local department of social services. James stated that they had an appointment in one week with Mr. S. Service.

Plan: Refer James to a cardiologist for an evaluation to determine current abilities and possible limitations relative to eligibility. James was also referred to a psychologist regarding his depression and the impact of depression relative to eligibility. I arranged for our next appointment in one week or concurrent with receipt of consultative reports.

Following initial interview: Call to hospital case manager: I called the hospital case manager and asked if she could pull James's file. After explaining James's situation, the case manager agreed that James did qualify for assistance under the Alabama Hospital Care Program. She stated that she could have paperwork ready for James to come by and complete. I asked if she could be present to assist James in completing the paperwork and she agreed. I called James and spoke with him about going by the hospital to fill out the paperwork as soon as he could. I asked James if he would like for me to meet him and assist him. James stated that he did not need me to be there and thanked me for my assistance.

Called mortgage lender: I called James's mortgage lender to ask if there was a possibility that James's mortgage payments could be deferred pending his rehabilitation. The bank officer was aware of James's situation, and she had contacted a local church that was willing to pay the bank interest only until James's rehabilitation was completed (approximately one-half of the payment is interest as James has approximately 50 percent equity in his home).

Called cardiologist: I spoke with the physician regarding James's concern about the sexual side effects of his current blood pressure medication. The cardiologist confirmed that James's medication did have that particular side effect. The cardiologist stated that he would address this issue at the next appointment. The cardiologist was asked several questions concerning James's condition in order to clarify issues regarding James's eligibility. The cardiologist asked me to send him a letter with my questions so he could address each of them when he sees James.

Letter to Cardiologist

Dear Dr. Cardiologist:

I am referring James to you for a medical evaluation to help in determining James's eligibility for Vocational Rehabilitation Services. Per our recent telephone conversation, I have listed several questions to assist me in the determination of eligibility and future planning for James. These questions are pertinent to James's current situation and to his future possibility of employment.

- What are James's functional limitations relative to mobility?
- Does he have any limitations in standing? If so what type?
- Would James have difficulty with temperature extremes?
- Will James have any stamina and/or endurance issues?
- Would James benefit from a cardiac rehabilitation program? What would be his prognosis?
- If you believe that James would benefit from cardiac rehabilitation program, is there a program available locally?

Thank you for your assistance with James and I look forward to working with you in the future.

Sincerely,

J. Chad Duncan

Rehabilitation Counselor

Response from Cardiologist

Dear Mr. Duncan:

Regarding our recent telephone conversation and your letter, I have come to the conclusion and recommendation that James would be a good candidate for a cardiac rehabilitation program. After talking about his options and travel situation, he would benefit from a local cardiac program. There is such a program at the hospital where James received his triple bypass surgery. This is not far from his home. Another benefit would be my ability to follow James's progress.

James was thoroughly examined at my office and his current prognosis would be highly improved with lifestyle changes and education regarding his medical condition. James's limitations have not changed significantly since the triple bypass. Specific Limitations for James:

- Walking: one-half to one mile
- Stairs: four flights
- Lifting: 10–20 lbs.
- Standing: 50 percent of the time
- Stooping, bending, twisting: Restricted
- Temperature extremes: Avoid

Regarding James's issue with his blood pressure medication, I have suggested a different medication that would not effect his sexual functioning, and discussed the potential side effects of this drug with him. James was very open and told me that he was seeing some other doctors about his other medical issues. If you have further questions concerning James's success in a cardiac program or his condition, please feel free to call me anytime.
Sincerely,
Dr. Cardiologist

Progress Note–May 15: (establishment of eligibility) James was prompt to this appointment. James seemed to be more candid and open about his current situation. James was very thankful for my assistance with the hospital. James stated that he will be seeing the cardiologist in a few days. We then went over the necessary steps and people that James may need to see to establish his eligibility over the next few weeks. James agreed to see several different specialists to help determine his eligibility. James agreed to see the following: a psychologist to evaluate him for the depression he is currently experiencing; an internist for a general medical examination and to further evaluate the hydrocele, and recurrent ear infections; a urologist to evaluate his hydrocele condition; an optometrist for his nearsightedness; a pulmonary specialist to evaluate his dyspnea, and an ENT doctor for evaluation of his left eardrum (hole)-recurrent infections in right ear with some hearing loss. James has already been referred to the cardiologist. During this session these appointments were scheduled.

Follow-up Note–May 17: The cardiologist responded to my questions concerning James's medical condition, limitations, and probable success in a cardiac rehabilitation program.

Follow-up Calls to James's Physicians

Optometrist: I spoke with the optometrist and it was confirmed that James indeed was nearsighted and that he would greatly benefit from wearing glasses. The optometrist stated that James's follow-up visit will be to select glasses upon approval from VR. After speaking with the optometrist a price was confirmed, and James will be able to pick up his glasses on the following appointment. The optometrist was asked to send a letter of his findings and recommendations for James's file.

Urologist: The urologist determined that James's hydrocele did not indicate any significant clinical findings. At this time, there is no need for treatment. The urologist was asked to send a letter of his findings for James's file.

Progress Note–May 27: James was again prompt for his appointment today. He seemed to be in high spirits and brought paperwork from all his physicians. I thanked James for being so thorough. After a long conversation about his wife and daughters, James said the meeting with the credit counselor was very helpful in assisting him and Sarah in understanding what was needed to pay his bills without filing for bankruptcy. James noted that talking with the credit counselor had lifted a huge weight off his shoulders.

On this date, it was determined, after thorough evaluation of all of James's records and physician reports, that he met the eligibility criteria to receive vocational rehabilitation services. James presents with a physical impairment (coronary artery disease) and mental impairment (depression) that constitutes substantial impediments to his ability to obtain and maintain employment. He cannot return to his former position. James will require VR services to obtain suitable employment.

Functional capacities/limitations: Due to James's current physical condition, he will not be able to return and maintain his previous employment. James has considerable limitations relative to employability. Physical limitations imposed by the cardiologist are:

- Walking: one-half to one mile
- Stairs: four flights
- Lifting: 10–20 lbs.
- Standing: 50 percent of the time
- Stooping, bending, twisting: Restricted
- Temperature extremes: Avoid

With these limitations, James will be unable to return to his previous occupation and place of employment. James is limited to jobs that are light duty.

Work skills: Due to James's educational level it will be beneficial and necessary for him to receive concrete instruction. James benefits most from instructions that are oral combined with short demonstration.

Significant attendant factors: There are several factors that affect James: (a) low educational attainment, (b) limited financial resources, (c) limited employment opportunities geographically, and (d) a narrow work history.

James's documented disabilities pose a substantial barrier to his ability to successfully obtain and maintain employment without necessary services from VR. James will also benefit considerably from physical restoration (cardiac rehabilitation). He will need to access services beyond three months that is not routine medical maintenance.

To assist in the development of the Individualized Plan for Employment (IPE), James was referred to a vocational evaluator to assist him in the determination of his interests and for occupational exploration. It was noted that James may need assistance in reading.

Letter to Vocational Evaluator

Dear Vocational Evaluator:

James has been declared eligible to receive VR services on the basis of his cardiovascular condition. I am referring him to you for assistance in occupational exploration. James has a good work history and he has primarily performed manual lifting tasks due to his exceptional strength. Unfortunately, he is unable to do this type of job any longer due to the impediments imposed as a result of his cardiovascular disease. James's current limitations imposed by the cardiologist:

- Walking: one-half to one mile
- Stairs: four flights
- Lifting: 10–20 lbs.
- Standing: 50 percent of the time
- Stooping, bending, twisting: Restricted
- Temperature extremes: Avoid

I would like for you to explore jobs that are similar to his past job of 15 years and others you may deem relevant given his educational and experiential background. He spoke very highly of his past job, and I believe that he would prosper in a similar environment. I also would like to evaluate James's math skills. From his records James performed very well in practical math, but not in reading. In my interactions with James, I believe that he is very capable of performing at a higher functional level than the WAIS-IV reported scores. As you will discover, James will do best in work that requires handling, sorting, tending, and/or manipulating activity.

James will be entering a cardiac rehabilitation program within the next week or so. This should give us time to research possible job openings in the area dependent upon your recommendations. James will also be receiving job placement services.

Sincerely,

J. Chad Duncan

Rehabilitation Counselor

After third session: Received report from the vocational evaluator. The report showed that James has strong interests in the area of mechanical abilities. The vocational evaluator noted that while James was adamant about not working in the areas of food or custodial services, he wanted to work and as a last resort he would consider custodial work. The vocational evaluator, however, reported that neither of these areas would lead to successful employment for James. The evaluator suggested that James seek employment in an industrial or shop setting that would allow him to work with others. The evaluator reported that James's perspective was hopeful for the future.

Progress Note–June 15: Made call to James's pulmonary specialist:

Pulmonary specialist: It was determined that James's dyspnea is due to his current heart condition and not for any other reason. James's dyspnea should not interfere with his ability to enter a cardiac rehabilitation program, gain, or maintain employment. In fact, it should help.

Received letter from ENT physician/audiologist: I received a letter from the ENT physician that confirms James does have a slight hearing loss in his right ear. The ENT physician also diagnosed an ear infection in James's left ear. Eardrops were prescribed to eliminate the infection. The audiologist recommends that James should avoid loud noise and, if exposed, use proper ear protection. It was also recommended that when James is listening to people talk that he has his better ear to the speaker. It was suggested that James maintain annual check-ups to monitor any further hearing loss. A letter documenting this was placed in James's case file.

Progress Note–June 30: James was seen today for the development of his IPE. After some discussion of the evaluator's report, and searching for similar occupations, it was determined that James would like to return to similar work where his limitations would not impede him and would be consistent with his physical ability. Accordingly, the vocational goal selected by James is Assembly Inspector, DOT Code: 763.684-010 or O*NET Code: 51-9061.05, Production Inspectors, Testers, Graders, Sorters, Samplers, and Weighers.

James is aware that he needs a job that has lighter duties to match his impediments. James is limited to light work within controlled environmental conditions. For James to succeed in obtaining this desired vocational goal he must undergo cardiac rehabilitation. The proposed cardiac rehabilitation program is a comprehensive program that will assist James in regaining his strength, teach him how to exercise properly, how to maintain a well balanced diet, how to stop smoking, how to deal with anxiety, and the importance of compliance with prescribed drugs.

James currently does not fully understand how to gain control of his health issues. He understands that there is a need and necessity for him to obtain and maintain his goal of work. This lack of understanding is currently creating a great deal of angst for James. James believes that this is a major contributing factor to his depression.

Proper releases were obtained prior to this session. James was referred to a psychologist to deal with his depression. This psychologist referred James and family to Family Life Counseling Services to help with family issues. The psychologist has arranged for future appointments to assist James with his depression and to learn methods that will facilitate his adaptation to his chronic health conditions.

James was referred to a cardiac specialist and it was recommended that he would benefit from cardiac rehabilitation. James decided on a program at the local hospital where transportation would not be an issue.

James's vocational goals have been discussed with job placement services. I have actively researched local industry to match James's interests and limitations with local employment opportunities. Job placement services are aware that James will undergo a cardiac rehabilitation program. Once James completes cardiac rehabilitation, he will meet with job placement services and me to seek appropriate job leads.

The IPE was reviewed and discussed with James. James was made aware that the IPE can be amended, if necessary. James was asked if he had any questions or concerns with the IPE. James stated that he had no questions and that he was looking forward to regaining his health and getting a job. James signed the IPE.

Progress Note–July 15: I was contacted by James today. He stated that he was beginning cardiac rehab today; and he also said that counseling was going well. James said that he was looking forward to this new chapter of his life.

Progress Note–August 10: James called to thank us for helping him obtain glasses. He states that it is amazing what he can see now. James mentioned that he is seeing his therapist once every two weeks for the next month and then he will have completed counseling. He states that he feels more up-beat and looks forward to returning to work. His relationships with Sarah and the girls are much improved.

Progress Note–September 23: James has completed cardiac rehabilitation. Today he is starting job placement classes at the Easter-Seals Achievement Center.

Progress Note–October 12: After one week of job placement classes, James reported that he feels more confident in finding a job. He stated that he has learned how to complete an application and how to look for jobs in the local market. James stated that he could sense a major difference in his home situation and it was for the better. He stated that everyone is eating more nutritiously, and that everybody understands that by doing this, they are helping him and themselves at the same time. James stated that he (and the employment specialist) had not yet found a suitable job. I told James that I would call his job placement worker about a possible job opportunity. I told James that I had been contacted by a local industry that was searching for an individual who was reliable and dependable.

Progress Note–October 27: I contacted the job placement specialist and told him about possible placement at a local business called Leonard Peterson. I explained that they make high end wood cabinetry and furniture for school science laboratories. I arranged for an interview with James's permission. This position meets the environmental conditions that James requires.

Progress Note–October 30: James and I met at Leonard Peterson. James was on time. I told James that I would help him with the application, but James stated that he felt like he could do it by himself. Following the interview, James said that he felt like he did well. He said the human resource manger would call him later this week. I told James that I had another job possibility, and although it is a similar job, it did not pay as well as Leonard Peterson. James stated that he would be interested if the job at Leonard Peterson did not come through.

Progress Note–November 5: I met with the job placement specialist concerning James's interview with Leonard Peterson. The human resource manager spoke highly of James, stating that he thought James had great potential. His only concern with James was his limited ability in reading, but that this job did not require reading as an essential function. I visited Leonard Peterson along with the job placement specialist and met with the human resource manager regarding his concerns in employing James. After some discussion regarding job duties, the willingness of the company to modify the job's lifting requirement from medium to light exertion (even though the job was classified as medium, the human resource manager acknowledged that this particular job could be modified because everything is moved by wheeled carts, and the load could be easily accommodated to a light exertional load without compromising production). I asked the manager about potential benefits. She stated that there was a health plan available for all employees after a 90 day trial work period, and that for this particular position compensation would be $10.00 per hour to start with yearly merit increases. She also noted that the career ladder for this occupational area was lead assembler and assembly supervisor and that openings occur on a regular basis.

Progress Note–November 11: James called me to say that he was hired on a probationary status. He said that with his background he was a good match, and with minimal training he should do fine. James was very excited and thanked me for helping him get the job. I told James that he did all the hard work and that I was excited for him. James stated he would start in one week. He mentioned that he was nervous, but at the same time that he has been blessed.

Progress Note–November 14: James came in today as he begins work tomorrow. James mentioned that he and his family had completed family counseling and that they were doing well. He was very thankful that we assisted him and his family at such a vulnerable time in their lives. I told James what to expect from the agency over the next ninety days. I told him once he successfully completed ninety days of employment, we would evaluate his case and mutually determine the closure date. James understood this and thanked us for helping him. I sent a letter of appreciation to the human resource manager at Leonard Peterson thanking her for hiring James, noting that he will be a reliable employee and, in time, an asset to the company.

Progress Note–December 16: James called to say the job is going well. He also mentioned that he has maintained smoke free status and he was using the skills that the psychologist taught him about stress reduction. I congratulated James on his successes and told him to keep it up.

Progress Note–March 15: I called James today about case closure. I told James I was very proud and excited for him and his achievements. James responded with thanking me and VR for being there for him and his family. James said that his health benefits have started, noting that this is the first health plan they have ever had. He is very much at ease with his life situation. James stated that he was given a one-dollar raise to $11.00 per hour following his ninety day review.

Job Placement

Rationale for Job

The job of assembler closely fit James's vocational interests and his desire to be in a factory setting. The job was considered medium duty work, but with an accommodation, the job was converted to light without any lost of productivity. Two essential functions for this position were identified: First, to assure that items produced meet or exceed quality standards; that is, there would be no imperfections in the product, and the second essential function was to keep an accurate accounting of the number of products being stored for delivery and the number of products being sent out each day. Both of these essential functions were well within James's ability. James can sight read words and with a short demonstration he was able to record the number of products stored and shipped without error.

Postemployment Services

It is not anticipated that James will need postemployment services. James was notified of the State of Alabama Client Assistance Program (SACAP) should he disagree with this decision.

Closure Memo

Upon successful completion of ninety days of employment, a letter was mailed to James (case closure had been discussed with James previously, and he agreed that it was time for his case to be closed) congratulating him on the successful attainment of his goal of employment. Other letters of thanks were sent to the director of the cardiac rehabilitation program and to the social worker who referred James to VR, acknowledging James's successful rehabilitation. A letter was also sent to his employer thanking the company for making the necessary accommodations that allowed James to be a successful employee.

Closure Letters

Dear James,

I would like to congratulate you on your success in obtaining and maintaining employment. It has been a pleasure working with a person who has such determination to succeed. At this time of great personal accomplishment I am, as we discussed, going to close your case as successfully rehabilitated. I commend you on your success and wish you and your family the best of luck and success in the future.

If you have any questions or concerns, feel free to contact me anytime.

Sincerely,

J. Chad Duncan

Rehabilitation Counselor

Dear Director of Cardiac Rehabilitation:

It has been a pleasure to see your cardiac rehabilitation program. It was certainly impressive and most successful for James. I look forward to working with your organization in the future. Your organization is definitely a valuable resource for our community. The professionalism and kindness of your staff was apparent and commented about several times by James. He stated that your therapists motivated him, even on the days he did not feel like doing anything. His wife is also happy that you have helped her husband understand the consequences of poor health habits, and that living and eating healthy is really better in all regards.

Thank you very much for being such an important factor in James's success.

Sincerely,

J. Chad Duncan

Rehabilitation Counselor

Dear Mr. Leonard Peterson:

Thank you for hiring James. I know that you have acquired an asset to your company. I would also like to thank you for listening to our suggestions in making accommodations for James's position. I feel that James is the right individual for your company and that your recent increase in his hourly wage demonstrates that confidence.

If you have any questions or concerns, please feel free to contact me anytime.

I look forward to assisting you and your company in the future.

Sincerely,

J. Chad Duncan

Rehabilitation Counselor

Postscript

The case that was presented to the instructor and classmates, in its entirety was over 100 pages in length. The final product was compiled in a three-ring binder with dividers separating each section addressed, and was presented to my classmates in a power-point format. To give this project a personal feel, a picture of what I thought James looked like was placed on the cover of my report, and was projected on a screen throughout the power-point presentation. By displaying a picture of how I thought James appeared gave his case a more human feel, and a primary reason to exhaust all possible options for James in his rehabilitation journey. I obtained forms from the Alabama Department of Vocational Rehabilitation to document the flow of James's case. I also used the internet extensively to research James's health conditions and other services that he required. Pamphlets describing services, e.g., cardiac rehabilitation, were tabbed and placed in sheet protectors and labeled within my final case analysis. I did not include the forms, information sheets, and pamphlets in the preceding narrative because this is an essential aspect of the resolution of the case that each person should research. Listed below are the various sections of my final product complete with the number of pages associated with each section denoting the comprehensiveness of documentation required for this project.

- Photocopy of the chapter/case of James—ten pages
- Alabama Department of Rehabilitation Services forms:
  - Alabama's Interagency Electronic Linkage System agreement—one page
  - Personal information—two pages
  - Consumer Guide—ten page booklet
  - Privacy Notice—two pages
  - Employment worksheet—two pages

- ○ Application intake worksheet–two pages
- ○ Medical history and questionnaire–two pages
- ○ Authorization, disclosure, and release of information–four pages
- ○ Individualized Plan for Employment–three pages
- ○ Plan review worksheet–one page
- ○ Job readiness worksheet–two pages
- ○ Employment worksheet– pages
- ○ State of Alabama Client Assistance Program (SACAP)–one pamphlet
- ○ Voter registration Application–two pages
- Miscellaneous worksheets/information:
  - ○ Guide on smoking cessation–six pages
  - ○ Fair Debt Collection Act–three pages
- Medical Information
  - ○ Information on dyspnea–one page
  - ○ Information on vision–one page
  - ○ Information on hydrocele–four pages
  - ○ Information on cardiac disease–thirteen pages
  - ○ Cardiac Rehabilitation Program brochure–five pages
  - ○ Information on depression–six pages
  - ○ Drug information–two pages
  - ○ Disability Handbook (information relating to impediments)–five pages
  - ○ Letters to and from professionals–twenty-six pages total
  - ○ Information on Actual Occupation–one page
  - ○ Job application–three pages
- DOT/O*NET Job description–seven pages

Final Thought

The experience of completing a project of this magnitude and the experience of reviewing and evaluating my peers' case presentations gave me considerable appreciation and insight into the complexities that rehabilitation counselors must address each and everyday in order to deliver quality services, as well as to convey the message of hope to vocational rehabilitation clients. This was a most beneficial experience that challenged me to do my best.

Chapter 8

THE CASE OF ALICE:
RHEUMATOID ARTHRITIS

Social Evaluation

Alice is thirty-one years of age and has one child, a son age seven. She and her son, David, live with her parents. David's father does not provide any support for his son. Alice received Temporary Aid for Needy Families (TANF) for two years following the birth of David. As a recipient of TANF, Alice was offered and enrolled in a special vocational training program in landscaping, a vocational area in which she had an interest. Since completion of this training program, Alice has not received any benefits from TANF. She quit this job which she said she "loved" because of increasing pain in her hands and wrists. She has for the past two years worked, on an occasional basis, as a waitress. She and David continue to live with her parents. Increasingly, the relationship between her parents, son, and herself has become strained. Her father wants her to move into an apartment and become self-sufficient. There appears to be a good relationship between the grandparents and David. Alice's parents, her father in particular, do not feel that Alice's complaints about pain and stiffness in her hands and wrists are completely true. Her father thinks Alice is too young to have arthritis.

Alice has not seen a physician about her complaints. She has been taking aspirin for the pain with some relief. She tends to have more stiffness and pain when the weather is cold and damp. The primary reason she quit her landscaping job was due to the variable weather conditions. She has stated that she would waitress full-time but the repeated use of her hands and wrists also tends to create pain and swelling. She has had morning stiffness for the last four years. She has not told her mother or father about the morning stiffness. There have been times-periods of three to six months-when she has been symptom free. It has been during these times that she worked full-time as a waitress. Alice very much wants to be independent of her parents and support her son and herself. She appears to be very sincere and motivated. She is very concerned and confused about her physical abilities; that is, why she cannot work consistently. She feels like her father does not believe there is a physical reason she cannot work full-time.

There has never been very much money for other than the basic necessities. Alice's parents, more often than not, have provided these. Recently, Alice's mother contacted the Department of Social Services asking them for medical assistance. Alice was referred to a medical clinic operated by the city for a complete evaluation.

Medical Evaluation

Alice has been in good health with the exception of pain and swelling in her hands and wrists which has increased to the point of seeking medical assistance. The onset of pain, stiffness, and swelling began approximately four years ago. She now complains that her hands remain swollen, that the pain is persistent, that she tires easily and that she has lost approximately twenty pounds in the past six months. She further noted that she is unable to satisfactorily perform some activities of daily living. She is, on occasion, unable to comb her hair, to brush her teeth, or to feed herself, and has great difficulty in dressing. She currently takes aspirin for relief of pain. This, however, has not always been effective.

Physician's Assessment

March: Physical Examination. Diffuse wrist swelling, particularly over the extensor retinaculum area of the wrist. The right wrist more severe than the left. No gross deformity is noted. X-ray Examination. X-rays are consistent with possible rheumatoid arthritis.
Diagnosis. Rheumatoid Arthritis
Medical Plan. Started on Indocin®. Return as needed.

April: Return to medical clinic for follow-up. Active RA is not controlled with Indocin. Patient to be referred to a Rheumatologist.

August: Referral to Rheumatologist

Review of Systems: Negative with the exception of hands and wrists. She has had recent weight loss of 20 pounds.

Physical Examination. Height: 5 feet 5 inches; Weight: 104 lbs. Blood pressure: 100/80.

ENT: Within normal limits.

Head and Neck: Normal Chest: Clear to P&A, Heart; Sounds are normal; rhythm is regular, no murmur, and no clinical enlargement.

Abdominal Examination: Negative.

Extremities: Findings are limited to the hands and wrists. Grip strength is 3/5. There is pain and swelling in the wrists and some limitation of motion in wrist flexion and extension. Slight hypertrophy of the metacarpophalangeal joint of both index fingers.

Medication Prescribed: Feldene®

Impressions: RA in remission at the present time.

Psychological Evaluation

The Department of Social Services referred Alice for psychological testing to include an intellectual assessment. The psychometric technician who evaluated Alice concluded that she was of bright normal intelligence. Her scores on the WAIS-IV were Verbal: 111; Performance: 114; Full Scale: 113. Because of her strong desire to enter the landscape training program, Alice was not given any vocational interest tests. All testing was completed as part of the Job and Training Division evaluation. Alice was accepted in the program and successfully completed the training. This evaluation was done approximately four years ago.

Vocational Evaluation

After graduation from high school, Alice worked as a door-to-door salesperson selling cosmetics. She did this for five years off and on. This work required her to have a car which she did not always have. Her father lent her his car, but never more than a day or two at a time as he needed the car to transport himself to and from work. Alice did not like this work although she said she enjoyed meeting new people.

Following the birth of her son, Alice was referred to the Job and Training Division for training in landscaping. The training program consisted of six months of on-the-job training with some classroom work. The classroom work focused on plant recognition, care, and basic landscape design. She was considered to be an excellent worker with much talent, particularly in being able to visualize a new design. Her specific responsibilities were to edge flower beds using shovels, edger tool, rakes, and grass snipers. She also mowed lawns, raked leaves, spread pine straw, grass seed, lime, and weeded the flower beds. The physical demands of the position required her to lift 50 pounds consistently and to lift 100 pounds with help occasionally. Additionally, the job required Alice to constantly stoop, bend, and reach as well as to use her hands and fingers. She quit this job because of the increasing pain, swelling, and stiffness she was having with her wrists and hands. The variable weather conditions, as well, tended to pose problems for her. Alice worked for approximately four years.

For the past two years Alice has, on an occasional basis, been a waitress in a local bar. She has been able to work this job for periods up to several months before her hands bothered her to such an extent that she would have to quit. The owner of this bar and grill has been very understanding and has allowed Alice to work as she is able. She has not been able to make very much money on this job as it is for tips mostly. A small daily wage is paid but it is less than minimum wage.

Educational Evaluation

Alice graduated from high school. She completed a general business course. Her grades were primarily Bs with a few Cs. Alice's school records indicated that she was very involved in extracurricular activities and excelled in sports. She was a track star, a long distance runner. She was encouraged by her academic counselor to go to college; however, she wanted to go to work as soon as possible.

Economic Evaluation

Alice's primary source of support has been from her parents. Through her work as a waitress she has been able to purchase clothing and other incidentals for her son. She has on occasion contributed to the household expenses (e.g., food, rent, and utilities) but this has not been consistent. Living arrangements are adequate for the time being. Alice and her son share the same room. Alice acknowledges that it would be better for her and her son to have separate rooms. Alice's parents are anxious for her to become more independent and to have her own place. They are willing to provide after school care for David once she gains employment. Alice's medical care is being paid by her father. Alice has no medical insurance for herself or for David.

Discussion Questions

Medical

1. What additional medical information or evaluations (e.g., physical therapy, occupational therapy, assistive technology) are needed? Why?
2. What activities, if any, should Alice avoid? Why? Is there any assistive technology available that would increase her ability to engage in instrumental activities of daily living (e.g., personal care needs, cooking, cleaning)?
3. What effects, if any, does Alice's medication have on her ability to participate in activities of daily living?

Psychological

1. What are the implications of Alice's WAIS-IV test scores?
2. What additional psychological information or evaluations, if any, are needed? Why?
3. Are there activities or situations that Alice should avoid? Why?

Social/Family/Community

1. What additional sources of family/social information are needed? How and from whom would these data be gathered?
2. What community resources (e.g., Department of Social Services, Housing, Child Care) may be utilized for the benefit of Alice and her son?
3. How could Alice's parents be exposed to more information

about her medical condition? From whom would these services be secured?

4. Are there any advocacy groups that may be of assistance to Alice?

Vocational

1. What information/data would be helpful in determining a vocational goal? Did Alice's previous work provide any transferable skills? If so, what are they?
2. Consider Alice's residual functional capacity to engage in work. Based on this assessment, what level or levels of work activity (sedentary, light, medium, heavy) can she perform? What impact does this information have on Alice's choice of occupations?
3. Consider Alice's nonexertional residual functional capacities (i.e., pain, lack of mobility during flare-ups of her RA) which may present a barrier to employment. What effect will this have on the selection of a vocational goal? Is there assistive technology that will increase her mobility or reduce the effects of pain?

Economic

1. Is Alice or her son eligible for any other governmental assistance?

Chapter 9

THE CASE OF ROBERT:
BACK INJURY

Social Evaluation

R obert is thirty-two years of age, married with one four-year-old son. This is Robert's second marriage. Robert's wife, Nicole, is employed as a sales clerk at a local convenience store. Her salary (which is minimum wage with no health benefits) is currently the major source of income for the family. Since Robert's accident (approximately one year ago), he has not been able to work. Because of this and the meager funds available to the family, there is some tension between Robert and his wife.

They reside in a small one-story frame house that appears to be adequate for their needs. The yard and house are well maintained. Nicole has had to assume responsibility for all yard work and routine maintenance around the home. This, too, is a source of tension between Robert and his wife. The family has one automobile which Nicole uses for travel to and from work. Robert's truck was completely totaled as a result of the accident. Nicole has borrowed substantial amounts of money from her parents in order to pay the monthly and other household expenses. Robert's relationship, as a consequence, with his in-laws is quite strained.

Prior to the accident, Robert and Nicole would engage in many social and recreational activities such as eating out, going to the movies, visiting friends and relatives, fishing, and bowling. There has been no social or recreational activity due to Robert's complaints of pain and his inability to sit or stand for more than one to two hours at a time.

Medical Evaluation

Robert sustained multiple contusions and a fracture of the L1 verte-bra when the truck he was driving was hit by a drunken driver. Robert's truck, on impact, was flipped several times and was com-pletely destroyed. Robert was hospitalized for a period of one week. The treating physician, an orthopedic specialist, fitted him with an anterior spinal hyperextension brace to be worn full-time following discharge from the hospital. He was, as well, given a prescription for Tylox® for pain control. Follow-up three months post injury noted that Robert was continuing to experience pain, although the pain was diminishing. His physician gave him a prescription for Phenaphen® #3 for pain relief and authorized refills of this medication for the fol-lowing three months. Robert no longer uses the brace but notes pain on prolonged sitting (greater than one hour) or standing or when lift-ing light weights (less than twenty five lbs.).

One year post injury, Robert still complains of pain and currently takes Motrin® on an as needed basis (PRN) for pain management. His physician has released him to return to work as a carpenter and esti-mated his permanent impairment from this injury to be 20 percent. The physician stated that "Robert will probably always have some dis-comfort in his back from the injury, aggravated by heavy work or heavy activity." This physician characterized Robert's exertional resid-ual functional capacity as noted below:

Physical Capacities Evaluation

- Sit: three hours Stand: three hours
- Walk: two hours
- Lift: 26 to 50 lb. frequently
- 51 to 100 lb. occasionally
- Bend: Frequently
- Squat: Frequently
- Crawl: Frequently
- Climb: Frequently
- Reach: Frequently

Robert returned to work but was unable to do the repeated bend-ing, stooping, and lifting requirements. He worked for two weeks and quit. He sought additional medical assistance and was told there was no physical basis for his pain, that it was "psychogenic." He was subsequently referred to a local psychologist who specialized in the treatment of pain.

Psychological Evaluation

During the initial interview Robert said that he has continued to have pain since the accident, although the intensity has diminished to the point that he only takes Motrin (800 mg) on an occasional basis; that is, every few days. He indicated that he sustains pain after sitting for only one to two hours and after working for a few hours. He related a recent incident where he worked for four hours and experienced pain for the next day and a half, pain to the extent that he could not work and his instrumental activities of daily living were significantly compromised. He currently experiences pain at least once a day, primarily associated with a physical task. He indicated that the intensity of the pain on a scale of 0–10 is initially 6–7 and then diminishes to a 4–5 (0 equating to no pain and 10 being intolerable to the point of seeking medical assistance). Pain, Robert noted, is caused by repeated bending, twisting, stooping, medium lifting (25 to 50 pounds), and prolonged sitting. Robert is very concerned about re-injuring himself; he thinks about it a lot. The Minnesota Multiphasic Personality Inventory (MMPI) was administered to Robert, but the results were considered to be invalid because he could not complete the test due to his inability to sit for prolonged periods of time. Robert was also given the Wechsler Adult Intelligence Scale-IV. Robert's full-scale IQ, 100, fell into the average range of intelligence. There was very little scatter in the subtests.

Vocational Evaluation

After dropping out of high school, Robert entered an apprenticeship program to become a carpenter. He successfully completed the program and has worked as a journeyman carpenter for the past ten years. He also has learned a lot about electrical and plumbing work, but has no certification or rating in either of these fields. For the past several years, as a second job, Robert had worked as a paperhanger on an independent contractor basis. He liked this work and thought that he may go into the wallpapering and painting business. As a journeyman carpenter, Robert's wages were very good and he always had at least one day of overtime wages per week. His income from the second job was extremely good, providing an additional income of approximately 40 percent to his principal job as a carpenter.

Educational Evaluation

Robert completed the eleventh grade prior to dropping out of high school. His school records indicate that he was an above average student. Robert's favorite subjects were industrial arts (consistently an A student) and mathematics/algebra (As and Bs). He participated in sports (lettering in basketball) and enjoyed a good reputation with school faculty and administrators. In fact, most teachers were surprised when he quit with just one year of school remaining.

Economic Evaluation

Robert and his wife are deeply in debt. His wife has borrowed substantial amounts of money from her parents to meet the monthly mortgage payment and other costs associated with the house. Robert's truck, which was completely destroyed in the accident, has not been replaced. At the time of the accident, Robert had just left the site of his second job (as an independent contractor) and was heading to another job site.

Discussion Questions

Medical

1. What additional medical information or evaluations, if any, are needed? There seems to be some conflict with Robert's account of his medical condition and the physical capacities evaluation. What are the implications of these two very different perspectives? Should you refer Robert to another orthopedic physician for a second opinion?
2. What activities should Robert avoid? What impact does pain have on Robert's ADLs, and his return to work or alternative vocational plans? Would a work hardening program be of assistance to Robert?

Psychological

1. What are the implications and relevance of Robert's psychological assessment? What impact does pain have on psychological testing (i.e., WAIS-IV and MMPI)?
2. Are there work or social situations that Robert should avoid? Would Robert and his wife benefit from counseling to deal with all the life stressors they both are currently experiencing?

Sociological/Family/Community

1. What additional sources of family/social information are needed? How and from whom would these data be gathered?
2. What community resources, if any, may be utilized for the benefit of Robert and/or his family? In particular, are there non-profit organizations that can help Robert and Nicole with their debt?

Vocational

1. What further information/data would be helpful in determining an alternate vocational goal? Did Robert's previous work provide any transferable skills? If so, what are they?
2. Consider Robert's residual functional capacity to engage in work activity. Based on that assessment, what level(s) of work activity (sedentary, light, medium, heavy) can he perform? Can Robert return to his former work?
3. Consider Robert's non-exertional residual functional capacities (i.e., his pain) that may present a barrier to employment. What effect, if any, will this have on the selection of an alternate vocational goal?

Economic

1. Is Robert eligible for Workers' Compensation, SSDI or any other disability related benefits? Is Robert's family eligible for assistance through any of the above noted sources or any others?
2. Are Robert and his family eligible for TANF, Food Stamps, or other social or medical services?
3. Because the other driver did not have insurance, does Robert

have any recourse to receive any compensation or consideration from a state operated uninsured motorist's fund?
4. Should Robert engage the services of an attorney?

Chapter 10

THE CASE OF JANET:
BLINDNESS AND VISUAL DISABILITY

Social Evaluation

Janet is forty-eight years old, married to Thomas, who is fifty-one years of age. They have been married for twenty-eight years and have two children, a son and a daughter who are both independent with families of their own. Janet was recently diagnosed as being legally blind as a result of glaucoma. Janet had been a cosmetologist for thirty years. Thomas is an automobile parts counter worker. They have a nice home in a comfortable suburban area near a large urban city. Moreover, with their children grown and self-supporting, they were beginning to enjoy a more luxurious lifestyle until Janet had to quit her job as a result of her vision problems.

Janet has primary open-angle glaucoma. Severe functional limitations of her vision occurred before the disease was detected. Although she was only vaguely aware of it, there was a family history of glaucoma. Her mother had been killed in an automobile accident as a young adult and had never developed any symptoms. However, her grandmother and great grandmother both had glaucoma. Janet's father remarried when she was a child, and she grew up, thinking of her stepmother more as her mother; consequently, she was not fully aware of the family history of glaucoma. Her adjustment to her blindness is complicated by the knowledge that she might have prevented the severity of the disability by more frequent visual examinations.

A very positive social feature in Janet's situation is that she has a strong marriage. Thomas is very supportive and prepared to do anything possible to help her adapt to her disability. Their grown son and daughter are also very supportive; they live nearby and want to be helpful to the extent possible considering their own family responsibilities.

Medical Evaluation

The diagnosis of Janet's eye condition is primary open-angle glaucoma. She just meets the criteria for legal blindness. She had only a few symptoms before she realized that she should have a visual examination at which time her ophthalmologist noted that irreversible damage had occurred. Janet had been wearing corrective lens for mild myopia since she was a child. There is a family history of glaucoma. There is also some family history of diabetes, although Janet shows no symptoms at the present time.

Psychological Evaluation

A clinical psychologist made some observations about Janet's basic personality and values based on a clinical interview and the results of the Auditory Projective Test. It was the psychologist's impression that Janet did not display any evidence of a serious mental disorder. She felt that her basic personality functioning was normal, and Janet was a person who had some very traditional feminine interests and preferences.

Nevertheless, the psychologist felt that she was having some difficulty adjusting to her disability which was confirmed by the Emotional Factors Inventory. Janet is particularly distressed about the fact that she might have prevented the severity of her disability. The psychologist felt that Janet could benefit from short-term counseling/psychotherapy. Counseling was recommended to help Janet accept the reality of her disability, but with the understanding that a meaningful life could still be available to her.

Vocational Evaluation

Janet completed her cosmetology training through a public school program that also provided her with a high school diploma. Although she worked part-time when her children were growing up, she has been performing cosmetology work for 30 years. She has enjoyed cosmetology very much and was considered to be an excellent and very creative stylist. She is not sure she would want to work in a related field because she is very disappointed that she can no longer perform in the manner that she has in the past.

Janet was administered the Penn Bi-Manual Worksample. Because she demonstrated excellent manual dexterity and coordination, it is understandable why she was so effective in cosmetology.

Educational Evaluation

Janet completed high school with a focus in cosmetology training. Her grades were average in the more traditional academic subjects such as math, English, and history. She has never been interested in reading literature or more general educational material. She was given the Otis Self-Administering Test of Mental Ability in high school and received an IQ score of 101.

Economic Evaluation

Janet worked for a well established cosmetology business. Her fringe benefits included health insurance. She purchased a supplemental disability retirement policy about two years ago. Her husband, Thomas, continues to work as an automobile parts counter worker. Her grown children have indicated that they will try to help economically, if necessary.

Discussion Questions

Medical

1. If Janet just meets the criteria for legal blindness, describe the possible characteristics of her residual visual capacity. What can Janet see, if anything? Is there assistive technology available that could increase Janet's field of vision?
2. What impact does this medical condition have on Janet's instrumental activities of daily living (e.g., dressing, cooking, mobility)?

Psychological

1. What additional psychological information or evaluations, if

any, are needed? Why?

2. Is Janet's guilt about the heredity effects of glaucoma justified? Does Janet need psychological counseling to gain a perspective on this situation? If so, what would be your recommendation?

Social/Family/Community

1. What additional sources of family/social information are needed? How and from whom would these data be gathered? What should Janet's children be told regarding the heredity effects of glaucoma?
2. What community resources or advocacy groups may be utilized for the benefit of Janet and her husband?

Vocational

1. What information/data would be helpful in determining an alternate vocational or educational or training program? Does Janet's current work provide any transferable skills? If so, what are they?
2. Consider Janet's residual functional capacity to engage in work (legal blindness–restricted field of vision). What effect will this have on the selection of a vocational goal? Based on this assessment, what level or levels of work activity (sedentary, light, medium, heavy) can she perform?
3. Does Janet really want to avoid anything to do with cosmetology, or is this just an initial reaction?

Economic

1. Is Janet eligible for services through the state-federal program for people who have visual impairments? What services, other than vocational rehabilitation, would Janet qualify to receive?
2. Is Janet eligible for SSDI benefits? What benefits would Janet receive through the disability retirement policy she purchased through her employer?
3. Are there any other local, state, or federal resources that Janet should consider?

Chapter 11

THE CASE OF JAMES:
CARDIOVASCULAR DISEASE

Social Evaluation

James is forty-four years old. He has been married for the past twenty years. James and his wife, Sarah, have three children, ages eighteen, sixteen, and fourteen. All children (girls) are currently in school with the oldest scheduled to graduate this year. She is described as a very bright and outgoing young person who very much wants to go to college. The other two girls are described as typical teenagers who, as well, appear to do very well in school. Both older children work part-time; buy their own clothing and other personal items. Interpersonal relations between the girls are described as warm and caring. James and Sarah, similarly, have an excellent relationship with their children and between themselves. Sarah works outside of the home as a maid for several different families. Sarah did not complete high school, although she plans to enroll in a GED program offered by the local school system. James completed the seventh (7th) and has no desire to ever return to school. He has difficulty with reading but is able to read a "little." His math skills are reported to be good, particularly as they relate to addition and subtraction (money management). He had been employed as a laborer in a machine shop. He characterized his work as "mostly lifting and carrying weights up to 150 pounds, consistently 75 to100 pounds" and some custodial tasks. Since his heart attack (six months earlier), James has not been able to work. His doctor told him he would never be able to do his former work, and that he would have to find work that was considerably lighter.

Since James has not been able to work, he has become progressively depressed. His relationship with his wife and daughters is slightly strained. The family's financial situation is such that mortgage payments have not been made for the past two months. The family's home is a small frame house that is sparsely but adequately furnished. James and his family have lived there for the past fifteen years. The children have volunteered their savings to help. The family has one automobile which is at least ten years old and frequently needs repair. James made the last payment on this car the month prior to his heart attack. James is a proud man who has achieved much given his humble beginnings. Sarah has sought help from the local Department of Social Services.

Medical Evaluation

James had a myocardial infarction at age forty-four with no previous history of heart disease. He had been in good health until that time with only the usual illnesses. Three months after his heart attack, James underwent triple bypass surgery. His recovery has been uneventful. Physicians at the hospital told him to change jobs; that is, to get a job where he could sit or one where he only had to lift light weights. They also told him to "change his personal habits." Following discharge from the hospital, James returned home and has not tried to work. The caseworker (that Sarah had contacted) referred James to a rehabilitation counselor. Approximately two months after referral, James was sent to a cardiologist for a medical examination. The following report was returned to the counselor:

Medical Examination and History (Significant Findings)

Hospital/Surgery: MI, triple bypass surgery: Patient sustained an anteroseptal MI. He subsequently underwent angiocardiography and was found to have severe coronary artery disease. Triple bypass surgery was performed. James progressed well following surgery and has recovered completely. High blood pressure. Treated with Aldomet®, onset at age 36. Patient indicates he has not always taken his B/P medication as directed. Genital urinary tract. Hydrocele. EENT; hole in left eardrum-recurrent infections in right ear some hearing loss; nearsighted–patient has no glasses; height: 5'8"; weight: 180 lbs.; blood pressure: 180/90; dyspnea on slight exertion; and two pack a day cigarette habit for 20 years.

Diagnosis
1. S/P anteroseptal myocardial infarction
2. S/P coronary artery bypass ×3
3. Class IIC cardiac disease
4. History of dyspnea

Functional/Environmental Restrictions
1. Walking: one-half to one mile
2. Stairs: four flights
3. Lifting: 10–20 lb.
4. Standing: 50 percent of the time
5. Stooping, bending, twisting: Restricted
6. Temperature extremes: Avoid

Psychological Evaluation

James was referred for psychometric evaluation by his counselor. Tests administered were WAIS-IV, vocational testing, and interview.

A. Behavioral observations: James is a forty-four-year-old male of small stature (height) with graying hair. His posture and gait were unremarkable. He entered the session with a pleasant and cooperative manner. He was able to communicate satisfactorily although he did appear to have a slight problem hearing less than normal conversation (volume). He attributed his hearing loss to his work which he described as quite loud. James had worked as a material handler for approximately fifteen years (prior to his MI).

B. Test results: James was found to be functioning in the borderline range of intelligence. He scored as follows: Verbal IQ: 72; Performance IQ: 74; and Full Scale IQ: 71. Little variation was found within James's verbal scores. Attention was his best area of verbal functioning. All scores in the performance area were within the borderline range except for planning abilities in regard to social situations which were average.

C. Vocational testing: Assessment focused on food service, custodial, and painting. James's work habits were considered to be quite good. He seemed to work best with verbal instructions. He needed assistance with written directions. He was a consistent worker and displayed initiative in his work and appeared to perform at his best. He expressed a strong desire to return to some type of employment. In tasks not so familiar to him, such as cooking, he did require some help. He was thorough in his work and used all tools appropriately. He appeared to cope well with these new job tasks.

D. Impressions/recommendations: James appears to be aware of his cognitive limitations. He has demonstrated that he is capable of self and family support. He did admit to some depression. It will be difficult to find a job that does not require heavy physical labor. James will do best in work that requires handling, sorting, tending, and/or manipulating.

E. Diagnosis: Borderline intelligence

Vocational Evaluation

James has worked consistently since he quit school at age sixteen. He has held a number of jobs all characterized by physical ability. His last position as a material handler had been as James has described it, "a very good job." He held this position for fifteen years prior to his heart attack.

As a material handler James was required to load and unload iron ore that could not be handled by machine. This required him to be on his feet all day, lifting weights up to 150 pounds, constantly lifting, and carrying weights of 75 to 100 pounds. He also did repetitive bending, stooping, and twisting throughout the work day. At slack times, he would perform custodial duties. James did not like this aspect of his job, preferring instead the more "manly" tasks.

Educational Evaluation

James left school without completing the eighth (8th) grade. School records indicated that James was held back in several grades. Teacher notations regarding his lack of progress suggested that he had trouble reading, and that he was particularly disruptive in class. He was sixteen years old when he quit school.

Economic Evaluation

James and his wife are currently purchasing the home they have lived in for the past fifteen years. Mortgage payments have not been made for the last two months; the bank has called several times in the last few weeks requesting payment. The bank loan officer has stated that if back payments are not received in the next sixty days, foreclosure proceedings will be initiated. They have exhausted all funds from a savings account established several years ago for college tuition for their daughters. These funds have been used to pay household expenses. Sarah's income from her maid's position is not enough to cover monthly expenses.

James's former position did not have health benefits and as a consequence, James's medical bills are very large. It appears doubtful that James will ever be able to pay these bills. His physicians have donated their services, but the hospital continues to bill him. Recently, the hospital had indicated that his bill will be turned over to a collection agency for payment.

Discussion Questions

Medical

1. What additional medical information or evaluations are needed, particularly with regard to James's other (aside from his cardiac condition) medical conditions?
2. What is Class II C cardiac disease? What effect will this have on his ability to participate in activities of daily living or his ability to return to his former work or other work?
3. What activities should James avoid? Would James benefit from a cardiac rehabilitation program?

Psychological

1. What additional psychological information or evaluations, if any, are needed? What are the implications and relevance of James's psychological assessment? Due to James's lack of reading ability, do you think his IQ testing was valid and/or reliable?
2. It would appear that James has been a good provider for his family. His current inability to work has affected his relationship, to some extent, with his wife and daughters. What psychological intervention would you provide to James and his family to help reduce the stress of this current situation?

Social/Family/Community

1. What additional sources of family/social information are needed? How and from whom would these data be gathered?
2. What community resources or advocacy groups may be utilized for the benefit of James and/or his family?

Vocational

1. What further information/data would be helpful in determining an alternative educational or training or vocational goal? Did James's previous work provide any transferable skills? If so, what are they?
2. Consider James's residual functional capacity to engage in work activity. Based on this assessment, what level(s) of work activity (sedentary, light, medium, heavy) can James perform?

Economic

1. Is James eligible for Workers' Compensation, SSDI, or any other disability-related benefits?
2. Is James's family eligible through the department of social services, such as, Temporary Assistance for Needy Families (TANF) or General Relief (GR) payments, Food Stamps, or any other services, e.g., assistance with mortgage payments, utilities, etc?
3. What intervention(s), if any, may be made with the hospital regarding the bill, the mortgage lender (late or no payments), and others?

Chapter 12

THE CASE OF ELLEN:
CHRONIC OBSTRUCTIVE
PULMONARY DISEASE

Social Evaluation

Ellen is fifty-two years of age. She has been married for ten years. This is her second marriage; the first ending in the death of her spouse. She has one son who is grown and is independent. There are no children from the present marriage. Ellen's husband, George, has been declared disabled by the Social Security Administration, and he receives a modest monthly disability payment and Medicare benefits. He has a "bad heart" and is unable to physically exert himself. He takes many medications each day. He is quite dependent on Ellen to care for his personal needs and is demanding of her time and attention. Approximately one year ago, Ellen began coughing uncontrollably and would pass out on occasion. She has had a "cigarette cough" for twenty years but nothing like these current "coughing spells." She sought medical treatment and was told she should stop smoking, that she had chronic bronchitis. Ellen did stop smoking (although George says she sneaks a smoke every now and again). Ellen has worked as a Food Service Worker for the local high school for the past twenty-five years. She has continued to work at this position but has been increasingly unable to carry out the tasks/duties required. Last week she was given notice that she was being "laid off" until her medical condition became better. Her doctor told her she needed to find other work that was less physically demanding and free of grease fumes. Ellen has been particularly upset and depressed since the loss of her job. She worries that she will not be able to return to work. Her husband's demands seem to be even greater now that she is home during the day. Household chores and maintenance have been neglected for the past year. As a consequence, the house and yard are in a moderate state of disrepair. The grass is overgrown and the house needs painting. Ellen has stated she just does not have the "wind" to do these necessary chores (or the money to hire someone to do them). Similarly, Ellen has not been able to do her own kitchen work (or cooking) or household cleaning (dusting, waxing, etc.) because the cleaners (fumes) make her cough and become short of breath. The inability to maintain her home has been very depressing for Ellen. She has always taken pride in her home's appearance.

Medical Evaluation

Ellen has been in reasonably good health all of her life. This past year has been an exception. She has been hospitalized several times for specialized pulmonary tests and has been seen by a number of physicians regarding her chronic bronchitis.

First hospitalization: Admitted: February 2 and Discharged: February 6

Discharge summary: This patient is a 52-year-old woman who was admitted for evaluation of a cough and history of depression. For the past 7–8 years she has had a history of nasal congestion, postnasal drainage, hoarseness, sore throat, and shortness of breath on light exertion. Also, she has had a severe cough which occasionally is productive. Symptoms are worst during active pollen seasons and during URI. Pulmonary function studies revealed moderate airway obstruction. She has symptoms of depression. Other significant physical problems are hiatal hernia with reflux, and obesity. During hospitalization, the patient was seen by a psychiatrist and it was suggested that her depression could be managed with Elavil®. The patient was told to follow a weight reduction diet. Surgical repair of the hiatal hernia was not recommended.

Impressions

1. Chronic Bronchitis with Bronchospasm
2. Respiratory Insufficiency
3. Depression

4. Hiatal Hernia with Reflux
5. Obesity
6. Urinary Tract Infection

Recommendations

1. Patient must be in an environment free of dusts, fumes, and gases.
2. Weight reduction program
3. Elevation of bed
4. Antibiotic treatment for UTI
5. Medications prescribed for chronic bronchitis: Theo-Dur®, 300 mg every 12 hours; Pro-vental® Inhaler, as needed; Breathine®, 5 mg every 8 hours
6. Medication prescribed for depression: Elavil®, 75 mg at bedtime.

Second hospitalization: Admitted: June 10 and Discharged: June 15

The patient was admitted after repeated complaints of dyspnea on exertion to what she calls emphysema and chronic bronchitis. Please note the Pulmonary Function Data Sheet for pulmonary testing.

PULMONARY FUNCTION DATA SHEET
NAME: Ellen
SEX: Female; Height: 5 ft. 2 in.; Age: 52; Weight 200 lbs. PREVIOUS STUDIES: Yes
SMOKING HABITS: Ever Smoked: Yes; Smoking Now: No; Stopped: 6 months ago; Smoked Cigarettes, 1 pack a day for 30 years.
RESPIRATORY HISTORY:
Dyspnea: Yes
How Long: 8 years
At Rest: No
With Exertion: Yes Cough: Yes
How Long: 20 years
Productive: Yes
OCCUPATIONAL HISTORY: Cook

PULMONARY FUNCTION STUDIES (6/10): Patient effort and cooperation was good. Results are consistent with moderate obstructive airways disease. Following inhalation of bronchodilators, there is significant improvement.

Ventilation Perfusion: *Ventilation.* There are multiple matched defects in both lungs. Washout is delayed. This is consistent with obstructive lung disease. *Perfusion.* There are matched defects in both lungs and this is consistent with obstructive lung disease. No evidence of pulmonary emboli.

PULMONARY FUNCTION STUDIES (6/13): The forced vital capacity and slow vital capacity are both reduced. Following bronchodilator administration there is improvement. These values are consistent with moderate to severe obstructive lung disease. A degree of restrictive impairment is suggested and may well be related to the obstructive disease and associated air-trapping.

FOLLOW-UP BY PULMONARY SPECIALIST, August: The patient should work in a clean environment free of grease and fumes. Her symptoms are controlled by medications, and at times, the wearing of a surgical mask to filter out concentrated fumes is recommended. The patient's hiatal hernia continues to bother her on occasion. The patient has gained weight and is presently 215 lb. She needs to lose weight. Acute exacerbations of her chronic bronchitis continue to be treated with Prednisone® (10 mg every day). Current medications include: Theo-Dur, 300 mg every 12 hours; Pro-vental Inhaler, as needed; Breathine, 5 mg every 8 hours; Elvail, 75 mg at bedtime.

Psychological Evaluation

Ellen was seen by a psychiatrist (as a hospital consultation) when she was first hospitalized. This physician gave her a prescription for Elavil. She continues to take this medication. Ellen has stated that her feelings of depression are "about the same." She does not report trouble sleeping.

Vocational Evaluation

After graduation from high school, Ellen attended a vocational technical college and received training in food service management. She did not complete this course of studies, preferring instead to marry and have a family. A few years after her marriage, she began to work part-time in the local high school as a cook helper and several years later as a food service worker on a full-time basis. In her position as a food service Worker, she was required to carry various pots and pans weighing between 15 and 40 lb.; helped cook, prepare meats, vegetables, make salads, wash dishes, sweep, operate the coleslaw machine, steam cooker, deep fat fryer, slicing machine; and to clean tables, chairs, trays, and the oven. She was constantly on her feet, walking short distances often carrying kitchen or cooking objects throughout the work day. She occasionally supervised the work of the cook helper. Ellen worked for the high school for the past thirty years (the last twenty as a full-time employee). She did not work during the summers.

Educational Evaluation

Ellen is a high school graduate. She did very well academically. School records indicated that she was active in several clubs and favored home economics. Ellen completed one year of a two-year course in Food Service Management prior to her first marriage. She has stated that she wished she had finished the program but thinks she is too old to return to this program after all these years. During the past twenty years, however, she has taken one or more classes at the local college each year. She has described these classes as liberal arts (literature, psychology, history, etc.). She has completed eighty-two semester credit hours but has never officially declared a major.

Economic Evaluation

Ellen and her husband own their home and have no outstanding debts of significance. Money has, nevertheless, become more important with less income and some things have had to be dropped. The house and the yard are in need of regular maintenance which, at the present time, goes beyond the money available to them. Ellen's medical bills while covered by insurance, her medications are not and are very expensive. George takes, as well, a large amount of medication. It is unclear if Ellen's hospitalization will continue. Neither Ellen nor George has any savings.

Discussion Questions

Medical

1. What are the medical implications of moderate to severe obstructive lung disease?
2. What effects do Ellen's medications have on her ability to participate in instrumental activities of daily living, e.g., cooking, cleaning, going to the store?
3. What are the effects of Ellen's other medical conditions, e.g., obesity, hiatal hernia?

Psychological

1. What are the implications and relevance of Ellen's psychiatric consultation? Should she continue to take the medication the psychiatrist prescribed?
2. Should Ellen seek psychological or psychiatric consultation for medication review or adjustment or treatment or could the family physician do this for Ellen?

Social/Family/Community

1. What additional sources of family/social information are needed? How and from whom would these data be gathered?
2. What community resources or advocacy groups may be utilized for the benefit of Ellen and/or her husband, e.g., household maintenance, for assistance with George?

Vocational

1. What further information/data would be helpful in determining an alternative educational, training, or vocational goal? Did Ellen's previous work provide any transferable skills? If so, what are they?
2. Consider Ellen's residual functional capacity to engage in work activity. Based on this assessment, what level(s) of work activity (sedentary, light, medium, heavy) can she perform? What effect will this have on the selection of an alternative goal?

Economic

1. Is Ellen eligible for Workers' Compensation, SSDI, or any other disability related benefits?
2. Is Ellen eligible for disability retirement from her employer (a state supported public school system)?
3. Is there any available assistance to help with the cost of Ellen's medications?

Chapter 13

THE CASE OF BARBARA: DEAFNESS AND HEARING DISABILITY

Social Evaluation

B arbara is eighteen years old, single, and she lives with her parents and two younger siblings. She has sensorineural deafness as a result of an infectious disease when she was a child. At present, she is in the process of making a decision about her future vocational plans as she has recently graduated from high school. Her father owns and operates a small shoe repair shop. Barbara's mother does not work outside of the home.

Barbara had cerebrospinal meningitis when she was five years old, and she has almost total hearing loss. However, she had been a very capable child prior to that time and has learned to adapt very well to the effects of her disability. Her speech skills are very good, considering her disability; moreover, she is exceptional for her disability group, at speech reading. She is well skilled in both Ameslan and Manual English. She has performed very well in school, graduating with honors. Her social adjustment is considered to be very appropriate, and she has demonstrated that she is an effective advocate for her disability group.

Barbara would like to attend a college or university. However, even with some scholarship money, her father cannot afford to send her to school away from home. Consequently, she is restricted to two universities in her home locality. Neither of these institutions has the kind of special resources for students with hearing impairments that were available to her in elementary, middle, or high school. Although she has been accepted academically at both institutions, school authorities have actually discouraged her from attending. Her father feels that it would be more realistic for her to consider learning a more specialized trade or craft.

Medical Evaluation

Barbara had cerebrospinal meningitis as a complication of measles when she was five years old. Antibiotics saved her life, but she was left with permanent damage to the inner ear resulting in sensorineural deafness. Although she has some capacity for hearing sound, it was determined that she would not benefit from hearing aid equipment. However, she had been in good health prior to the illness and was not permanently injured in any other way. Her cognitive abilities did not seem to be affected, and her vision, and larynx are within normal limits. She recently had a physical examination and was judged to be in excellent health.

Psychological Evaluation

Barbara was administered a special adaptation of the Wechsler Adult Intelligence Scale IV and received the following scores: Verbal IQ-124; Performance IQ-126; and Full Scale IQ-126. Therefore, her intelligence was assessed as being in the superior range on both the verbal and performance scales. She has never been administered any personality instruments other than a vocational interest inventory (see Vocational Evaluation section below). The clinical psychologist indicated that there was no evidence of psychopathology based on his clinical interview. Moreover, he described her as appearing to be a very conscientious and responsible individual who was effectively motivated toward productive achievement.

Vocational Evaluation

Barbara has never worked; she has mainly concentrated on developing the social and technical communication skills and behaviors that would help her in later employment. While Barbara was in high school, she was administered a special adaptation of the Strong-Campbell Interest Inventory. She scored very high in the general categories of Social and Artistic and all the specific teaching categories within these general categories. As indicated in the Psychological Evaluation section above and the Educational Evaluation section below, she clearly has the ability to achieve a college or university objective. However, because Barbara is also considering a craft or trade objective, she recently took some vocational aptitude tests related to a goal of this nature. The results indicated that she has very good abilities in regard to dexterity, mechanical, spatial, and similar areas. It appears that she could be successful in a variety of clerical, technical, and precision production occupations.

Educational Evaluation

As previously indicated, Barbara has developed very good skills in regard to speaking, speech reading, and manual communication. She has also performed well in school, obtaining a 3.7 (4.00 system) grade point average. She was named to the National Honor Society and graduated with honors from high school; her scores on the Scholastic Aptitude Test were above the average for college preparatory students. Her best subjects in high school were English and the social sciences.

Economic Evaluation

Barbara has been offered two scholarships that would help with tuition at distant universities (out of state) that have good logistical and educational resources for assisting students with disabilities, including hearing impairments. However, she is dependent on her parents for the remainder of her tuition and other expenses. Her father simply does not have the income to finance her attending a university out of state and away from home. He owns a shoe repair shop which provides him with a modest income. He also has to be concerned about Barbara's brother and sister who are only a few years younger. He cannot borrow any more money because he is already at his maximum limit of credit. Barbara has applied for a long-term student loan, based on financial need; but it does not appear that it would be enough to finance out-of state university schooling.

Barbara and her parents have calculated that they could afford to send her to either one of the two universities in their locality. She could continue to live at home and possibly find some part-time work to help with the finances. However, neither of these institutions have adequate resources to assist students with hearing impairments. Moreover, individuals in authority at these institutions have actually discouraged her from attending for the latter reason. Consequently,

Barbara is giving consideration to a more specialized type of trade, craft, or clerical curriculum at the nearby community college, or a similar training facility in the locality.

Discussion Questions

Medical

1. What additional medical information or evaluations, if any, are needed? Why?
2. What assistive technology does Barbara need or would need if she was to relocate to another geographic location?

Psychological

1. What additional psychological evaluations or evaluations, if any, are needed? Why?

Social/Family/Community

1. What additional sources of family/social information are needed? How and from whom would these data be gathered?
2. What community resources or advocacy groups may be utilized for the benefit of Barbara and her parents?

Vocational

1. What additional information/data would be helpful in determining a career or vocational goal?
2. Consider Barbara's nonexertional residual functional capacities that may present a barrier to employment. What effect will this have on the selection of a career or vocational goal?
3. What resources would be needed to achieve the vocational goal? How long would it take?

Economic

1. Is Barbara eligible for SSI benefits?
2. Is Barbara eligible for educational grants?
3. Are there any other economic or governmental resources that Barbara should consider?

Chapter 14

THE CASE OF ERIC:
LEARNING DISABILITY

Social Evaluation

E ric is a twenty-five-year-old college student. He is not married but is seriously involved with a young woman he has been dating for the past two years. He anticipates that they will marry once they complete college. He is a senior, and she is in her third year of college. Both have double majors: English and psychology. Eric has always been considered to be very bright, although his grades in high school did not reflect this potential. Eric's teachers in elementary, middle, and secondary school took an interest in him and made every effort to provide for his educational needs in order for him to succeed. Even though his teachers were accommodating, Eric did not understand why he was unable to do as well as his classmates; he felt dumb. Eric's parents were also understanding; hoping he would outgrow his school problem. When this did not happen, Eric's parents, his father in particular, became convinced that Eric's problem was the result of his laziness. They thought he would be alright if he just spent more time on his studies.

Today, Eric's relationship with his parents is somewhat strained. His father has now refused to contribute any further to Eric's college education. He does not approve of Eric taking a reduced course load which is delaying the completion of his degree program, putting him beyond the age one is supposed to be graduated from college. Eric's mother does send him a little money each month and calls him frequently. For the past year, Eric has been working part-time and taking only two courses a semester. His grades have shown great improvement with this limited schedule. He found that when he attempted to take more than three courses, his grades dropped dramatically; resulting in an academic suspension. Eric's parents saw his suspension as the consequence of "socializing" too much. Eric continues to try communicating with his parents, but has met with limited success, particularly with his father.

Eric's girlfriend, Robin, cares a great deal for Eric and she is convinced that he has a learning disability. She encourages him to refer himself to the university's learning disability specialist for testing. Finally, Eric has agreed, but only reluctantly.

Medical Evaluation

Eric met his developmental milestones at age expectancy despite questionable perinatal hypoxic brain damage which was noted in his medical records. Aside from this one entry, his medical history is relatively free from any significant illnesses or injuries sustained during childhood or adolescence. Eric's most recent general physical examination concluded that he was in excellent health with normal vision and hearing.

Psychological Evaluation

Eric was referred to the university's learning disability specialist for testing and recommendations regarding his ability to learn. Eric has had six advisors during the five and a half years he has been at the university. His current advisor, Dr. Harris, is very supportive of Eric and has, among other things, recommended that Eric take a reduced course load, use tape recorders to tape lectures, and has helped him manage his time more efficiently and effectively. Eric has developed a strong relationship with Dr. Harris. Eric's previous advisors felt he was not applying himself, working too much, enjoying the social environment of the university too much, and several faculty members have questioned Eric's intellectual ability to handle college level work.

A. Tests administered: WAIS-IV, Woodcock-Johnson Psycho-Educational Battery, and Interview.

B. Clinical observations: Eric was very cooperative during the testing and interview phases of the evaluation. Considerable time was spent in discussing the purpose of the evaluation and the anticipated outcomes of the evaluation. Eric impressed this interviewer as being a very bright, articulate, and knowledgeable person. Eric admitted that he had, throughout his life, been made to feel inadequate and "dumb" at times, particularly when math and other quantitative subjects were studied. He has, for example, taken and failed college math five times. Statistical concepts according to Eric are a "mystery." Similarly, he has failed formal logic twice. Before working with Dr. Harris, his current advisor, Eric seemed to spend all his time trying to organize his life without much success. Eric is motivated to succeed.

C. Test results: The results of the WAIS-IV indicated that Eric has above average potential for academic success. A significant scatter was found in the various subtests; Eric's greatest strengths were in his verbal abilities, but a marked weakness was found in the quantitative area. The results of the Woodcock-Johnson also showed deficits in processing quantitative data. His aptitude for mastering mathematic concepts and skills needed for everyday life is adequate, but deficient for college level mathematics. Eric's greatest strengths were in his verbal abilities; although he did need to use a tape recorder to support processing abstract concepts and to efficiently and effectively organize his thoughts. It was recommended that Eric continue to use a tape recorder to tape lectures (particularly when abstract concepts are being discussed) and to continue utilizing time management and organizational skills taught to him by Dr. Harris. In order to further enhance these skills it was further suggested that Eric use a computer with word processing capabilities. Finally, it was recommended that Eric's math and quantitative course requirements be substituted with course work in computer usage, provided the required courses are not essential to his degree program.

Vocational Evaluation

Eric has never worked full-time. His work experience has been part-time and he has consistently worked a variety of jobs to help out with college. Currently Eric is working a twenty-hour week (college work/study program) as a copy machine operator for the university's print shop. His supervisor at the print shop has stated that Eric is a good worker; however, he does have some problems in organizing his work, but this has improved. Eric has worked in a number of fast-food restaurants. He did not like handling money, and made many mistakes, which caused him to be fired from most of these jobs.

After graduation, Eric would like to work in some area of mental health that would allow him to have contact with people. He would ultimately like to go to graduate school, major in psychology and become a counseling psychologist. He has performed well in his psychology courses (a B+ average) although his courses in quantitative subject matter has been average to below average, and his overall grade point average is a C.

Educational Evaluation

Eric's high school grades were average in most subjects with below average grades in math. His teachers felt that he was a bright young man with limited motivation; he was described as devoted to having fun. Some of his teachers said he was not very smart, but very glib. Eric excelled in extracurricular activities; he was vice-president of the senior class. He was a highly visible and vocal (and quite articulate) person on campus. He spent a considerable amount of time with the Key Club and was actively involved in sports; he lettered in baseball and track. In general, Eric was a very popular high school student.

Eric's tenure at the university has been marked by flashes of brilliance and periods of failure. He was admitted to the university on an exception basis (he was heavily recruited by the track coach). The athletic department was very attentive and supportive of Eric as long as his eligibility was valid. They interceded with his professors and provided him with tutors. One and a half years ago, when his eligibility ended, Eric was suspended for one semester because of his poor academic grades. When he returned after his suspension period, Dr. Harris became his advisor. It was at this point that Eric began to follow Dr. Harris's advice, reducing his course load, using a tape recorder for class lectures, and using a computer based program to organize his schedule. Gradually his grades began to improve.

Economic Evaluation

Since losing eligibility to run track (he exhausted the maximum number of years of eligibility), Eric has had to rely on college loans, part-time work, and limited money from his mother to pay for tuition and other associated costs. Money earned from his work study job and money he receives from his mother is used to pay for his apartment and food. There is very little money remaining for other activities; Eric's girlfriend generally pays the cost of their social life.

Eric's father, as noted earlier, has refused to pay Eric's tuition or any other costs because he does not believe that Eric is really putting forth good effort. They are cordial to one another, but remain distant.

Discussion Questions

Medical

1. What additional medical information or evaluations, if any, are needed? Why?
2. What does the medical notation "perinatal hypoxic brain damage" imply and what is the current relevance of this notation?

Psychological

1. What are the implications of Eric's test results? What activities or situations, if any, should Eric avoid?
2. What are the implications for academic accommodation relative to Eric's learning disability?
3. Does Eric need personal adjustment counseling to adapt to his learning disability?

Social/Family/Community

1. What additional sources of family/social information are needed? How and from whom would these data be gathered?
2. What community resources or advocacy groups may be utilized for the benefit of Eric, particularly regarding the poor relationship Eric has with his father?

Vocational

1. What information/data would be helpful in determining a career or vocational goal? Do Eric's current work and his previous work provide any transferable skills? If so, what are they?
2. Consider Eric's nonexertional residual functional capacities (i.e., lack of organizational ability, impulsivity, and math problems)

that may present a barrier to employment or activities of daily living? What effect will this have on the selection of an educational, training or vocational goal?

Economic

1. Is Eric eligible for any governmental or social services?

Chapter 15

THE CASE OF WILLIAM:
MENTAL RETARDATION

Social Evaluation

William is an eighteen-year-old who lives with his parents and two younger siblings, Mary, age thirteen and Roy, age four. William's father has a master's degree in public administration and is employed in state government. The mother is employed on a part-time basis as a public health nurse. Both parents are very warm, concerned, and actively involved in William's care. They have some difficulty in accepting his limitations but are open to realistic interpretations and willing to do all they can to help William achieve his potential. William is reported to have a good relationship with his sister. They are very protective of each other but also fight over little things. Mary understands and accepts William's impediments. William's relationship with his younger brother is described as very warm and giving. William's contact with his peers is reported to be nonexistent; he does not see or call any friends. The only socialization William has is with his family, adaptive swimming instruction, and limited recreational activities with the city's special populations program. William expresses interest and considerable knowledge regarding rock music and enjoys watching television. William has assigned chores around the home (yard work, feed and water the dogs, clean his room, and vacuum), which he does willingly and regularly. He accomplishes his chores satisfactorily but is slow.

Medical Evaluation

William was born after nine months of uncomplicated pregnancy. Delivery was normal under general anesthesia because rotation was necessary. Meconium staining of the amniotic fluid was noted. Birth weight was seven pounds and seven ounces. Hospital/nursery course was uneventful.

William's general health has been good with the usual notation of childhood illnesses. His parents noticed staring spells beginning at age two (lasting 10 to 15 seconds), particularly when he was tired. These episodes have completely diminished over the years. William's early development was slightly slow and the parents were concerned about his inability to talk well since he was two years old. He started talking in sentences around age four, but has been hesitant to communicate at school. His speech currently reflects an economy of words; that is, short responses with little explanation or detail. Currently he is independent in matters of self-care, such as, bathing, shaving, and dressing. His fine motor dexterity and gait appear to be impaired slightly.

Psychological Evaluation

William has undergone psychological testing/evaluation at ages thirteen, fifteen, and eighteen through the auspices of the public school system. In each instance, William was evaluated to assess his current level of intellectual functioning for placement and/or continuance in the special education program.

I. PSYCHOLOGICAL ASSESSMENT–AGE 13

A. Tests administered: WISC-III, WRAT, and Bender-Gestalt.

B. Observation/results/interpretation: William, a thirteen-year-old, is currently functioning within the overall EMR range of intelligence. Relative strengths were found in word knowledge which indicates his overall potential is higher. Severe weaknesses were evident in abstract reasoning, attention to detail, and sequencing. Perceptual-motor scores were below expectancy at this time; William experienced difficulty with proper integration and directionality.

C. Impression/recommendations: William is to continue in an EMR class setting.

II. PSYCHOLOGICAL ASSESSMENT–AGE 15

A. Tests administered: Bender, Draw-A-Person; and WISC-III.

B. Observations: William is a slim boy of average height and weight. He cooperated on all tasks.

C. Results and interpretation: William's overall verbal and non-verbal scores were in the TMR to EMR range with scores, respectively, of 42–50, 49–58, and 42–50. His individual subtest scores were all below average. William did, however, show strength on a verbal subtest that measures general fund of information. William's Bender reproductions and Draw-A-Person results were commensurate with his intellectual functioning.

D. Impression/recommendations: William is to continue in his EMR class placement.

III. PSYCHOLOGICAL ASSESSMENT–AGE 18

A. Tests administered: WISC-IV, Bender-Gestalt, Revised, and student interview

B. Observations: William was somewhat hesitant about the testing; when the purpose was explained, he appeared to relax. He did not engage in conversation although he did respond appropriately when questioned. He is undecided about his vocational interests but would like to have a job. During testing it was noted that William would occasionally stare into space and become blank looking for a few seconds. Verbal reorientation did bring him back to the task. He appeared unaware of many of his errors. On a pencil and paper task, William held his pencil tightly and worked close to the paper.

C. Results and interpretation: WISC-IV Scaled Scores: Information 3, Picture Completion 1, Similarities 5, Picture Arrangement 2, Arithmetic 2, Block Design 1, Vocabulary 6, Object Assembly 2, Comprehension 3, Coding 4, and Digit Span 1. Verbal Scale IQ = 62; Performance Scale IQ = 46; Full Scale IQ = 50.

BENDER-GESTALT TEST, REVISED: Perceptional Development Age = 6.0 to 6.5

William's IQ of 50 puts him on the borderline for the educable and trainable mental retardation classifications. Because of the disparity between the verbal and performance scales, it is felt that William's abilities are more equivalent to the educable classification of mental retardation. The Bender-Gestalt test is in line with William's performance IQ. His difficulty with visual-motor skills is reiterated by the Bender-Gestalt test results. William evidenced great difficulty with pencil manipulation and awareness of the designs. Scored errors included rotations, distortions of shape, integration of parts and preservation of designs.

Impression/recommendations: William is functioning between educable and trainable mentally retarded classification. There is some indication that his abilities lie more in the educable range. He is to continue in his present placement (EMR class) with the goal of vocational training. William has a good attitude and will put forth effort, both of which are good traits for employability.

Vocational Evaluation

William was given the MESA Vocational Evaluation by the city's vocational-technical center. The following are those results:

A. Perceptual/neurological skills (testing for skills that are basic to almost all occupations): Six tasks were administered which assessed perceptual and neurological skills. William demonstrated below average ability in tasks measuring vision screening, size discrimination, eye/hand coordination, eye/hand/foot coordination, and color discrimination. William experienced difficulty when completing these tasks. William appeared to be attentive when directions were being given, but his ability to follow through and comprehend were demonstrated as extremely weak. During assessment of this skill area, William needed prompting and constant supervision as an effort in keeping him on task.

B. Manual dexterity/motor coordination/tool use (sample normal tool use skills): Tasks were administered which assessed manual dexterity, motor coordination, and tool use skills. Overall performance in this skill area was ranked significantly below average at the 5th and 10th percentile. William experienced difficulty with tool usage, tool recognition, problem solving, assembly, and following directions. William's work required constant assistance and monitoring. Other related deficits observed were in understanding positional directions, organization of work station, and communication skills.

C. Finger dexterity/fine assembly (deals with manipulation of small parts and use of small tools using both hands): William demonstrates higher performance when completing tasks involving use of the dominant hand. Performance is indicated as being higher in tasks which involve working with large parts. William experienced difficulty completing fine assemblies and manipulating small tools and parts. William became very nervous and frustrated when completing this type of task.

D. General ability (measures upper level problem solving and abstract skills): Performance in the area of general ability ranged from low to low average. Problem-solving ability, reasoning, visual memory, and communication skills were assessed as extreme weaknesses. These skills were observed as extreme deficits in isolation and also when interrelated with other skills. Ability to follow directions was ranked low-average. On a task which assessed a combination of related skills: reading, a visual diagram, tactual discrimination following multiple instructions, and assembly performance was ranked low. William experienced extreme difficulty staying on task and following instructions.

E. Impression: The MESA Vocational Screening reveals that William's vocational strengths are in finger dexterity using the dominant hand. Identified weaknesses were in the following areas: vision screening, size discrimination, shape discrimination, eye/hand coordination, eye/hand/foot coordination, color discrimination, manual dexterity, motor coordination, tool use, fine assembly, solving, reasoning, instruction following, communication skills, and independent perceptual activities. The overall vocational screening reveals that William has very limited aptitude and vocational potential at the present time. Task behaviors and following directions are very weak and may hinder success in training and vocational preparation. William's work requires constant monitoring, supervision, and prompting. Attention skills and listening skills were observed as being satisfactory but comprehension factors and ability to follow through were extremely deficient. Work speed, pace, and work quality were observed as being below average. These related factors may also hinder success in specific vocational programs and in training.

F. Recommendations:
1. William should do career exploration/research into the following occupational clusters: Leading/Influencing; Protective; Artistic*; Selling, Plants/Animals, Service; and Education.* High interest indicated on both MESA Interest Assessment and the

Case Interest Inventory.

2. William should receive counseling on working in a group, peer relations, seeking help when needed, and working independently after training has been provided.

3. William's vocational training should incorporate educational activities that will address vocational awareness skills, working conditions, educational requirements, physical requirements, and salary.

4. Based on the vocational screening, training of new concepts is better presented if the new task or concept is presented orally, and oral presentation is paired with visual stimuli, demonstration, or visual diagram. Steps or skills in the task should be presented very concretely and deliberately: William will need constant monitoring during a training phase to assure that he is on task, following directions, and fully comprehends what is to be done.

5. Summary: Based on the vocational screening, William has limited vocational aptitude and potential at the present time. When considering vocational preparation and future vocational goals, emphasis should be on work that is concrete, routine, and organized; that is, work that follows a pre-established pattern.

Educational Evaluation

William has attended public schools his entire life. He has always been in a self-contained special education class (EMR placement). This is his last year in public school and his parents have requested that he be referred to the supported work program. During his sophomore and junior years, William was placed on a job site where he worked cleaning tables and other associated kitchen duties (two half-days a week). The purpose of this placement was to develop work tolerance and good work behavior. William's supervisor rated his activities as adequate but "slow and without much attention to detail."

Economic Evaluation

William is dependent upon his parents.

Discussion Questions

Medical

1. What additional medical information or evaluations, if any, are needed? What effect are the seizures that William had when he was younger?
2. What is the proper or appropriate classification/diagnosis for William's medical condition?

Psychological

1. What additional psychological information or evaluations, if any, are needed?
2. What are the implications of William's diagnosis/classification?

Social/Family/Community

1. What additional sources of family/social information are needed? How and from whom would these data be gathered?
2. What community resources or advocacy groups may be utilized for benefit of William relative to recreation and leisure activities?
3. What services would William be eligible to receive from the community mental health, mental retardation program?

Vocational

1. What vocational or prevocational experiences has William had? Would these be transferable to jobs in the competitive labor market?
2. Consider William's nonexertional residual functional capacities that may present a barrier to employment. What effect will this have on the selection of a vocational goal?
3. What options does William have other than sheltered employment? Is supported employment a viable option for William?

Educational

1. Has William's educational placement been appropriate?
2. Are there other related services, resources that may be utilized by William? If so, what are they?

Economic

1. Is William eligible for SSI?
2. Given that William is eighteen years of age, should William's parents continue to financially contribute to his habilitation?

Chapter 16

THE CASE OF LINDA: MOOD DISORDER

Social Evaluation

Linda is twenty-two years old, single, and has no children. Although she has good training and skills for secretarial work, she is currently unemployed. She lives with her mother who has a good job as a bookkeeper for a large bookkeeping and accounting firm. Linda's father died about ten years ago. Linda finished a business/clerical high school certificate program with good grades about four years ago. However, she has had an unstable employment record since graduation from high school. She has worked for a number of small business firms, although she has never stayed with one employer more than three months. Usually, she has voluntarily resigned but she has been fired by two employers in the past year.

According to her mother, Linda was quiet and introverted as an adolescent, but did not really begin to experience unusual problems until after graduation from high school. Her mother admits that she had probably overprotected Linda and restricted her activities too much during her adolescence. However, she thought she had helped Linda to become more outgoing during her last year or two of high school. Nevertheless, shortly after Linda began her occupational career, she began to restrict her own activities. She would turn down opportunities to socialize with other female friends or to date. She would tend to neglect her appearance and experienced a poor appetite as well as insomnia. She complained of feeling "down" most of the time.

The symptoms that Linda has been experiencing have become more severe during two separate two-week periods in the past six months.

She experienced a severe reaction that included suicidal thoughts about six months ago. Her family physician put her on some medication (Prozac®) that seemed to help her symptoms; however, she recently had another episode that resulted in hospitalization. After medical treatment, she seems to have improved although her physician has decided to refer her for professional counseling/psychotherapy.

Medical Evaluation

Linda's family physician considers her two episodes to be major depression. A psychiatric consultation has suggested that Linda has been experiencing dysthymia for some time prior to experiencing her first major depressive reaction. Although antidepressant medication (Zoloft®) has helped the major depressive reactions, both her family physician and the psychiatric physician consultant believe that Linda should be referred for professional counseling/psychotherapy. They have requested a psychological evaluation for further confirmation and suggestions.

Psychological Evaluation

The results of the Minnesota Multiphasic Personality Inventory as well as a projective instrument, the Thematic Apperception Test, support the medical observations concerning dysthymia and major depression. This clinical psychologist suggested that therapy should particularly concentrate on her unnecessary feelings of worthlessness and inappropriate guilt. He recommended that cognitive-behavioral techniques might be particularly helpful to Linda. The psychologist also administered the Wechsler Adult Intelligence Scale-IV to Linda and obtained the following results: Verbal IQ-110; Performance IQ-114; and Full Scale IQ-112. Therefore, she is considered to be in the bright normal range of intelligence.

Vocational Evaluation

As indicated previously, Linda completed a business/clerical high school certificate and made good grades, obtaining a 3.5 (4.00 System) average. She has good skills in such areas as typing (computer word processor), bookkeeping, filing, and related clerical skills. However, her recent emotional reactions have interfered with her concentration and caused her to perform in an inconsistent and incompetent manner at times. Her employment record does not appear very good because she has chosen to change jobs often and has been terminated for her poor performance on two occasions. However, she likes secretarial work and would like to continue in that vocation if she can feel better.

Educational Evaluation

Linda was a slightly better than average student in high school in general academic subjects such as math, English, and history. However, she was not interested in the college preparatory curriculum and did not excel until she entered the business/ clerical certificate tract. She is not interested in reading literature or novels but has recently developed an interest in reading materials on personal growth and development.

Economic Evaluation

Linda has not been able to save any money, and she is currently unemployed. Consequently, she is dependent on her mother for financial support. Her mother has a good job and wants to help Linda to become self-supporting, as well as be able to have a stable emotional life.

Discussion Questions

Medical

1. What additional medical information or evaluations, if any, are needed? Why?
2. Should Linda be referred for a medication evaluation?

Psychological

1. What are the implications of Linda's psychological assessment? What accommodations may be needed by Linda in the performance of a job?
2. What additional psychological information or evaluations, if any, are needed? Why?

Social/Family/Community

1. What additional sources of family/social information are needed?
2. What community resources or advocacy groups may be utilized for the benefit of Linda and her mother? Should Linda be independent from her mother?
3. What type of cognitive-behavioral counseling techniques would be most helpful with Linda? For example, would you recommend assertiveness training?

Vocational

1. What further information/data would be helpful in determining an educational, training or vocational goal?
2. Consider Linda's nonexertional residual functional capacities (i.e., emotional reactions, inability to focus or concentrate) that may present a barrier to employment. What effect will this have on the selection of an educational, training or vocational goal?
3. Could Linda benefit from supported employment services?

Economic

1. Is Linda eligible for governmental supported services?
2. Should Linda and her mother consider application for any other type of local, state, or federal financial support?

Chapter 17

THE CASE OF JOSEPH:
PERSONALITY DISORDER

Social Evaluation

Joseph is thirty-three years old and divorced and has no children. He is currently employed as a laborer in the construction industry and is being paid the minimum wage. He lives alone in a low-rent housing district. Because he has a bachelor's degree in business administration (having graduated eleven years ago) and has demonstrated his potential for higher income and responsibility at various times, Joseph is considered underemployed. He has drifted from one job to another and has periodically received unemployment compensation. Although Joseph is motivated to go for therapy at a community mental health center, his therapist is frustrated with him because he does not seem to want to accept responsibility for his contribution to his problems. He blames other people and the world for his lack of achievement of his potential.

Joseph is the oldest of three children. He has one brother four years younger who is a practicing attorney and is married and has a family. His sister is seven years younger and is a secondary education teacher and has recently married. His father has been a claims adjuster for many years and his mother was a stay at home mom and homemaker. Joseph's parents admit they made mistakes in raising him which they were able to correct with the other children. They were overindulgent and helped to create unrealistic expectations about life. Joseph was particularly envious of his younger brother and was very competitive with him. Moreover, Joseph feels that he will eventually be more successful than his younger brother as he has a grandiose sense of importance about himself that makes him feel he is destined for unusual success.

Joseph's feelings for his family vacillate between extremes of positive and negative. However, he feels he is entitled to their support and attempts to exploit them materially and financially. This is characteristic of most of his personal relationships. He was married for about a year and has had many short term relationships with women. However, his moods, impulsiveness, and problems with anger along with other characteristics have contributed to estrangement in these relationships. He generally feels empty and confused about his identity.

Medical Evaluation

Joseph is basically in good physical health. Because of his moods, he has requested medication at times to help him with sleeping or functioning on the job.

These medications (Ambien® and Adderall XL®), however, have only been of limited benefit to him. He has consistently relied on alcohol to help him feel better and this may have become a substance abuse problem. In general, he does not try to take better care of his physical health. He is slightly obese, does not adhere to a balanced diet, and rarely exercises.

Psychological Evaluation

On the Wechsler Adult Intelligence Scale-IV, Joseph received a Verbal IQ of 121, a Performance IQ of 122, and a Full Scale IQ of 122. There was no unusual scatter on the various verbal and performance subtests scale scores. His intelligence scores are in the superior range and suggest that he has the cognitive potential to perform at an above average level in educational, social, or occupational pursuits. However, the examiner hypothesized that Joseph may have a personality disorder based on his initial interview as well as Joseph's social history. This hypothesis was supported by Joseph's results on a personality inventory, the Millon Clinical Multiaxial Inventory, as well as projective testing using the Thematic Apperception Test and the Holtzman Inkblot Technique. Joseph appears to have a combination of a borderline personality disorder and a narcissistic personality disorder. He also appears to have an alcohol abuse problem, but this seems to be secondary to his personality disorder.

Vocational Evaluation

Joseph has held a number of jobs since his graduation from college 11 years ago. He initially entered a management training program with a national department store chain. However, he decided that their policies and procedures were too rigid and resigned after six months. He then worked as a sales representative for a small computer company. Although he functioned fairly well in this capacity, he became bored and decided to travel to the west coast as he had lived on the east coast all his life. He initially had difficulty finding employment and delivered newspapers for a while. However, he eventually obtained an excellent position in a management capacity with a small manufacturing company. He became very egotistical in this position and eventually clashed with the president of the company and was fired. He then tried to start his own business but failed at that endeavor. In the past few years, Joseph has had more difficulty finding employment compatible with his education and cognitive ability. Employers are not impressed with his employment record. He was recently forced to take a job as a laborer with a construction company.

Educational Evaluation

The quality of Joseph's grades was variable in high school. However, he did finish with an overall B average and scored above average on the Scholastic Aptitude Test. He was accepted into a small four-year college. Vocational inventories in high school and college had not been helpful to him in pinpointing a major; he seemed to have some inconsistent interests. He eventually drifted into a major in business administration. Joseph decided this would be a very practical education and would help him to eventually become wealthy. His grades were also variable in college, but he did graduate with a 2.5 average (4.00 scale). Although he scored well on the Graduate Record Examination, he did not consider graduate school because his grades were not very competitive and he was bored with school.

Economic Evaluation

Joseph recently took the laborer position because he needed the money. He has had a good income at times during his employment history. However, he has never managed his finances very well and has often had to borrow money from family or friends. His parents have been willing to provide him support whenever he needed it, and he has infrequently paid them back. He has always paid back his brother and sister and most of his friends. He has managed to receive unemployment compensation a few times.

Discussion Questions

Medical

1. What additional medical information or evaluations, if any, are needed, why? What are the implications of Joseph's mild obesity and his use of alcohol?
2. How could Joseph be encouraged to take better care of his health?

Psychological

1. What additional psychological information or evaluations, if any, are needed? Why?
2. What are the implications of Joseph's psychological assessment? What are the impediments of his psychological condition?

Social/Family/Community

1. What additional sources of family/social information are needed?
2. What community resources or advocacy groups may be utilized for the benefit of Joseph?
3. What services, if any, would Joseph be eligible for from the local community mental health agency?

Vocational

1. What further information/data would be helpful in determining a vocational goal?

2. Consider Joseph's residual functional capacity to engage in work. Based on this assessment, what level(s) of work activity (sedentary, light, medium, heavy) can he perform? Did Joseph's previous work provide any transferable skills? If so, what are they?

3. Consider Joseph's nonexertional residual functional capacities (i.e., his need to be in charge, his need to be right) that may present a barrier to employment. What effect will this have on the selection of a vocational or training goal?

4. If Joseph's condition is, as noted in the *DSM-IV-TR,* resistant to change and not readily helped by psychological interventions, how can Joseph's personality become a positive attribute from a vocational perspective? Or is that possible?

5. What kind of behavioral intervention strategies would be helpful to Joseph in regard to a career goal?

6. What type of personal adjustment counseling or therapy will best help Joseph to function in an occupational role?

Economic

1. Is Joseph eligible for any type of governmental assistance?

Chapter 18

THE CASE OF PATRICIA: SEIZURE DISORDER

Social Evaluation

Patricia is thirty-two years old. She and her husband of fifteen years separated approximately two years ago. He left for work one day and did not return. Their relationship had, over the past five to six years, deteriorated to the point that they rarely spoke to one another. Their three children (a fourteen-year-old son and two daughters, ages ten and eight) remain in the custody of Patricia. Patricia is not angry or bitter at her husband. The children miss their father, but prefer his absence to the previous level of tension within the household. It was tough for awhile after his departure, particularly in terms of finances. Patricia is currently receiving Temporary Assistance to Needy Families (TANF) and Food Stamps. These funds seem barely enough to subsist on. There is no money for new clothes or shoes, or for any recreational activities. Patricia's relationship with her children may be described as warm and caring. Each child has assigned chores, and all share in the work of the household.

Patricia wants to find a job and get off TANF. She does not, as she has stated, want to become a "welfare mother." She has never worked outside of the home; her marriage and family were the focus of her life. Patricia completed the eleventh grade. During the past twenty-five years she has had occasional seizures. Her first seizure was at five years of age. She had averaged one to two seizures per year for the past five years. Recently, she began to have one to two seizures per week. As a result of these seizures, her children report that Patricia is tired most of the time and stays depressed much of the time. They believe she is taking her medications as prescribed. She has, nevertheless, withdrawn from her family and will not go outside of the house for fear of falling (as a result of a seizure) and hurting herself. She stopped driving, as well, out of concern she might hurt someone. Patricia is scheduled to be hospitalized for a complete medical evaluation.

Medical Evaluation

Patricia has been in good health with the exception of having an occasional seizure. She is safety conscious. Recently, she began to have one or two seizures a week.

Hospitalization: Admitted April 7, Discharged April 16.

Admission Diagnoses:

1. Seizure disorder, presumed idiopathic
2. Dilantin® toxicity

Summary of hospitalization: The patient has a history of grand mal seizures since age five. She has taken Dilantin and another drug (which she could not name and did not currently have) intermittently for control. She was seen by her family physician shortly after the seizures recurred. He prescribed Dilantin and Phenobarbital®. The Phenobarbital was discontinued because it made Patricia drowsy. The Dilantin dosage has been changed several times. Observed seizure activity has been described as clonic/tonic activity, salivation, and fecal/urine incontinence. The seizure activity lasts approximately four to five minutes. Patricia states she does not have any warning or aura. Following the seizure, she states she is very tired and must sleep for several hours. The patient's medical history is positive for high blood pressure, past history of alcohol abuse, and a positive family history of seizure activity in the patient's mother and one sibling. She had a total abdominal hysterectomy and appendectomy approximately six years ago. Physical examination of the patient was within the normal limits. She is obese (5 feet, 200 pounds). During the course of the patient's hospitalization, she was given an EEG (both awake and sleeping). The awake recording was normal; however, during sleep, a medium amplitude sharp wave was noted in the left temporal head region and was considered epileptiform. The patient was started on Tegretol® and Dilantin, and after therapeutic levels were established, she has remained seizure free.

Discharge diagnosis: Seizure disorder with focus in the left

temporal region.

Medications prescribed at discharge: 1. Dilantin, 300 mg per day and 2. Tegretol, 200 mg per day.

Follow-along by neurologist: Patricia has been seen on a monthly basis by her neurologist, primarily to check blood levels for therapeutic range of medications. She continues to be seizure free six months post hospitalization. Her driver's license was revoked by the Department of Motor Vehicles (DMV) because of her seizure disorder. The physician with the DMV has stated that Patricia must be seizure free for a period of one year before her license will be reinstated.

Psychological Evaluation

The Department of Social Services referred Patricia for a psychological evaluation to include a WAIS-IV only. Patricia was neatly and appropriately dressed for the interview. She was very cooperative and motivated and approached the testing situation seriously. It is felt that her performance accurately mirrors her current functioning. Patricia's Verbal IQ of 80, her Performance IQ of 72, and her Full Scale IQ of 78 placed her in the borderline range of intelligence.

Vocational Evaluation

Patricia has never held a full-time job. She has, on occasion, done babysitting and has worked as a counter attendant at a fast food restaurant. She wants to work, but does not feel she is capable because of her seizure disorder. Even though she has been seizure free for six months, she feels that no one will hire her. Additionally, she does not want to work for minimum wage. She feels she would lose her Medicaid if she works. She applied for Supplemental Security Insurance benefits approximately seven months ago. She recently was notified that her claim was being denied. Her denial letter stated that her medical condition was not severe enough to warrant disability payments. They suggested that she seek work where she would not be expected to be around moving machines, to climb, or to work at heights. They noted that the following jobs were representative of occupations that she could perform:

- Patcher, Electrical Equipment, DOT Code 723.687-100

- Stem Mounter, Electrical Equipment, DOT Code 725.684-018
- Focuser, Electrical Equipment, DOT Code 725.687-018

Educational Evaluation

Patricia completed the eleventh grade. She quit school to get married and have a family. Patricia's school records indicate that she was an average to below average student. She did not excel in sports or other extracurricular activities.

Economic Evaluation

Patricia's sole source of income is the TANF payment and Food Stamps she receives from the Department of Social Services. Her housing costs are reduced through another governmental program; consequently her rent and utilities are proportionally based on the amount of cash benefits she receives. Patricia has clear title to her automobile. Her car is in good operating condition. She, however, cannot drive for approximately six months provided she continues to be seizure free. Patricia's and her children's medical needs are covered by Medicaid.

Patricia is worried about her future. She wants to work and earn more money than she receives from Social Services, but feels she is not qualified for jobs that pay more than the minimum wage. She also wonders about the loss of TANF benefits/Food Stamps/housing assistance/Medicaid if she got a job.

Discussion Questions

Medical

1. What additional medical information or evaluations, e.g., obesity, alcohol use, are needed? Why?
2. What is Dilantin toxicity?
3. What effects, if any, do Patricia's medications have on her ability to participate in activities of daily living or to participate in an educational or training program?

Psychological

1. What are the implications and relevance of Patricia's WAIS-IV test scores? Does Patricia have the ability to undergo an academically based training program, e.g., child care services, at the local community college?
2. What additional psychological data or evaluations, if any, are needed? Why?

Social/Family/Community

1. What additional sources of family/social information are needed?
2. What community resources or advocacy groups may be utilized for the benefit of Patricia and her children?

Vocational

1. What information/data would be helpful in determining a career or vocational goal? Did Patricia's previous work provide any transferable skills? If so, what are they?
2. Consider Patricia's nonexertional residual functional capacities, e.g., periods of unconsciousness, and side effects of medications, that may present a barrier to employment. What effect will this have on the selection of a vocational goal?

Economic

1. Is the receipt of TANF/Food Stamps/Housing Assistance/ Medicaid a disincentive regarding Patricia's desire to work?

Chapter 19

THE CASE OF JOHN:
SPINAL CORD INJURY

Social Evaluation

John is twenty-one years old and single and has no children. He lives with his parents in a small rural community. John has a spinal cord disability as a result of an automobile accident about a year ago while on active duty in the U.S. Army. His disability is considered to be service connected; consequently, he receives a military service retirement pension. His father owns and operates a successful small town hardware store business. His mother is a homemaker. John is the only child. They live in a nice home on several acres of well kept property.

After John finished high school, his parents wanted him to enter college and study mechanical engineering. He had always been effective in the use of mechanical equipment, and he also had a good understanding of the principles behind their operation. He was particularly interested in automobiles. John did pursue studies at a nearby community college for two semesters, but then dropped out to enter the U.S. Army. Although he was assigned to infantry duties, he had been hoping to eventually receive training in something more related to his interests and abilities. He was on leave when he had an automobile accident; his car went off the road and hit a tree. The final determination was that it was a freak accident that was not his fault.

John's parents had been rather indulgent in their early child rearing behavior. Although John could do well when he applied himself, he often had unrealistic expectations about what should be available to him in the world. Because of his current condition, his parents tended to be reinforcing this behavior. He should probably go to an evaluation facility in order that his physical and social rehabilitation potential can be more effectively evaluated. However, he feels that he can be adequately evaluated in his own home. His mother tends to be overprotective about his condition, and she works hard to make sure his physical needs and social preferences are met. John's father feels that his primary responsibility to his son, at this time, is to make sure that his financial needs and interests are met.

Medical Evaluation

John's injury is very high in the spinal cord at the level of the C5 vertebra. He is paralyzed from the neck down and is totally dependent for personal hygiene, movement, dressing, writing, driving, and so forth. Although he needs assistance in obtaining his food, he does have nearly full eating skills. If his injury had been higher in the spinal cord, he would have had difficulty in breathing; however, he does not need respiratory equipment. John received good medical treatment, but he requested that he be released before his full potential in regard to medical rehabilitation could be assessed. Moreover, his potential in regard to physical rehabilitation had hardly been explored when he returned home. For example, he does not make use of even the simplest of adaptive devices such as a mouth stick. Although John recognizes that he might benefit from further medical and physical rehabilitation, he feels that it can be accomplished at home. He feels that spinal cord injury centers are dehumanizing and ego deflating places. Moreover, he doesn't believe that he has much further medical rehabilitation potential and that his family physician can help him in that area. His family physician has indicated that his medical potential may be at its limit, but that there is no way to know without a more thorough assessment at a comprehensive facility. John is not willing to take the risk because of what he perceives as a potentially hurtful social and psychological experience. He is interested in exploring further physical rehabilitation possibilities such as an electronic wheelchair. However, he feels that the kind of physical rehabilitation alternatives he would be interested in could be managed at home and coordinated by the Veterans Administration and state vocational rehabilitation representatives.

Psychological Evaluation

John did have an opportunity to engage in some psychological testing during his hospitalization. He was given the verbal portion of the Wechsler Adult Intelligence Scale-IV and was assessed as having an IQ of 135, which is considered to be in the very superior range. Therefore, he appears to have excellent intellectual potential in regard to academic success. However, projective testing revealed emotional immaturity and self-centeredness. He was described as having a very demanding attitude with a low tolerance for frustration. His disability seems to have exacerbated these personality characteristics.

Vocational Evaluation

John left the hospital before there was an opportunity to do any vocational-educational testing or assessment. However, during one interview, he had expressed his interest in mechanical engineering and how he had always been effective in using mechanical equipment as well as understanding the principles behind their operation. In spite of his automobile accident, he still seemed interested in automobiles. Due to the functional limitations of his disability, he was uncertain as to how he might be able to apply these interests in the future. John's only real work experiences have been serving as an infantryman in a peacetime U.S. Army, and helping out in his father's hardware store.

Educational Evaluation

John had always scored exceptionally high on scholastic aptitude tests; however, his performance in school represented an underachievement. He completed high school with an overall B average. He had some very good grades in mathematics and natural sciences; although he had some low grades in social sciences and humanities. His high school guidance counselor recommended that he attend a community college for awhile before considering a four-year institution. However, his scholastic performance pattern continued at the community college. He dropped out after two semesters and entered the U.S. Army for a four year tour of duty. He thought he might be ready for college after his enlistment. Also, he hoped to get some specialized training in the military service related to his interests that might be helpful to him later.

Economic Evaluation

With a service-connected disability rated at 100 percent, John has a military retirement that pays him an income higher than the average four-year college graduate. He also has other benefits such as commissary privileges, medical care, and Veterans Administration Vocational Rehabilitation Services. His father is considered to have a successful hardware store business for a small community. He owns his home and has indicated that John can stay there indefinitely.

Discussion Questions

Medical

1. What additional medical information or evaluations, e.g., PT, OT, AT, are needed?
2. With special equipment, what are John's possibilities regarding physical rehabilitation, instrumental activities of daily living, and to participate in an educational or training program?
3. Due to John's disability, is he at risk for certain reoccurring medical complications?

Psychological

1. What are the implications of John's verbal IQ score on the WAIS-IV?
2. How would you help John prevent his personality characteristics from interfering with his total rehabilitation?
3. What additional psychological information or evaluations, if any, are needed? Why?

Social/Family/Community

1. What additional sources of family/social information are needed?
2. What community resources or advocacy groups may be utilized for the benefit of John and his parents?
3. What opportunities are available to John in regard to avocational/ recreational pursuits?

Vocational

1. What further information/data would be helpful in determining an alternative vocational goal? Did John's previous work provide any transferable skills? If so, what are they?
2. Consider John's residual functional capacity to engage in work. Based on this assessment, what level(s) of work activity (sedentary, light, medium, heavy) can he perform? What effect will this have on the selection of an alternative career or vocational goal?
3. What assistive technology needs would John require if he were to enroll in an educational program? What accommodations would be required in an educational environment? Would these accommodations be transferable to an employment setting?

Economic

1. What benefits and services are available to John through the Veterans Administration Vocational Rehabilitation Program? Other benefits from the VA?
2. Is John also entitled to services from the state vocational rehabilitation program?
3. Is John eligible for SSDI benefits?

Chapter 20

THE CASE OF CHARLES: SUBSTANCE ABUSE DISORDER

Social Evaluation

Charles is twenty-seven years old, married to Sally, who is twenty-five years old, and they have a three-year-old daughter, Jennifer. Charles is a career federal civil service employee at the managerial level. He was recently promoted to a unit manager position with the Department of Labor. Sally is a high school English teacher and has a teaching position with a well known private school. Consequently, they enjoy a good income between them and live in a nice upper middle class neighborhood.

Charles is beginning to worry about his drinking. He and Sally have enjoyed reasonable social drinking since they met in college. However, Charles has been experiencing some problems with his drinking in the past two or three years since the birth of Jennifer and the increased responsibility in his work. He has drunk too much on a number of occasions and has felt "hung over" the next day. He has had a few close calls while driving and drinking. Sally has begun to drive them home from social events when it appears that Charles has had too much to drink. He has not missed any work and continues to do well in his work. However, he often does not feel well and is not as happy in his work. He often feels depressed at home and will drink to feel better. He and Sally are beginning to have arguments about his drinking.

Charles likes to drink and does not really want to give it up. He comes from a family where social drinking was considered enjoyable, but there was never any evidence of alcohol abuse. However, Charles cannot seem to moderate his drinking and it appears to be getting pro-

319

gressively worse. He has studied some Alcoholics Anonymous literature and even attended one of their meetings. However, he does not
agree with some of their principles and beliefs. Although he seems to
meet the minimum criteria for addiction, he just does not see himself
as an alcoholic in the sense depicted at these meetings.

After being given a warning by a police officer about his driving and
drinking, he decided to talk to his family physician. They talked about
the possibility of tranquilizers or other medication. However, Charles
had experimented with similar drugs in college and had not liked their
effect. The physician decided to refer Charles to a licensed professional counselor who does personal adjustment counseling/therapy
with mental health and substance abuse issues.

Medical Evaluation

A recent comprehensive physical examination indicated that
Charles was in excellent physical health. Thus far, there appear to be
no irreversible effects of his drinking. He reports periodic withdrawal
symptoms and other physical symptoms consistent with addiction.
However, his physician feels that he would only have mild physiological problems for a few days if he were to completely stop drinking. He
has cautioned Charles that continued excessive abuse can have a
cumulative effect and cause serious physical problems. His physician
has suggested that tranquilizers and similar medications (e.g., Xanax®
or Buspar® and Ambien®) would be much less physically dangerous
than alcohol.

Psychological Evaluation

Charles has never really had a comprehensive psychological evaluation. He took some aptitude, interest, and personality tests at the
counseling center when he was in college. He achieved an IQ of 133
on the Otis Lennon Mental Ability, a group intelligence test. The
Strong-Campbell Interest Inventory, a vocational interest inventory,
helped him to recognize his interest in public government and administration. Personality inventories developed for use with normal populations, such as the California Psychological Inventory, basically indicated that Charles is a very conscientious individual who has a need
to achieve well in traditional settings in our culture.

Vocational Evaluation

A vocational interest inventory helped Charles to realize his interest in public government and administration. Upon graduation from college, Charles was immediately accepted for a management training position with the Department of Labor, which is part of the federal civil service system. He has performed his responsibilities well and has advanced at a normal pace. He was recently given greater administrative responsibility. If he performs his responsibilities well in this position, he may be able to advance at a faster pace. However, one of his supervisors, during his management training, advised him that he needed to relax more. His assessment of Charles's managerial potential was excellent. However, he felt that Charles might not be as happy in a position of very high responsibility unless he learned to better cope with stress.

Educational Evaluation

Charles has always done well in school. He finished close to the top of his class in high school and made excellent scores on the Scholastic Aptitude Test. He graduated with honors with a 3.7 (4.0 system) grade point average from college and scored well on the Graduate Record Examination. He obtained his bachelor's degree in political science. The Department of Labor has been sponsoring him on a part-time basis for a Master of Public Administration degree, which he should complete in another year.

Economic Evaluation

Charles and his wife, Sally, make a good income between them. They live very comfortably and they have managed their finances well. They have a mortgage on their house and a few other loans, e.g., car, furniture, and they have no serious financial problems. Charles has decided, for the time being, not to use his health insurance for the personal adjustment counseling/therapy as he would like to avoid having a mental health problem listed on health insurance records. Consequently, he plans to pay cash for his therapy visits.

Discussion Questions

Medical

1. What additional medical information or evaluations, if any, are needed? Why?
2. Do you think that Charles should give greater consideration to taking a tranquilizer or similar medication because his physician has indicated that it would be a safer alternative than alcohol?

Psychological

1. What additional psychological information or evaluations, if any, are needed? Why?
2. Do employee assistance programs assure confidentiality to their clients? Why is this an issue for Charles?

Social/Family/Community

1. What additional sources of family/social information are needed?
2. What community resources or advocacy groups may be utilized for the benefit of Charles?
3. Do you think the general mental health counselor should refer Charles to a counselor who specializes in alcohol and drug abuse problems?
4. What type of mental health counseling techniques or approaches would you recommend to help Charles with his alcohol abuse problem?

Vocational

1. What types of behavioral techniques or strategies would help Charles to better cope with stress on the job?
2. If Charles continues to have too much difficulty with stress related to his work, what kind of modifications would you recommend in regard to his career plans?
3. Do you think Charles is in jeopardy of losing his job?

Economic

1. Under what circumstances would Charles be eligible to receive vocational rehabilitation services?

Other

1. If Charles were denied VR services, what would be the basis for denial?
2. Would the results of the eligibility determination process be beneficial to Charles? In what ways?

INDEX